Federated Intelligent System for Healthcare

Scrivener Publishing
100 Cummings Center, Suite 541J
Beverly, MA 01915-6106

Publishers at Scrivener
Martin Scrivener (martin@scrivenerpublishing.com)
Phillip Carmical (pcarmical@scrivenerpublishing.com)

Federated Intelligent System for Healthcare

A Practical Guide

Edited by

S. Rakesh Kumar
Department of Computer Science and Engineering, GITAM University, Bengaluru, India

N. Gayathri
Department of Computer Science and Engineering, GITAM University, Bengaluru, India

and

Seifedine Kadry
Department of Applied Data Science, Noroff University College, Norway and Artificial Intelligence Research Center, Ajman University, United Arab Emirates

Scrivener Publishing

WILEY

This edition first published 2025 by John Wiley & Sons, Inc., 111 River Street, Hoboken, NJ 07030, USA and Scrivener Publishing LLC, 100 Cummings Center, Suite 541J, Beverly, MA 01915, USA

For more information about Scrivener publications please visit www.scrivenerpublishing.com.

Wiley Global Headquarters
111 River Street, Hoboken, NJ 07030, USA

For details of our global editorial offices, customer services, and more information about Wiley products visit us at www.wiley.com.

Library of Congress Cataloging-in-Publication Data

ISBN 978-1-394-27135-1

Front cover image courtesy of Adobe Firefly
Cover design by Russell Richardson

Set in size of 11pt and Minion Pro by Manila Typesetting Company, Makati, Philippines

Printed in the USA

10 9 8 7 6 5 4 3 2 1

Contents

Preface

This book explores the integration of federated learning and intelligent systems within the healthcare domain, providing an in-depth understanding of how these systems enhance healthcare practices. It details their principles, technologies, challenges, and opportunities, with a particular focus on secure, privacy-preserving medical data sharing. Additionally, it examines the role of artificial intelligence and machine learning in healthcare, along with the ethical considerations surrounding these advanced technologies.

With an emphasis on practical implementation and real-world use cases, this book equips healthcare professionals, researchers, and technology experts with the knowledge needed to navigate the complexities of federated intelligent systems and harness their potential to transform patient care and drive medical advancements.

This volume serves as a platform for researchers to present their ideas on unlocking the future of healthcare with cutting-edge insights, transforming healthcare, embracing federated intelligence, and shaping the future. It features both novel technological advancements and conceptual, visionary scenarios.

The editors extend their deepest gratitude to the contributing authors for their invaluable expertise and dedication, which have significantly enriched this work. We also thank Martin Scrivener and the team at Scrivener Publishing for their continuous support throughout the book's preparation.

S. Rakesh Kumar
N. Gayathri
Seifedine Kadry

1

Introduction to Federated Intelligent Systems in Healthcare

Naseem Ahmad

Dr. Rehabilitation Psychologist, Amroha, Uttar Pradesh, India

Abstract

Federated learning is an extensive technique that helps organisations protect patients privacy. Training of deep learning model on federated healthcare data has been evaluated through this learning method. Evaluation and transfer of medical data have been justified potentially with the involvement of federated learning techniques. Decentralised training of the deep learning model has been ensured with the involvement of the federated learning technique. The acting of the hospital-to-client model has been ensured with the involvement of the FL technique. While conducting collaboration between different medical institutions secure preservation of patient information has been ensured with the implementation of this method. Enhancement of patient and institutional access to high-quality healthcare service has been ensured with better utilisation of federated learning techniques. Great promise for healthcare applications has been ensured due to the presence of the FL method. Improving the quality of data and reducing the risk of incorrect data annotation-related problems are solved successfully with the utilisation of federated learning technique. Data vulnerability and data breach-related problems are also solved successfully with better utilisation of this federated intelligent system. Instrumental and environmental noises are also solved potentially with better implications for federate intelligent systems. This study demonstrates the role of a federated intelligence system in ensuring the standardisation of medical datasets. Data partition-related aspects of the medical industry have been evaluated efficiently with the successful use of federated learning programs in healthcare. Conducting training on the collaborative machine learning model fl helps to create secure pool of information of multiple clients. The intelligence of the healthcare field has been emphasised with the successful implementation of federated learning. Security privacy, stability and reliability of the

Email: drnaseem1974@gmail.com

S. Rakesh Kumar, N. Gayathri and Seifedine Kadry (eds.) Federated Intelligent System for Healthcare: A Practical Guide, (1–24) © 2025 Scrivener Publishing LLC

healthcare industry have been increased potentially with the involvement of federated learning techniques. The development of an entire healthcare management system has been confirmed successfully by evaluating different potential components of federated learning techniques. In addition, comprehensive changes in the operation of the medical field have been ensured with the involvement of federated learning and the internet of medical things that can. The growth and development of healthcare services have been ensured with the involvement of these technologies. Implementation of a federated intelligence system contributes to improving the ability to sense and transmit health updates successfully. Potential biomedical image analysis and security of information have been evaluated authentically due to the presence of IOMT or federated learning method. Distributed learning for the machine learning model of the medical industry has been highlighted due to the presence of federated learning in healthcare.

***Keywords*:** Federated learning, internet of medical things, medical data, machine learning, security privacy, healthcare services, medical dataset and deep learning

1.1 Introduction

Federated learning is used by healthcare federated intelligent systems to train models at the same time across different healthcare data sources, all the while keeping patient information safe. To find out what cooperative learning in medicine can do, where it came from, and what problems it has, we must examine it closely. It is called secondary study when we review and analyze books and research papers that have already been written. The results show that healthcare data can be used to learn useful things for shared smart systems without putting patients' privacy at risk. Still, there are many ways that data and privacy issues are still a problem. In conclusion, for federated learning to fully realize its promise of personalized patient care, it needs unity between different healthcare sectors, new technology, and strong data governance processes. Healthcare professionals can use Federated Intelligent Systems to make the most cutting-edge decisions based on data. These systems can maintain data privacy and accelerate joint model training across multiple separate data sources by using collaborative learning. Using this method, which keeps patient data safe and secure locally, helps to lower the privacy concerns that come with processing and storing data in one place. Wearable tech and digital health records have made the healthcare business generate more data. In response, more complex statistics and personalized care plans have been created. For example, in healthcare, shared intelligence systems can get useful information from patient data without revealing the patients' identities. Together, these technologies allow healthcare institutions to create more accurate diagnosis tools and prediction models. Treatment works better, and is of higher quality. Big data is used in healthcare to create shared intelligence systems that keep patient data safe. This piece examines group learning in healthcare by exploring its current state, problems, and potential future developments. Shared learning is a creative way to keep data private while using multiple data sources to train machine learning models. To get the most out of shared learning, our study aims to guide healthcare managers how to optimize data while ensuring and protecting patient privacy. To make shared learning more useful in healthcare, it's important to know how it can be used in real life. In studies and tests that have led to better patient tracking, sickness prediction, and individual treatment plans, federated learning has been useful. These cases show that strict privacy rules can be followed while shared learning is used to handle complicated and varied healthcare data.

Cancer study centers and hospitals use cooperative learning to make it easier to diagnose cancer. These companies could work together to make models that are more accurate and reliable by sharing changes to models instead of raw patient data. And this allows models to learn from the diverse types of patients and the knowledge of the participants. We can detect and treat cancer faster if we work together, ultimately for the benefit of the people. Scientists are also investigating how joint learning can be utilized to develop programs capable of predicting long-term illnesses [15].

Federated learning can better tell when a patient's state is about to get worse by mixing data from different healthcare sources, like smart tech and electronic health records. This allows doctors to assist the patient sooner, which could improve their health and lower costs. With the help of AI, shared learning, and the Internet of Things (IoT), the future of healthcare looks bright. By letting computers learn from multiple data sources at the same time, this combination could make medical care more accurate and efficient. Federated learning is a huge step forward in the healthcare business because it lets you use huge amounts of data safely without putting patients' privacy at risk. The healthcare industry can't work without strong teamwork, strict obedience to the law, and a steady flow of new ideas. If these problems are fixed, shared learning could make healthcare systems around the world better and personalized treatment even better.

1.2 Evolution and Principles of Federated Learning in Healthcare

Federated learning is a game-changing way to keep private patient data safe when healthcare needs to analyze data together. This new idea strikes a good balance between the strict privacy and data security rules in the healthcare industry and the advantages of big data analytics [16]. The idea behind collaborative learning is decentralized model training. Federated learning saves data close to home, while centralized machine learning uses data from many places to teach a model [1]. Healthcare devices, hospitals, and even clinics use their own data sets to help them learn. These small groups use their own data to train a shared model. They only send the changed model results to a central server, not the original data. There are many good things about this independent model teaching method. First, it makes sure that privacy rules like HIPAA in the US and GDPR in Europe are followed. This makes data breaches much less common. Sensitive patient data probably wouldn't get out while being stored or transported because raw data never leaves the local area. The only thing that is given to someone is the model choices, which are usually less private and nameless.

Central computers can help you keep track of changes to models. To create changes, it combines locally calculated modifications from several devices or institutions into the global model. The local groups receive this combined model back so they may retrain it using their own data. The world model may learn from many different data sources and improve over time if the data is kept hidden. The healthcare sector may gain greatly from federated learning as it allows models to be trained from a variety of data sources [10]. These differences happen because of the different types of patients, healthcare data sources, and patient groups. Federated learning allows teachers from various schools to work together on model lessons. The models are more useful now that they live longer and show a wider range of illnesses and patient results. With federated learning, it's also easier to look at other kinds of data. Smaller or less data-rich businesses may be able to get past data walls by using a global model built on a bigger dataset. This link could lead to better ways to predict the future, come up with treatments, and make diagnoses. When it comes to healthcare, learning to work together might be harder than usual. A number of technological challenges remain, such as making local devices faster, fixing issues with model convergence and bias, and keeping model update secrets safe while they're being sent [2]. People and groups with different goals and ideas about data governance find it hard to work together and trust each other. Even with these issues, it looks like collaborative learning will be very useful in the future. To make shared learning systems more reliable and safer, researchers are exploring how to use block chain technology, differential privacy, and secure multiparty computation. As shared learning spreads, it's likely that more healthcare businesses will use it. This will pave the way for further growth and progress. Federated learning changes how healthcare data is used for model training and forecast analytics [21]. It opens the promise of big data in healthcare by letting people work together to analyze data and protect privacy. This makes medical outcomes safer, more tailored to each person, and more accurate.

In healthcare, shared learning is becoming more and more common, so technical and real problems need to be fixed. Technology has trouble making conversation reliable and useful. Federated learning needs to be changed so that it can work with big setups without using more time or data. This is because both local hubs and central computers are always changing the way they share information. To make model training on spread-out networks better, researchers are looking into asynchronous updates and gradient compression. It is very important for shared learning to happen in healthcare that training data is correct and uniform. Healthcare data often comes from more than one place and isn't always of the same quality, style, or standard. This uncertainty could hurt learned models and show biases. To keep this from happening, federated learning systems need complicated ways to prepare and normalize data before they can join datasets for training. Models are stronger and can be used in more healthcare situations when they use federated average and meta-learning.

A lot more needs to be said about how to keep data safe and in control for shared learning. Strong privacy and data security rules must be followed by healthcare companies [14]. To meet these needs, federated learning needs to be carefully planned and put into action. Legal deals, rules on how to use data, and tracking tools are needed to keep an eye on joint learning. To safely share and handle data, businesses need the newest cryptography methods, such as homomorphic encryption and secure multiparty computing. Another problem is that shared learning doesn't work with all systems. Since different healthcare systems and gadgets use different methods and standards, it may be hard to combine and share data. Standardized data sharing forms and APIs are needed to make healthcare systems more open and help people talk to each other [22]. More standard and easy ways to share healthcare data are being made possible by FHIR. This is very important for group learning to work.

Even with these problems, cooperative learning could be good for healthcare. Predictive analytics can be used in healthcare in interesting ways. In joint learning, healthcare professionals can guess how patients will do, what problems they might have, and the best way to help them. These models might give doctors more accurate and complete data, which could help them treat patients better and make better decisions. A lot of different groups taught them about different things. Medical study might be helped by federated learning. Researchers can get more information without putting patients' privacy at risk. This allows them to do more study and come up with new ideas. Federated learning could help big genome projects that need genetic information from more than one source. By combining data from different study groups, federated learning could speed up personalized medical research. When AI and IoT are added to shared learning, it works better in healthcare. AI systems can look at any data and give useful information. IoT gadgets collect info about patients and give it in real time. Putting these two things together might make healthcare systems more adaptable and better able to meet the needs of patients and provide better care.

In the future, federated learning might be good for health. As healthcare companies work together and technology gets better, federated learning will become more common [17]. Federated learning systems are getting better and more reliable; thanks to research. They are also looking into new uses and ways to solve problems that already exist. Today's healthcare will be better, more accurate, and more tailored to each patient if shared learning programs grow. Federated learning is a new way to teach models use healthcare data. It improves healthcare by letting people work together to learn while keeping patient information safe. Federated learning should be used a lot; but first, problems with organization, law, and technology need to be fixed. The possible benefits make the work worth it. As long as healthcare companies use this technology, shared learning will shape personalized care that is based on data. Figure 1.1 shows evolution and principles of federated learning in healthcare.

1.3 Applications of Federated Learning in Healthcare

Finding the best treatment plan for each patient has become much easier; thanks to federated learning. It has also made it easier to identify diseases and rate their seriousness. This new technology gives clinicians safe access to a huge number of various kinds of information. This solves one of the most important problems in healthcare right now. Most of the time,

Figure 1.1 Evolution and principles of federated learning in healthcare. *(Source: Self Developed).*

cooperative learning is used in medicine to find and evaluate illnesses. A lot of different data sources are used by federated learning algorithms to find trends and make accurate predictions about the future state of health [7]. A system that puts together EHRs from different sources might be able to figure out how likely it is that a patient will get diabetes or heart disease. This is why it's so important to stop chronic diseases before they begin and to act swiftly to mitigate their effects if they do arise. Also, shared learning makes it simple to create AI-powered systems that help doctors make decisions. These tools can help professionals better evaluate cases, make care plans, and make suggestions based on proof. Using picture data from multiple modes, a learning model made by a group of doctors might help find cancer and other problems more quickly. When genome data from several study groups is put together, it might be possible to find genetic markers that are linked to certain illnesses. It is possible to do a more exact and focused study because of this [4]. Table 1.1 shows the applications of federated learning in healthcare.

Doctors may use joint learning to make sure they meet the specific needs of each patient. Federated models bring together data from different sources to make sure that every patient gets the best care possible. If a person has a certain type of cancer, a multisite oncology model might decide not to give them chemotherapy based on their genetic make-up, medical background, and how they responded to earlier treatments. A custom plan like this could lead to better outcomes with fewer side effects and more patient agreement. Federated learning enables professors from different universities to collaborate on projects without putting patients' privacy at risk. Privacy laws like GDPR and HIPAA make it possible for scientists to work together to train models on private data without sharing the real data [12]. The medical sector would gain from this partnership's potential to expedite medicinal breakthroughs. Operations performance

Table 1.1 Applications of federated learning in healthcare.

Aspect	Description
Improved Treatment Planning	Federated learning facilitates personalized treatment plans by analyzing diverse patient data sources.
Disease Prediction	Algorithms can predict the likelihood of diseases like diabetes or heart disease by analyzing electronic health records (EHRs).
AI-Based Decision Support	AI-based tools assist doctors in evaluating and planning treatments based on available data.
Faster Disease Detection	Radiologists use learning models to detect tumors and other abnormalities faster using image data.
Personalized Study Possibility	Combining genomic data from different study groups enables the discovery of genetic markers for illnesses.
Personalized Care Plans	Federated models ensure that all patients receive optimal care by considering data from various patient groups.
Privacy-Preserving Collaboration	Allows collaboration among researchers without compromising patient privacy, in compliance with privacy laws.
Operational Efficiency Improvement	Helps hospitals predict patient admissions and optimize resource utilization based on data from multiple hospitals.
Technological Challenges	Issues include maintaining model update secrecy, reducing computing load on local devices, and addressing model biases.
Potential Healthcare Transformation	Federated learning could revolutionize healthcare by enabling data-driven decision-making while safeguarding patient privacy.
Enhanced Medical Research	Predicts diseases, suggests personalized treatments, and improves diagnostic accuracy and operational efficiency.

(*Continued*)

Table 1.1 Applications of federated learning in healthcare. (*Continued*)

Aspect	Description
Expected Growth in Healthcare	As technology advances, federated learning is expected to gain traction and expand its applications in healthcare.

(Source: Self Developed)

is impacted by federated learning. Hospitals may operate more efficiently, anticipate which patients will require admission, and make better use of their resources by using federation models. A pooling learning system might be able to forecast the number of patients admitted based on information from many hospitals. This aids managers in scheduling the usage of their workforce and assets.

Even though it has benefits, setting up group learning in healthcare is hard. Technology problems include keeping model update secrets confidential while they are being sent, making sure that local devices don't have to do too much work, and fixing issues with model bias and convergence. However, improvements in edge computing, differential privacy, and secure multiparty computation are making these problems better [13]. Federated learning has the potential to transform the delivery of healthcare by enabling data-driven decision-making while safeguarding patient confidentiality. Federated learning improves several aspects of medical research and patient results, including operating efficiency and diagnostic accuracy, as well as illness prediction and individualized therapy ideas. Federated learning in healthcare is likely to grow as technology advances and fosters new ideas.

Federated learning is causing a huge change in the healthcare industry because it allows people to work together to analyze data quickly and securely, while also meeting strict privacy standards. The goal of this new method is to protect patient privacy while giving researchers access to the huge amounts of data that current medical processes create. Federated learning could change healthcare in many ways in the future. It could speed up processes, help find and predict diseases, and create personalized treatment plans, among other things. One great thing about shared learning is that it could help the medical field get better at making predictions. FEMI may be able to find trends and patterns that would be hard to see in a single file by combining data from different schools [18]. Many electronic health records (EHRs) may be used together with pooled learning algorithms to help better predict when long-term diseases like diabetes and heart disease will start. If doctors can find diseases early on, they might be able to stop them from happening, which could lower the number of cases and the seriousness of these issues. One more benefit of shared learning is that it might help improve the formulas that are used to group threats. By drawing attention to people who are more likely to have problems, this could help healthcare workers in optimizing the use their time and resources. This method of learning could be useful for advanced diagnosis tools and analytical tools that make predictions. In many areas, like imaging, cooperative learning has shown promise. By using a range of picture data sources to teach models, radiologists could make systems that can correctly find cancer and broken bones. Testing tools that are run by AI could help patients get better care by making assessments faster and more accurately. Another possible benefit of federated learning is that it may make it easier to find DNA traits that are linked to diseases. By putting together DNA data from many study centers, scientists may be able to find trends that help make personalized care better [23].

Individualized health plans are another area where joint learning is making big changes. Many times, common sense says that all people should be handled the same, no matter what makes each one special. In pooled learning, data from many sources about a patient is put together to make personalized treatment plans. A merged model with information from several cancer centers may look at a patient's genes, medical history, and response to previous treatments, among other things, before prescribing chemotherapy [19]. This personalized way makes it easier for patients to take their medications as prescribed, which is good for their health and behavior. Because shared learning fosters collaboration, medical researchers can also benefit from shared insights and ideas. Privacy laws like HIPAA and the General Data Protection Regulation (GDPR) are met by federated learning, which allows experts to collaborate on shared models without sharing raw data. This joint tool speeds up the process of medical finding by putting together data and information from many different sources. Federation-based learning could be useful for large-scale clinical studies with many subject groups. As a result, experts can arrive at more comprehensive and valuable findings.

Federated learning could help healthcare groups work better. A big problem for healthcare centers is how to effectively manage the flow of patients while getting the most of the resources they have. When pooled learning models are used to predict how many patients will be accepted, it's easier for the management to plan how to share staff and resources. With these methods, it may be possible to find trends and patterns in data from a number of hospitals. This makes the hospital run more smoothly, care for patients better, and make better decisions. Federated learning can be helpful in healthcare, but it's not always easy to put it into practice. Technical problems that need to be fixed include fixing model bias and convergence, making local devices' computers less busy, and making sure that changes to models are kept secret while they are being sent. Some of these issues are starting to be solved; thanks to progress in edge computing, safe multi-party processing, and differential privacy. Edge computing cuts down on delay and boosts efficiency by handling data closer to where it comes from. Secure multi-party computing allows more than one person to work on a calculation at the same time without sharing any personal data. In addition to hiding information that could be used to identify a person, this adds noise to the dataset.

As technology improves, it looks like shared learning will become more important in healthcare. Recent progress in artificial intelligence, blockchain technology, and private computers will make shared learning systems much safer and more effective [24]. As AI systems get better, they will be able to diagnose and predict things better. Blockchain technology might be able to keep a lasting record of all data transfers. This makes collaborative learning methods more transparent and trustworthy. Patient info will be kept safe; thanks to improvements in private computer technology. Federated learning could change healthcare by letting decisions be based on data while still protecting patient privacy. Its application in areas like organizational performance, personalized care planning, diagnosis accuracy, and prediction analytics demonstrates its wide-ranging impact. As new joint models and tools come out, federated learning will greatly improve both medical study and patient results. This new method could make treatment of patients more accurate, individualized, and efficient all over the world. This would be very good for the healthcare business.

1.4 Challenges and Limitations of Federated Learning in Healthcare

Federated learning has a lot of potential to change the world, but it has a lot of problems in healthcare. There are some problems that need to be fixed before shared learning processes and their health benefits can be fully realized. Data that are not all the same is a big problem. EHRs, medical images, smart tech, and DNA data are some of the places where healthcare data comes from. Formats, layouts, and quality vary across different sources.

It might be harder to train collaborative learning models when there is heterogeneity because the models have to be able to handle a lot of different, possibly inconsistent data [6]. Institutional differences as to how data is labeled and pre-processed make this problem worse, and they need complicated strategies to be harmonized and standardized. Communication waste is still a big problem. Federated learning sends changes to models from local devices or institutions to a central computer on a regular basis. The primary server puts together updates to make the world model better. This can take a lot of time and energy when working with large models or many partners. To keep federated learning working in healthcare settings, one needs effective communication channels and optimization methods that cut down on delay and data use.

Another problem is the difficulty of combining models. Putting together information from different sources could lead to model divergence and chaos. Differences in how the data is distributed locally can lead to poor model performance or prevent it converging altogether. Researchers are looking into adaptive aggregation algorithms, customized federated learning, and weighted average as ways to fix these problems [9]. However, getting many healthcare systems to work consistently and reliably is still a problem. Because of GDPR in Europe and HIPAA in the US, data safety and security are very important in shared learning. Federated learning stores data locally, which makes it less likely that data will be stolen; nonetheless, model changes are still a security risk. Advanced encryption, safe multi-party computing, and differential privacy methods are needed to keep data private and secure while it is being sent and gathered.

To solve these problems, people from different fields need to work together. To build and use federated learning systems, engineers, data scientists, healthcare workers, and lawyers must all work together. This partnership could lead to the creation of data formats that are special to healthcare data, privacy-protecting processes, and useful communication methods. Edge computing, which does computations closer to the data source, and blockchain technology, which handles data in a public and safe way, look like they could help improve collaborative learning [8]. To keep up with the changing needs of shared learning in healthcare, new ideas and better ways of doing things need to be explored and researched all the time. Federated learning could change how healthcare decisions are made based on data, but it needs to get past some problems first. Federated learning methods may work best in healthcare if people from different fields work together and think creatively. This will make sure that they are used safely and effectively to improve patient outcomes and medical study. Figure 1.2 shows the challenges and limitations of federated learning in healthcare.

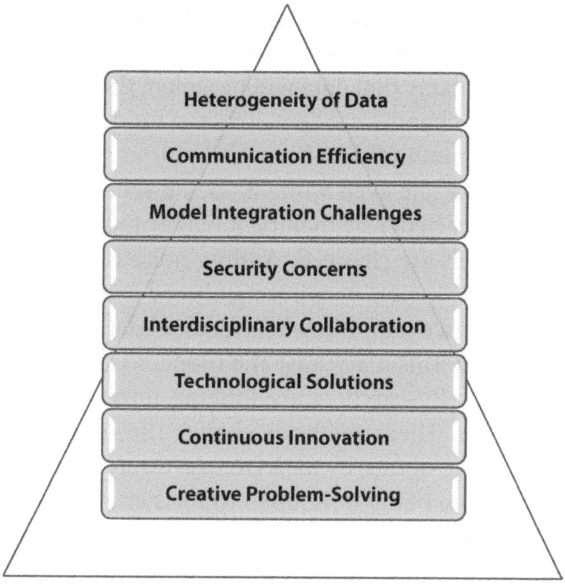

Figure 1.2 Challenges and limitations of federated learning in healthcare. (*Source: Self Developed*).

To use healthcare's full potential for shared learning, we need to keep coming up with new ideas and working together across different fields to solve important problems. It is hard to send model changes quickly between central computers and local nodes, so it's important to use communication methods that are both long-lasting and scalable. Because healthcare data is so big and different, it is very important to make these communication methods better, so that delay and bandwidth use go down. Researchers are looking into ways to speed up communication, like gradient compression and efficient update timing, because shared learning is becoming more useful in real-life healthcare settings. Getting different data sources to work together and balance is another big problem. Healthcare data can come in a lot of different ways, such as genetic patterns, random medical pictures, and organized electronic health records. To keep connection in a shared learning system, each type of input needs its own set of preparation and standardization methods [20]. To solve the problems and make it easier for different datasets to work together, we need more advanced ways to harmonize data, like ontological mapping and global information standards. Effective data enrichment methods may possibly make model training better by getting more full and accurate data from more sources. It is not possible for federated learning to happen if patient information is not kept private and secret. Even though keeping data locally in collaborative learning makes it less likely that data will be stolen, there may still be problems with how model changes are sent. To keep model changes safe, more advanced encryption methods like homomorphic encryption can be used. This keeps private data safe even while it's being sent. Differential privacy methods make security better by making it harder to figure out who someone is when the models are changed. Adding noise to the data makes this possible. Due to technological constraints, shared learning models cannot be combined. Divergence happens when regional data trends are different from the world model. This may cause the model to either fail to converge or to perform poorly. Researchers are looking into different ways to do adaptable aggregation. These methods change the update weights when the amount and quality of nearby data change. Strategies for personalized shared learning are also being developed to further enhance performance and accelerate the merging of models [25]. These approaches allow the global model to be fine-tuned to better suit the local situation.

Besides technical problems, organizational and legal difficulties make shared learning even harder to use. For getting around in the regulatory world, which has strict data security rules like GDPR and HIPAA, one needs detailed legal systems and compliance processes. All healthcare organizations should have a clear strategy for keeping data safe. These need to include ways to share data, keep track of changes, and get permission. Following all the rules and creating an environment where people trust each other and work together are important for joint learning to work. We can't say enough about how important it is for experts from different areas to work together to solve these issues. Shared learning in healthcare has caused a lot of complicated problems that need to be solved by data scientists, engineers, doctors, and judges working together. Working together with people from different fields is more likely to lead to new healthcare data forms, better ways to communicate, and software that protects users' privacy. Shared learning is more likely to work for healthcare companies if they work together to make rules and guidelines. It's hard to say 'no' when you think about the cool new ways that cutting-edge tech like blockchain and edge computing can be used for group learning. Edge computing makes model changes more efficient and cuts down on delay by examining data closer to where it comes from. Using edge devices, healthcare companies might be able to speed up and improve learning processes while also reducing the working load on core systems. Blockchain technology could be a safe and open way to control the flow of data. It is separate and can't be undone, so it could be useful for shared learning. Federated learning systems could be made even safer and more reliable by using smart contracts on the blockchain to automatically check for compliance and apply rules about how to use data. To keep up with the changing needs of healthcare shared learning, it is important to keep coming up with new ideas while studying. Federated learning will get better as new algorithms are made, old methods are improved, and new ways of combining technology are explored. Pilot projects and real-world uses can give useful information that can be used to improve and test these technologies, which can lead to more research and development. Healthcare might be able to get past its current issues and enjoy the advantages of shared learning if it encourages new ideas and teamwork. Federated learning has a big chance to make things better for patients and get people to make decisions about their care based on data. Before we can fully enjoy these benefits, a few things need to be fixed. Federated learning is able to get past these problems and become an important part of modern healthcare by working with people from different fields and constantly coming up with new ideas and using new technology. Because of this, medical study will be held to a higher standard, and healthcare solutions will be safer, more accurate, and of higher quality.

1.5 Future Directions and Innovations in Federated Healthcare Systems

Federated healthcare systems need tools that can be scaled up or down and connected to other systems so that different parties can work together. Systems that can safely handle a lot of healthcare data are necessary for both patient care and medical study. One of the best ways to make joint learning more private is to use private, high-tech methods. It seems like a good idea to use differential privacy and homomorphic encryption. Differential privacy safeguards individuals' privacy by ensuring that a single data point does not significantly alter the study's conclusion [3]. Differential privacy allows one to obtain insights without allowing private information to leak by adjusting data noise. Rather, homomorphic encryption enables mathematical operations on encrypted data without requiring its decryption. It doesn't matter if the data is intercepted during transmission; it remains secure and inaccessible to unauthorized users.

Healthcare systems that are linked together are likewise influenced by shared learning algorithms. Algorithms that can manage healthcare data, ensure model consistency, and address bias are critical. Customized federated learning modifies the global model to match the local data patterns [5].

Because of this, the model works better and is more exact. Researchers are looking into adaptive aggregation methods that change how much weight local updates have based on how well they work and how well they are made. This would make models more stable and reliable. A better system can help get models out there and teach people how to use them in medical settings. Edge computing lowers delay and internet consumption by processing data closer to its source. This makes joint learning more useful and able to grow. Deploying tasks to edge devices could enable healthcare companies to implement new models more quickly. Table 1.2 shows the future directions and innovations in federated healthcare systems.

Interoperability is also needed for federated healthcare systems. Protocols make it possible for systems and businesses to work together. No matter how skilled they are, interoperability makes it easy for healthcare professionals from different backgrounds to work together on projects.

Table 1.2 Future directions and innovations in federated healthcare systems.

Aspect	Description
Scalable Tools	Federated healthcare systems require scalable tools that can be adapted to various stakeholder needs.
Data Privacy	High-tech methods such as differential privacy and homomorphic encryption safeguard patient privacy.
Adaptive Algorithms	Customized federated learning and adaptive aggregation methods improve model accuracy and stability.
Edge Computing	Edge computing reduces delays and broadband use by processing data closer to its source.
Interoperability	Standardized methods and interoperable systems facilitate collaboration among healthcare entities.
Collaborative Efforts	Close collaboration among experts, IT professionals, and healthcare workers is essential for success.
Technological Advancements	New technologies enhance infrastructure and encryption methods to improve security and privacy.
Improved Healthcare Outcomes	Federated healthcare systems are poised to enhance security, privacy, medical research, and outcomes.

(Source: Self Developed)

The goal of this group effort is to combine the skills and information of many people to make models that are more correct and complete. Experts, IT engineers, and people who work in healthcare must all work together for shared learning to work. We can build strong, adaptable, and cooperative federation learning systems with their help. These tools could help improve privacy, security, medical study, and patient results in the future. Sooner, shared healthcare systems will work well; thanks to new technologies. Data will be safe with homomorphic and differential encryption, and it will be easy to build and train models with new technology and methods [11]. The use of compatible technology, which enables people work together, will make healthcare better and faster.

Federated learning can only be fully used in healthcare if there is a well-thought-out plan that looks at both the present and the future. Creating strong algorithms, putting in place cutting-edge privacy-protecting technologies, building systems that can grow and work with others, and creating places where different groups can work together are all parts of this process. Federated healthcare systems can only work if they can grow as needed and talk to each other. We say that a system is flexible when it can handle changing amounts of data and work in a range of healthcare situations, from small offices to big hospital networks. On the other hand, interoperability makes it easier for systems and groups to talk to each other and work together. For systems to work together, they need to use the same methods and data types. By making different data sources more consistent, these standards make it possible for a more integrated approach for working together to learn. Electronic health data can be shared; thanks to the Fast Healthcare Interoperability Resources (FHIR) standard, which was created by HL7. These rules might be much more helpful for shared learning programs if they were used by the whole healthcare business. Along with connection, new privacy-protecting strategies are needed to make sure that patient data is safe and stored securely. Differential privacy and homomorphic encryption are two well-known ways to protect privacy. Differential privacy adds noise to the data, so adding or removing a single data point doesn't have much of an effect on the research result. This could be a good way for researchers to get useful information without putting people's privacy at risk. On the other hand, heuristic encryption allows one to do mathematical functions on protected data. This means that no one will be able to read the data, even if they are stolen on the way, which is not likely to happen. Federated learning systems are more likely to run safely and keep private health information safe if these steps are taken. Sharing knowledge in healthcare will only work if complex programs are made to handle the huge amounts of different and confusing healthcare data.

The global model is changed by algorithms for customized shared learning to make it more like the trends in the local data. In turn, this means that the models work better and are more accurate. Adaptive aggregation methods give local changes different amounts of weight based on how useful and good they are. This enables us to know that the world model is using the best data available. Because healthcare data are so complicated and varied, these methods are necessary to fix issues with bias and model agreement. Researchers are always coming up with new ideas and getting better at old ones to make joint learning models more consistent and reliable. A strong framework is needed to set up and train shared learning models in real hospital situations. Edge computing is very important in this case because it studies data close to where it came from. This makes group learning more efficient and flexible by cutting down on internet use and delay. By moving computing chores to edge devices, medical facilities might be able to speed up the operation and training of models. They will be ready to act quickly, if any new health problems come up. Edge computing could make data safer by cutting down on the amount of data that needs to be sent to central computers.

An important part of healthcare shared learning is for stakeholders to talk to each other and work together. For shared learning systems to work, people who are good at IT, data science, healthcare, and the law need to work together. We can make sure that the whole system is managed, from its scientific core to its adherence to rules, if we all work together. Stakeholders may combine their resources, knowledge, and data to improve the level of healthcare and spur new ideas. Also, cutting edge technology like blockchain could make shared learning systems much safer and more open. Blockchain technology provides a shared record that can't be changed. This makes all activities open to the public and easy to check. This method could be used to keep an eye on model changes, deals for sharing data, and privacy rules being followed. Using blockchain technology and shared learning, someone could make a reliable and safe tool for medical study involving many people [20]. The opportunities and risks of shared learning are always changing, so new research and improvements are needed to keep up with them. Both pilot projects and full versions are useful ways to test new ideas and make present methods better. These projects found a lot of useful information that could be used to lead future work and help create the best shared learning practices for healthcare. Federated learning systems can stay ahead of the curve with help from the healthcare business, which can pay for more study and push for tests.

Federated learning is very good for the healthcare business because it enables professionals to work together on data analysis while still protecting patient privacy. Some of the big issues that need to be dealt with before this promise can be kept are size, connectivity, data security, and program development. Federated learning could have a big effect on modern healthcare by using edge computing, strong algorithms, better data protection methods, and flexible models for working together. Better, more specialized, and faster care for patients around the world might be possible if new technology is widely used and the healthcare business as a whole encourages professionals to work together. Federated learning could be very helpful for the healthcare business in the future, but everyone will have to work together to get there. The government should protect people's data and privacy while also making it easy for them to use shared learning. Healthcare companies should make sure they have all the tools they need and train their staff before using shared learning systems. To fix the issues that healthcare data brings up, researchers and writers must always come up with new concepts and improve methods and techniques that are already in use. If these companies work together to make a strong and flexible shared learning environment, it could lead to better patient results, faster medical research, and lower healthcare costs.

It is important to keep a close eye on the benefits and effectiveness of shared learning methods as they change. It might be helpful to look at the systems often to see how they can be made better, so that they meet the needs of both healthcare professionals and people. It is very important to get feedback from end users, especially from patients and doctors, to make shared learning models work well and are easy to use. Taking a proactive and flexible approach to developing and implementing shared learning may help the healthcare industry get the most out of it and make sure it lasts. Federated learning is the most up-to-date way to use data to make healthcare better. It could make things easier, make treatment plans more personalized, and make diagnoses more accurate. But the healthcare sector needs to solve some problems with algorithm creation, data protection, interoperability, and scaling first before it can fully enjoy these benefits. Using new tools, encouraging collaboration between different groups, and always coming up with new ideas may all help shared learning make modern healthcare easier, which could lead to better patient results and more efficient healthcare delivery. We still have a long way to go before shared learning in healthcare pays off in full, but if everyone works together, the trip will be well worth it.

1.6 Conclusion

In the future, connected smart technology could use shared health data to keep patients' information safe. Problems with joint learning need to be dealt with by education, health, and the law. Strong rules for data, cross-disciplinary study, and participation of all stakeholders are needed for federated healthcare systems. Federated learning will empower healthcare organizations to develop innovative tools and solutions, making it easier to personalize care to each patient. We need joint study funding to get around the problems with healthcare group learning. If lawmakers, data scientists, doctors, and lawyers all work together, they might come up with new ideas and ways to do things. Robust measures must be implemented to protect data to keep sharing it safe. Members of the same healthcare system can share data and work on study projects together through partnerships and consortiums. Lastly, health professionals might have to pay a lot for the software and hardware they need to work together to learn. Through shared learning and clever system interaction, healthcare groups make it possible for secure exchange of patient data. This idea says that professionals from the fields of medicine, law, and education should work together on issues related to group learning. Federated healthcare systems need a strong law foundation, a lot of money to be spent on study, and support from everyone who needs it. If the law doesn't make it clear, healthcare companies can't use joint learning. For shared learning to use medical data, lawmakers need to pass laws that protect those data. These rules keep medical information safe. Permission, safety, and privacy should all be in the rules. Laws that protect data, like GDPR and HIPAA, must be followed. By applying these best practices for data security, we can establish shared learning protocols that protect patient privacy and allow data-driven progress in healthcare. Second, to fix the practical and technical problems with healthcare collaborative learning, we need to support cross-disciplinary study. Data scientists, doctors, legal scholars, and lawmakers should all work together on funded projects. Interdisciplinary study could lead to new ways to use collaborative learning. Lawyers must check that these methods follow laws about protecting personal information. Data scientists may, however, work with doctors to create fast programs that sort medical data. By working together, we might be able to make data standards better, protect privacy, and make joint learning models for healthcare that are more realistic.

For shared healthcare systems to work, data need to be managed quickly and correctly. Data control options that help medical study and patient care must find a good mix between sharing and protecting data. Strong data governance systems need clear rules about who can view, use, and share data with others on joint teams. First, make deals about sharing data that spell out everyone's rights and responsibilities. Partnerships and consortiums help people work together toward common goals, share resources, and figure out the best way to use pooled learning, which speeds up the process. Strong data control that encourages openness and responsibility could make people more interested in and confident in shared healthcare programs. For the infrastructure, shared learning costs a lot of money and technology. For healthcare companies to meet their shared learning computing goals, they need to buy safe multiparty computation and edge computing options. By processing data locally, these options cut down on delay and improve model training. To keep patient data safe while it's being sent or collected, we must give priority to securing data transport technologies like differential privacy and homomorphic encryption. If workers have the right tools, federated learning might work better in healthcare.

For federated learning to work in healthcare, all stakeholders must be involved and enthusiastic. Policymakers, techies, patients, healthcare workers, and academicians are all part of this group. Patients might be more willing to give information for medical study if they know about the benefits and safety of shared learning. Lawmakers can support shared learning by passing helpful laws and making funding options available. Help could come from tech companies that make shared learning in healthcare situations easy to use. Healthcare federated learning needs a multimodal approach with strong legal rules, funds for research across disciplines, good data control, big investments in technology, and active involvement from stakeholders. Federated learning could improve patient results, speed up medical research, adjust medicine, and keep patient data safe if three major problems are fixed. As new tools and ideas develop, everyone involved must work together to make shared learning work best for improving healthcare.

References

1. AbdulRahman, S., Tout, H., Ould-Slimane, H., Mourad, A., Talhi, C., Guizani, M., A survey on federated learning: The journey from centralized to distributed on-site learning and beyond. *IEEE Internet Things J.*, *8*, 7, 5476–5497, 2020.
2. Boulemtafes, A., Derhab, A., Challal, Y., A review of privacy-preserving techniques for deep learning. *Neurocomputing*, *384*, 21–45, 2020.

3. Dwork, C., Kohli, N., Mulligan, D., Differential privacy in practice: Expose your epsilons! *J. Privacy Confidentiality*, *9*, 2, 12–50, 2019.
4. Hassan, M., Awan, F.M., Naz, A., deAndrés-Galiana, E.J., Alvarez, O., Cernea, A., Fernández-Brillet, L., Fernández-Martínez, J.L., Kloczkowski, A., Innovations in genomics and big data analytics for personalized medicine and health care: A review. *Int. J. Mol. Sci.*, *23*, 9, 4645, 2022.
5. Marfoq, O., Neglia, G., Vidal, R., Kameni, L., Personalized federated learning through local memorization, in: *International Conference on Machine Learning*, 2022, June, PMLR, pp. 15070–15092.
6. Mendieta, M., Yang, T., Wang, P., Lee, M., Ding, Z., Chen, C., Local learning matters: Rethinking data heterogeneity in federated learning, in: *Proceedings of the IEEE/CVF Conference on Computer Vision and Pattern Recognition*, pp. 8397–8406, 2022.
7. Nguyen, D.C., Ding, M., Pathirana, P.N., Seneviratne, A., Li, J., Poor, H.V., Federated learning for internet of things: A comprehensive survey. *IEEE Commun. Surv. Tutor.*, *23*, 3, 1622–1658, 2021.
8. Nguyen, D.C., Ding, M., Pham, Q.V., Pathirana, P.N., Le, L.B., Seneviratne, A., Li, J., Niyato, D., Poor, H.V., Federated learning meets blockchain in edge computing: Opportunities and challenges. *IEEE Internet Things J.*, *8*, 16, 12806–12825, 2021.
9. Qi, P., Chiaro, D., Guzzo, A., Ianni, M., Fortino, G., Piccialli, F., Model aggregation techniques in federated learning: A comprehensive survey. *Future Gener. Comput. Syst.*, 150, January 2024, 272–293, 2023.
10. Rieke, N., Hancox, J., Li, W., Milletari, F., Roth, H.R., Albarqouni, S., Bakas, S., Galtier, M.N., Landman, B.A., Maier-Hein, K., Ourselin, S., The future of digital health with federated learning. *npj Digital Med.*, *3*, 1, 1–7, 2020.
11. Syed, D., Refaat, S.S., Bouhali, O., Privacy preservation of data-driven models in smart grids using homomorphic encryption. *Information*, *11*, 7, 357, 2020.
12. Thapa, C. and Camtepe, S., Precision health data: Requirements, challenges and existing techniques for data security and privacy. *Comput. Biol. Med.*, *129*, 104130, 2021.
13. Yao, A., Li, G., Li, X., Jiang, F., Xu, J., Liu, X., Differential privacy in edge computing-based smart city Applications: Security issues, solutions and future directions. *Array*, 19, 100293, September 2023.
14. Sollins, K.R., IoT big data security and privacy versus innovation. *IEEE Internet Things J.*, *6*, 2, 1628–1635, 2019.
15. D'Ignazio, C., *Counting feminicide: Data feminism in action*, MIT Press, Cambridge, Massachusetts, United States, 2024.
16. Savova, G.K., Danciu, I., Alamudun, F., Miller, T., Lin, C., Bitterman, D.S., Tourassi, G., Warner, J.L., Use of natural language processing to extract clinical cancer phenotypes from electronic medical records. *Cancer Res.*, *79*, 21, 5463–5470, 2019.

17. Hu, Y., Niu, D., Yang, J., Zhou, S., FDML: A collaborative machine learning framework for distributed features, in: *Proceedings of the 25th ACM SIGKDD International Conference on Knowledge Discovery & Data Mining*, 2019, July, pp. 2232–2240.
18. Olukoya, O., Assessing frameworks for eliciting privacy & security requirements from laws and regulations. *Comput. Secur.*, *117*, 102697, 2022.
19. Vorisek, C.N., Lehne, M., Klopfenstein, S.A.I., Mayer, P.J., Bartschke, A., Haese, T., Thun, S., Fast healthcare interoperability resources (FHIR) for interoperability in health research: systematic review. *JMIR Med. Inf.*, *10*, 7, e35724, 2022.
20. Alzahrani, A.G., Alhomoud, A., Wills, G., A framework of the critical factors for healthcare providers to share data securely using blockchain. *IEEE Access*, *10*, 41064–41077, 2022.
21. Rahman, M.M., Kundu, D., Suha, S.A., Siddiqi, U.R., Dey, S.K., Hospital patients' length of stay prediction: A federated learning approach. *J. King Saud Univ. Comput. Inf. Sci.*, *34*, 10, 7874–7884, 2022.
22. Borgogno, O. and Colangelo, G., Data sharing and interoperability: Fostering innovation and competition through APIs. *Comput. Law Secur. Rev.*, *35*, 5, 105314, 2019.
23. Hoeyer, K., Data as promise: Reconfiguring Danish public health through personalized medicine. *Soc. Stud. Sci.*, *49*, 4, 531–555, 2019.
24. Bellagarda, J.S. and Abu-Mahfouz, A.M., An updated survey on the convergence of distributed ledger technology and artificial intelligence: Current state, major challenges and future direction. *IEEE Access*, *10*, 50774–50793, 2022.
25. Peng, H., Ma, S., Spector, J.M., Personalized adaptive learning: an emerging pedagogical approach enabled by a smart learning environment. *Smart Learn. Environ.*, *6*, 1, 1–14, 2019.

2

Federated Autonomous Deep Learning for Distributed Healthcare System

Rakesh Mohan Pujahari[1]*, Rijwan Khan[2] and Satya Prakash Yadav[3]

[1]Lloyd Institute of Engineering and Technology, Greater Noida, India
[2]Department of Computer Science and Engineering, ABES Institute of Technology, Ghaziabad, UP, India
[3]Department of Computer Science and Engineering, Madan Mohan Malaviya University of Technology, Gorakhpur, UP, India

Abstract

Federated autonomous deep learning has caused a dramatic revolution in the healthcare sector. Large amounts of data have been collected and stored by smart devices, helping people manage their health. In several sectors, artificial intelligence (AI) has demonstrated considerable potential not only for storing and analyzing health-related data but also for supporting early disease detection. However, communication breakdowns pose challenges to the efficacy of AI devices. The potential for data sharing across devices raises questions about data security.

Federated learning (FL) has been highlighted as a technique that can significantly reduce issues related to sensitive data security by minimizing data transfer. Combining techniques from Explainable Artificial Intelligence (XAI), FL, and AI can help alleviate a variety of systemic challenges. This chapter highlights the applications of federated learning (FL) in healthcare. Numerous studies provide insights into FL and its application in medical treatment. This paradigm is now being effectively used by specialists for diagnostic purposes.

***Keywords*:** Federated learning (FL), artificial neural networks (ANN), deep learning (DL), vertical federated learning (VFL), horizontal federated learning (VFL), electronic health records management (EHRs), cyber security, medical imaging

**Corresponding author*: rpujahari@gmail.com

S. Rakesh Kumar, N. Gayathri and Seifedine Kadry (eds.) Federated Intelligent System for Healthcare: A Practical Guide, (25–60) © 2025 Scrivener Publishing LLC

2.1 Introduction

Technology in the modern era has changed the globe in ways never seen before. It now includes more than just PCs, laptops, and cell phones. An abundance of internet-connected devices has led to the development of increasingly efficient "smart devices." Due in large part to its most well-known and readily available feature, "the Web," which provides desktop information in an intuitive way, the Internet has expanded rapidly in many domains [25]. A computer and an internet connection are all that are needed to access information from anywhere in the world. In terms of social networking, online banking, and educational purposes, the Internet has entered a golden age [26].

Household appliances can now be connected to a network, enabling them to function autonomously [26]. AI has been used to create intelligent conversational user interfaces for Siri, Alexa, and various other voice command devices. The real world and the healthcare sector have similarly experienced a technological surge. The Internet of Medical Things (IoMT) is another term for IoT in the healthcare sector. The reliance of the healthcare sector [43] on IoMT and AI has increased daily, aiming to lower healthcare costs while simultaneously improving the effectiveness and quality of care. IoT ensures that healthcare services are personalized by protecting each patient's digital identity. However, many health problems in traditional healthcare systems remain undetected due to their inaccessibility. Nonetheless, sophisticated, widely used IoT-based sensors [1] have made it possible to effortlessly monitor and evaluate patient data. This ensures that government systems treat the patient community equitably and reduces the monopoly held by private hospitals [17]. Sensors used in diagnostics are integrated with various wearable devices intended for patients receiving care in hospitals, regularly monitoring oxygen saturation and pulse rates [4].

Surgeries and other tasks are performed using trained robots, including patient care afterward and remote monitoring. This strategy can greatly minimize issues related to sensitive data security. Combining Explainable Artificial Intelligence (XAI), Artificial Intelligence (AI), and FL approaches can reduce a number of systemic constraints and difficulties.

As health-related data are highly sensitive and is shared for research, diagnostic processes, and illness analysis and recording, the healthcare sector is particularly susceptible to cybercrime and privacy concerns. The datasets from remote hospitals are often unbalanced, and their clients' interactions with the global server of federated learning are sporadic [12].

Federated learning benefits both patients and specialists in this situation. It provides patients with peace of mind, knowing that their private information won't be compromised by sharing it with unaffiliated organizations [5]. Moreover, it effectively anticipates hospitalizations related to cardiac events through signal processing of disease or patient data [30]. Additionally, federated learning models have proven effective in COVID-19 calculations and diagnostic analyses. They can identify a variety of anomalies by analyzing imaging models, such as CT scans and X-rays [23, 46].

This chapter summarizes the use of FL in healthcare. A variety of studies provide insights into FL and its application in medicine. Specialists are currently using this paradigm method effectively for diagnostic purposes. Universities have also begun incorporating FL into their curricula to educate students about its applications in healthcare. Nonetheless, many research endeavors have been unable to elucidate the weaknesses inherent in this methodology that may impact its efficacy.

2.2 Background

The Internet of Things, or IoT, is a new kind of Internet and a new generation of services [43]. It symbolizes a global information-gathering network that disseminates data over the Internet. In the United States, Kevin Ashton initially proposed the concept of the Internet of Things in 1999 [26]. Both the Internet of Things (IoT) and artificial intelligence (AI), often referred to as the "fourth industrial revolution," employ computer technology to simulate human decision-making. John McCarthy initially presented this cutting-edge technique in 1956 [1]. In the realm of research, the terms artificial intelligence and machine learning are sometimes used interchangeably [2].

Although machine learning techniques can discern patterns from available data, they rely on human understanding to differentiate between features [17]. Artificial neural networks (ANN) are utilized in deep learning (DL), a subfield of machine learning (ML), to mimic human brain function and extract information directly from raw images. These two technologies are now significant in every field [8]. Additionally, household appliances can function autonomously when linked to the network. AI has been used to create intelligent conversational user interfaces for Siri, Alexa, and other voice command devices [10].

The real world and the healthcare sector have likewise experienced technological growth [17]. The Internet of Medical Things, or IoMT, is another name for IoT in the healthcare sector [30]. Various wearable devices have integrated medical sensors for hospitalized patients, routinely monitoring oxygen saturation and pulse rates.

Using AI technology, even robots have been trained to perform operations and other tasks, including patient care and remote monitoring [3, 30]. As a result, sophisticated computing methods are needed for accurate processing, analysis, and storage [11].

To manage the process of data interpretation and utilization, strict regulations such as the Health Insurance Portability and Accountability Act (HIPAA) have been developed [13]. However, these sophisticated approaches were not designed to access massive volumes of data, and this vast volume presents several challenges [19], particularly for deep learning (DL) and machine learning (ML). The use of federated learning (FL) reduces the amount of data transmitted, significantly addressing issues related to sensitive data security [7]. Several systemic limitations and challenges can be mitigated by combining Explainable Artificial Intelligence (XAI), FL, and AI techniques [28]. The machine learning (ML) algorithm was first introduced by Google AI in 2016 [46]. Several authors have suggested using FL to train an ML model without gathering data samples from all users. In this way, malware that exploits various devices connected to the Internet of Things (IoT) can be discovered [31]. Mobile apps, transportation, healthcare, and military applications are just a few of the industries that employ FL, as shown in Figure 2.1 [44]. These applications can analyze data from the Internet of Things in real time. This process executes complex machine learning algorithms one at a time using powerful processing units with full operating systems [18]. This further reduces the need for communication by enabling asynchronous transmission [34].

FL is categorized into three divisions based on the increasing growth in this field: horizontal federated learning (HFL), federated transfer learning (FTL), and vertical federated learning (VFL) [30]. This study offers a review of the literature on federated learning systems and techniques, with an emphasis on how they are used in the medical field. This approach's primary difficulties, ramifications, problems, and possibilities for the healthcare sector are delineated. FL employs the concept of in-person learning for devices.

2.3 Use of Federated Learning

Related to its fundamental qualities, federated learning (FL) finds extensive use in sectors that employ smart devices (Figure 2.2). Here, we focus on a few of those important areas:

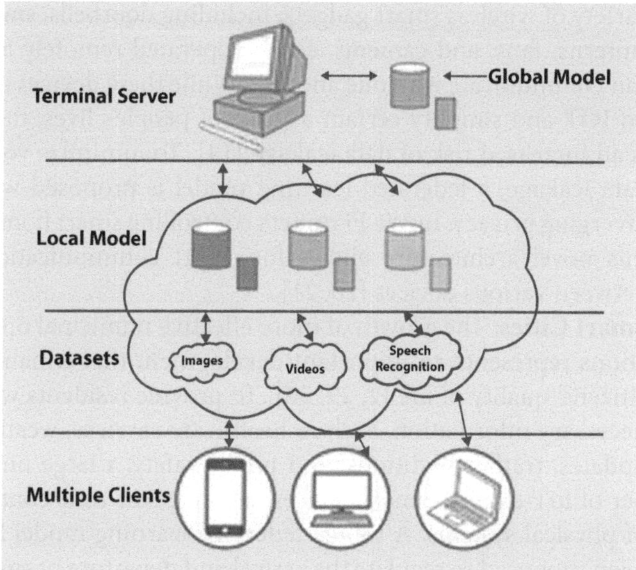

Figure 2.1 A frame of the algorithm that shows the federated learning process steps. FL is a decentralized ML technique for training and data privacy.

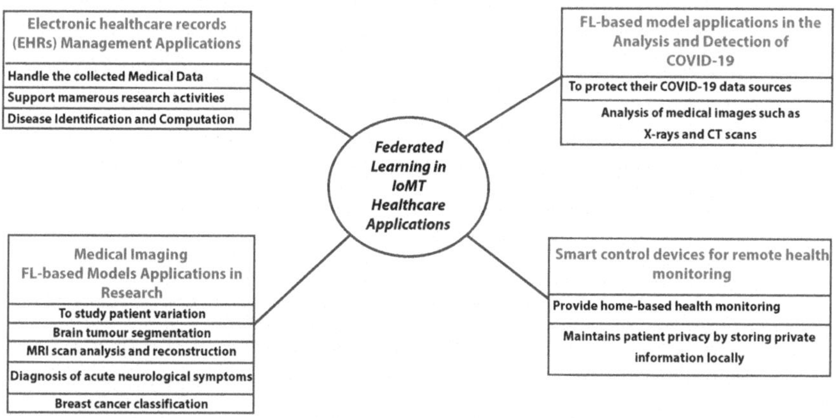

Figure 2.2 Internet of medical things (IoMT) and federated learning applications in healthcare.

1. **Smart homes:** Because of the comforts they offer, smart homes with integrated smart devices are much sought after. Additionally, they raise people's standards of living [15]. Through smartphone applications and microcontrollers, a

variety of wireless smart gadgets, including doorbells, smart lanterns, fans, and cameras, can be operated remotely and can communicate with one another. While these devices run on IOT and simplify certain aspects of people's lives, there is an increased risk of data leakage [14]. To minimize vocal data leakage, a federated learning model is proposed with diverging privacy. In Wi-Fi routers controlling smart homes, this novel architecture allows for smart communications between various devices [20, 21].

2. **Smart Cities:** The growth of more effective municipal operations represents an important development that enhances citizens' quality of life [2, 29, 36]. To provide residents with necessary information, such as healthcare services, weather updates, traffic conditions, and public safety, a large number of IoT-enabled smart devices facilitate real-time control of physical systems. A robust federated learning model has been proposed to regulate the arrival and departure of smart dynamic bus systems in the city, considering significant factors such as real-time traffic conditions and weather.
3. **Cybersecurity Issues:** Cybersecurity attacks, or cyberattacks, are becoming more frequent as smart networks spread faster. The use of fake cameras and forged routers in the Mirai attack serves as an example of the potential vulnerabilities. The highlighted security attacks emphasize the need for analysis related to devices used for diagnostics and medical purposes. Federated learning (FL) can be utilized to design and test models that protect smart devices from intruders and hackers [27]. A federated learning model specifically designed for smart devices has been proposed for near-future implementation, using algorithms developed with FeDML calculations. The purpose of the model is to detect unusual traffic patterns; thus, the recommended structure was evaluated based on Raspberry Pi to ensure continuous utilization.
4. **Driving on Auto Mode:** Because vehicles run on IoT, the day when autonomous driving becomes a standard feature of daily life is drawing nearer. Reliable autonomous driving system development requires constant real-time data interchange with the surroundings [29]. However, there may be privacy and data leaks from this transaction. Additionally, communication issues may arise.

This could result in the driving system reacting improperly to a moving car. Federated learning (FL)-dependent edge computing can help autonomous driving systems overcome these problems. With FL's assistance, foundational frameworks for models can be developed to accurately account for fluctuations in vehicle behavior.

The integration of technologies like blockchain related to vehicular networks enables the seamless exchange of commonly used local models for vehicles operating in autonomous mode, thus offering more reliable frameworks. There are several architectural layers at which blockchain and FL may be combined [30].

5. **New Generation Innovation in Industry:** The rapid growth of the Industrial Internet of Things (IIoT) has significantly impacted how ICT is utilized in the industrial sector [33]. The concept of Industry 4.0 emerged due to the availability and interconnection of real-time data [40]. The two primary challenges facing the Industry 4.0 ecosystem are inadequate data flow at unique sites and economic data inconsistencies despite the value provided through various IIoT implementations. To overcome these challenges, a secure permission-based network connected to various IIoT devices allows for the safe sharing of local models at the original stations and intelligent industrial equipment. These business companies are referred to as "super nodes" because they incorporate storage and computing capacity [35]. In permissioned blockchains, there are two types of transactions: sharing and retrieving data. Due to storage restrictions and privacy concerns, permission-based blockchains utilize federated learning to access linked data, monitoring all data sharing. The benefits of using FL in IIoT are validated by the projected model's outcomes [30].
6. **Healthcare:** Federated learning can also be applied in healthcare to address challenges associated with maintaining privacy while training models. It allows for the creation of sensitive and responsive models tailored to local conditions and real fluctuations in vehicle activity [37]. The authors developed an FL training technique that enables any institution to train IoMT models using its own records, thus ensuring the confidentiality of medical information [22]. Furthermore, a specialized federated learning framework

has been established so that medical facilities can collaborate in training model activation and interpreting CT scans of patients designated as testing positive for COVID-19 [41].

2.4 Smart and Efficient Healthcare Systems: Various Types of Federated Learning

The most recent advancements and applications in intelligent healthcare have led to the classification of FL algorithms into three categories:

(i) **Horizontal Federated Learning (HFL):** HFL client nodes train a distributed shared common model using local datasets. The feature space of each of these local parties' datasets is the same, but their segment spaces differ. The surrounding FL nodes may thus employ a similar artificial intelligence algorithm to train their datasets. Without specifically referencing local data, the server aggregates local updates provided by local clients to generate a global model. Within smart healthcare, one typical use case for HFL is the identification of speech abnormalities [39].

(ii) **Vertical Federated Learning (VFL):** Methodologies based on entity alignment, along with encryption techniques related to local dataset training, can be utilized to alleviate overlap in segment for distributed clients [42]. A collaborative learning model among insurance companies and hospitals in a smart healthcare context provides an example of VFL applied to IoT-based applications. For instance, two healthcare providers and an insurance company with different data qualities but similar patient bases can collaborate to train a single AI model. Data that may be utilized to support improved healthcare decisions include prior hospital medical records and insurance company healthcare bills [45].

(iii) **Federated Transfer Learning (FTL):** The process of computing feature values from many feature spaces into a single copy is known as transfer learning. Following that, local datasets may undergo training using this technique for presentation. When clients operate at the distributed level and exchange gradients at the server, encryption techniques are utilized to secure privacy. Through partnerships at the global level, multiple institutions can aid many patients by employing a wide spectrum of treatment options for diseases. Federated transfer learning is increasingly necessary for diagnosing illnesses in smart healthcare scenarios. This approach can enhance the effectiveness of the collective AI model, increasing the model's diagnostic accuracy.

2.5 Healthcare Integrated Learning in IoMT Apps

Federated learning plays a noteworthy role and contributes significantly to IoMT uses and applications within the healthcare sector. As illustrated in Figure 2.3 below, FL is beneficial in various fields, such as medical imaging, electronic health record (EHR) maintenance, sickness detection and diagnosis, and remote patient monitoring [47].

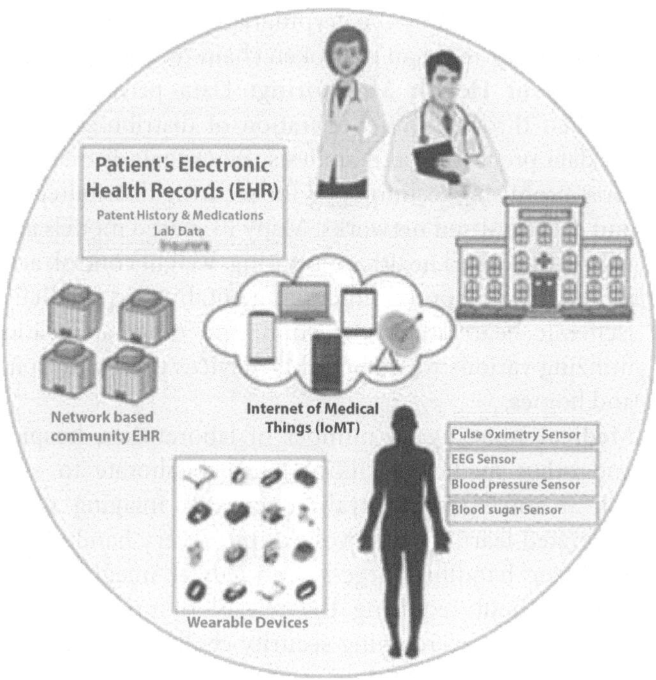

Figure 2.3 Uses of Internet of medical things (IoMT) and federated learning in the healthcare sector.

(i) **Electronic Health Records Management (EHRs):** The bulk of healthcare data and medical indicators are collected using IoMT devices positioned in various locations. EHRs are utilized in the healthcare sector to assist in various research projects, calculations, and illness diagnoses, in addition to managing the obtained medical data. A common issue with traditional AI approaches is the privacy and security threats associated with data analysis and transmission. Given its high precision and sensitivity, merely deleting information is often insufficient to protect patient confidentiality, which is crucial in the healthcare system since different entities may access the database for their own purposes. More reliable models related to medical data analysis, especially for highly sensitive data, can be obtained from FL. The collaboration of distributed entities for data processing and analysis ensures data privacy. Among the process steps, the greatest capability to protect decentralized networks and dispersed data is offered by blockchain. The blockchain stores data as a series of blocks connected by the cryptographic hash of the previous block, forming an unbroken chain [6, 24].

(ii) **Display of Health Monitoring:** Data privacy is safeguarded through the cooperation of distributed entities for data processing and analysis. Blockchain is one of the most promising technologies for securing distributed data and decentralized networks. Many FL-based models assist with lifestyle and health monitoring, weight control, activity detection, mood prediction, mental illness prediction, ischemic heart attack detection, and other applications utilizing various wearable IoMT devices used in hospitals and homes.

(iii) **Medical Imaging:** A number of laboratories, hospitals, and other medical facilities must collaborate to establish an intelligent, centralized medical imaging system. Federated learning has evolved into a very handy framework for handling large-scale medical imaging operations without requiring the release of private medical data, thereby overcoming security challenges. Since face-to-face FL model training requires more bandwidth due to the utilization of visual data, it also helps reduce network congestion. However, there is reported variation in the precision and accuracy of models based on federated learning for various purposes, including patient data variation, brain tumor segments, MRI analysis, neurological symptom analysis, MRI reconstruction, MRI studies, and breast cancer classification.

(iv) **COVID-19 Detection and Data Analysis:** Globally, the COVID-19 pandemic has impacted every nation and has progressed to the point that most countries now consider it a serious health risk. Remarkable results were achieved in the early diagnosis of this disease thanks to a number of innovative tactics. However, during the epidemic, concerns about patient privacy made it challenging to collect the large volumes of data needed to refine COVID-19 detection algorithms. It was discovered that federated learning (FL) was the best workable paradigm for preserving user privacy in a distributed model training environment. Consequently, through model training, certain companies could safeguard their COVID-19 data sources. In FL-based models, only gradients are conveyed, not whole datasets.

Many models based on federated learning have been developed for the diagnosis of medical images, such as CT scans and X-rays, in order to identify different abnormalities that aid in the diagnosis of COVID-19.

2.6 Federated Learning Based on Federated Mechanisms and Difficulties in Healthcare Applications

In the healthcare sector, learning through federated mechanisms offers a number of advantages, including cross-institutional collaborative model training, all while safeguarding patient privacy. However, it also has a unique set of challenges and concerns (Figure 2.4) [9, 16, 32].

2.6.1 Data Security and Breach

(a) **Privacy and Security of Data:** Healthcare data are extremely sensitive and subject to strict privacy regulations, including the Health Insurance Portability and

Accountability Act (HIPAA) in the United States, which covers personal health information (PHI). Throughout the workflow of federated learning, it is crucial to ensure the confidentiality of patient data. Federated learning can also create new opportunities for security flaws, such as model inversion attacks, where adversaries use the trained model to infer private patient data. Preventing these hazards is a difficult task.

(b) **Adversarial Attacks:** When incorrect parameters, such as batch size, epochs, or learning rate, are learned by deep learning and machine learning models, it can lead to insufficient or inaccurate learning. The accuracy of predictive healthcare models has been scrutinized since machine learning models are created using historical patient data and then evaluated on new patients. This is due to the growing possibility that adversarial instances may be generated using various data distributions. Furthermore, machine learning (ML) and deep learning (DL) models may be compromised by adversarial attacks, as well as other security and privacy-related problems.

(c) **Poisoning Attacks and Inference:** Using an adversary, an inference attack aims to obtain private data about a person or patient from a trained federated learning model.

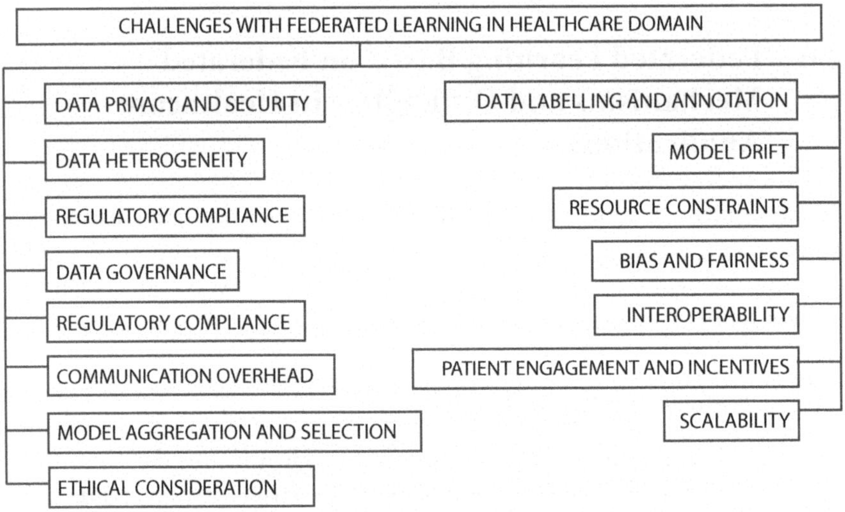

Figure 2.4 Shortcomings and various hurdles of federated learning.

This can be extremely concerning in the healthcare environment, as it could result in the unauthorized exposure of individuals' personal health information. In healthcare federated learning, three types of inference attacks are employed: model inversion, membership, and property inference. Malevolent players carry out poisoning attacks by altering their local data or model updates to undermine the federated learning process as a whole. Poisoning attacks can have a significant impact on the healthcare sector by jeopardizing the model's recommendations and forecasts.

(d) **Evasion Attacks:** Evasion attacks, also known as exploratory attacks, are among the most widely used adversarial tactics and are typically employed at the inference level. Unlike attacks on training data, the case may not involve altering the dataset used to train the model. A hostile actor attempts to outsmart the deployed model by presenting fictitious data samples or discovering the model's features during inference. The success of these attacks is contingent upon the adversary's knowledge of the model. Numerous strategies have been put forth to strengthen federated learning models' defenses against evasion attacks.

(e) **Insufficient Training Models:** Models based on machine learning can exhibit a range of flaws during training. Issues may include contaminated models, inadequate or inaccurate instruction, privacy violations, and unauthorized access. When epochs, batch size, and learning rates of ML/DL models are chosen incorrectly, inadequate or erroneous learning occurs. Human judgment is essential when utilizing ML/DL models. Therefore, during this stage, it is crucial to emphasize fairness, accountability, and system resilience. Challenges such as evasion attacks, system interruptions, network-related issues, and more may arise during the deployment phase.

(f) **Inversion Attack on Gradients:** This method of attack increases the likelihood of recovering and reconstructing input data by utilizing gradient information derived from model parameters in both trained and untrained cases. It verifies how configuration and various parameters impact the difficulty of reconstructing an input image related to increasing data and demonstrates that any input directed to a fully connected layer can be analytically reconstructed, regardless of other model design components.

(g) **Cases of Inversion Attacks on Gradients:** This attack method increases the probability of obtaining and replicating received data by using the data gathered from both trained and untrained model parameters. It examines how the data is analyzed and affects the complexity of modifying an input image from gradient data and demonstrates that any input routed to a fully connected layer can be analytically reconstructed, irrespective of other model design aspects. Genetic analysis allows medical professionals to customize interventions and therapies based on each patient's unique genetic makeup. This could lead to earlier diagnosis, more personalized medicine development, better treatment outcomes, and fewer side effects. To increase treatment efficacy and minimize adverse effects, it can also enhance medication selection and dosing. Researchers and legislators are continually developing innovative strategies to safeguard individuals' genetic information while enabling significant medical advancements.

2.6.2 Heterogeneity of Data

(a) **Data Sources Variability:** Data in the healthcare field are collected from a variety of sources and vary significantly between healthcare organizations and providers in terms of organization, quality, and format. These sources include genetic data, medical images, wearable technology data, and electronic health records (EHRs). Variability must always be considered to create a coherent and significant model in federated learning.

(b) **Imbalanced Data:** Some diseases or medical conditions may be rare in the healthcare sector, leading to unbalanced statistics. Federated learning algorithms need to be capable of effectively managing and handling these unequal distributions of data. This is particularly important as it affects the model's capacity to accurately forecast and recommend actions for these uncommon circumstances. It is imperative to utilize specialized strategies for handling imbalanced or balanced data distribution to ensure the efficacy and equity of federated learning-based healthcare applications.

2.6.3 Compliance Regulatory Mechanism

Regulatory and Legal Complexities: When adopting federated learning in the healthcare sector, compliance with regulations such as GDPR (General Data Protection Regulation) in Europe or HIPAA (Health Insurance Portability and Accountability Act) in the United States is crucial. Ensuring that the technology complies with regulatory standards can be a complex process that requires legal expertise. The healthcare sector cannot compromise compliance with healthcare regulations in order to secure patient data and maintain legal integrity. Federated learning must adhere to these regulations.

2.6.4 Data Governance

It is essential to establish clear governance frameworks and procedures for data ownership, access, and sharing across various healthcare organizations. This entails setting up permission processes and data usage agreements.

(a) **Agreements on Data Sharing:** The process of developing data sharing agreements (DSAs), which specify the conditions and terms under which healthcare organizations exchange federated learning data, begins with an examination of legal frameworks and best practices. These agreements cover data usage, security, privacy, and legal compliance.
(b) **Process of Giving Consent:** Examine the authorization processes that allow affected parties to freely agree to have their data used for federated learning initiatives. It is crucial to understand the ethical and legal implications of patient consent.
(c) **Ownership of Data:** Investigate data ownership from a federated learning perspective. Discover how ownership is impacted by data governance and how each participating healthcare facility defines, shares, and manages data.
(d) **Control, Security, and Access:** Explore methods for implementing security measures and access restrictions to safeguard shared medical data. Recognize the strategies

employed to protect data against breaches and unauthorized access.

(e) **Privacy-Preserving Techniques:** Investigate methods that maintain confidentiality while addressing data exchange and training issues, such as secure multi-party computing and differential privacy.

(f) **Regulatory Compliance from Legal Perspectives:** Ensure that processes and governance frameworks comply with applicable healthcare laws, such as GDPR in Europe and HIPAA in the United States. Recognize the limitations and regulatory obligations for the use and exchange of healthcare-related information.

(g) **Data Committees for Governance:** Consider establishing boards or committees dedicated to overseeing data-sharing procedures, resolving disputes, and ensuring compliance with data-sharing regulations.

(h) **Standardization of Data:** Ensure that healthcare institutions prioritize data standards and interoperability for data transmission and integration into federated learning systems.

(i) **Accountability and Transparency:** Explore ways to keep data-sharing procedures transparent and hold individuals accountable for any violations or misconduct. This could include reporting systems and audit trails.

(j) **Ethical Considerations:** Examine the ethical implications of data sharing, including justice, fairness, and the potential for bias in federated learning initiatives. Recognize the influence these factors have on governance decisions.

(k) **Documentation and Record-Keeping:** Investigate methods for documenting data-sharing operations and tracking access, consent, and usage of data to ensure compliance and transparency.

(l) **Stakeholder Engagement:** Involving a variety of stakeholders, including data scientists, legal professionals, patient advocates, and healthcare practitioners, is essential for the creation and management of data sharing protocols.

2.6.5 Process of Communication Overhead

(a) **Limitations on the Process of Communication:** To update the global model, federated learning requires frequent communication between participating institutions. This communication process can be challenging, particularly for universities with inconsistent network connections or bandwidth restrictions.

(b) **Bandwidth Restrictions:** Examine how restricted bandwidth affects the effectiveness of federated learning. Investigate methods for enhancing model updates and communication in settings with limited bandwidth.

(c) **Network Reliability:** Explore the difficulties caused by erratic network connections, such as packet loss and delay, and how these impact federated learning's ability to synchronize model updates.

(d) **Computing at the Edge:** Examine the concept of edge computing and how federated learning systems may utilize it to reduce network congestion and reliance on centralized data centers.

(e) **Protocols Related to Communication:** Analyze technologies and protocols designed to perform effectively in high-latency or low-bandwidth networks. Learn how these protocols can improve the effectiveness of federated learning.

(f) **Differential Updates:** By broadcasting only updates or model revisions, differential updates are a research technique that helps lower the volume of data transferred over the network.

(g) **Aggregation of Local Models:** Investigate strategies to reduce the amount of information that must be exchanged between institutions throughout the federated learning system by more efficiently aggregating local model changes.

(h) **Network Optimization:** Explore network optimization techniques, such as data compression, data prioritization, and adaptive communication protocols, to enhance communication reliability in federated learning.

(i) **Asynchronous Federated Learning:** Examine asynchronous techniques related to federated learning that may alleviate the burden on institutions by avoiding the need for real-time update synchronization concerning network resources.

(j) **Data Partitioning:** Consider the idea of partitioning data locally to lessen the volume of data that needs to be shared among various institutions during federated learning cycles.

(k) **Resource-Constrained Environments:** Conduct studies on the most effective ways to implement federated learning in resource-constrained environments, including remote areas or rural medical institutions.

(l) **Edge Device Integration:** Investigate how federated learning frameworks integrate edge devices, such as mobile or Internet of Things devices, and how this affects communication needs.

2.6.6 Model Selection and Aggregation

(a) **Secure Aggregation:** One of the most important components of federated learning is the secure and privacy-preserving aggregation of model changes. This procedure, which can be complex, employs methods to prevent information leakage, including multi-party computing and differential security.

(b) **Multi-Party Computing and Security:** To lessen the amount of data that needs to be shared among various institutions during federated learning cycles, consider the idea of partitioning data locally.

(c) **Differential Privacy:** Examine how differential privacy methods can protect the privacy of certain data during the summarization of model-related updates. Determine how this approach addresses individual contributions to the data by adding noise.

(d) **Homomorphic Encryption:** Investigate homomorphic encryption and its application in performing calculations on encrypted data, enabling the aggregation of model updates without disclosing private information.

(e) **Federated Averaging:** Learn about the process of federated averaging, which is commonly used in federated learning to aggregate model changes. Consider how privacy-preserving techniques may enhance this process.

(f) **Privacy-Preserving Aggregation Algorithms:** Investigate federated learning-specific privacy-preserving aggregation algorithms. The goal of these methods is to securely merge model changes while minimizing information leakage.

(g) **Centralized vs. Decentralized Aggregation:** Examine the differences between centralized and decentralized aggregation methods in federated learning and the security and privacy implications of each approach. Recognize the trade-offs associated with each method.

(h) **Quantification of Privacy Guarantees:** Analyze how to compare the levels of privacy protection offered by various approaches. Understand the methods for comparing and assessing the privacy safeguards provided by different techniques.

(i) **Scalability:** Evaluate how scalable privacy-preserving aggregation methods are, particularly when working with a large number of clients or collaborating institutions.

(j) **Privacy vs. Accuracy Trade-offs:** When selecting an overall approach, consider the trade-offs between privacy protection and model accuracy. The model's performance might suffer due to noise introduced by certain operations.

(k) **Real-World Cases:** Explore use cases in applications such as mobile devices using federated learning, healthcare, and finance, where model upgrades are critical.

(l) **Industry Standards and Studies:** Stay updated on the latest findings and recommendations from the industry, along with recent studies on federated learning, its integration with privacy preservation, and aggregation techniques.

2.6.7 Annotation and Labeling of Data

Obtaining tagged healthcare data for supervised learning within the federated learning architecture can be challenging.

(a) **Labeling at the Local Level:** Investigate ways to protect patient privacy while producing labels locally at each healthcare facility. This method might involve automatic tagging algorithms or local annotation by medical experts.

(b) **Secure Label Sharing:** Examine safe protocols that allow participating institutions to share locally generated labels or labeled data without jeopardizing patient privacy. Secure multi-party computing and encryption are two examples of this.

(c) **Aggregation of Labels:** Develop methods for fusing labels generated locally into a coherent dataset so that federated learning can be utilized to train the global model. This process must safeguard the data's accuracy and confidentiality.

(d) **Label Quality and Consistency:** Consider strategies for ensuring the quality and consistency of labels produced locally, as discrepancies in labeling procedures throughout institutions may affect the success of the global model.

(e) **Data Labeling Standards:** Investigate the implementation of standardized data labeling procedures or standards to encourage uniformity and precision in label creation between healthcare facilities.

(f) **Active Learning:** Examine how federated learning may employ active learning approaches to strategically choose samples for labeling to maximize labeling efficiency.

(g) **Research Privacy-Preserving Labeling Techniques:** These techniques protect patient privacy while facilitating the generation and exchange of labels.

(h) **Collaborative Labeling Efforts:** Consider collaborative labeling solutions that involve multiple healthcare institutions working together to share efforts and knowledge in order to classify data.

(i) **Review and Quality Control:** Establish quality control and review processes to ensure that labels produced locally adhere to the required standards for accuracy and relevance.

(j) **Moral and Legal Considerations:** Recognize the necessity of obtaining patient consent, adhering to laws like GDPR and HIPAA, and understanding the ethical and regulatory ramifications of data labeling in the healthcare sector.

(k) **Data Augmentation:** Examine methods for augmenting data that can enhance data handling, even when the initial dataset is small.

(l) **Benchmark Datasets:** Investigate whether the healthcare sector has any benchmark datasets that may be used to pre-train or fine-tune models, thereby reducing the amount of local labeling that is necessary.

2.6.8 Model Drift

Due to changing patient demographics, medical practices, and recommendations, healthcare-related data are subject to change over time. To prevent model drift, federated learning models need to be designed with flexibility in mind.

(a) **Changing Medical Guidelines and Practices:** Healthcare is a dynamic field where procedures, treatment recommendations, and medical practices are always evolving. For instance, new drugs, surgical methods, or diagnostic standards could be developed over time. Federated learning models may produce poor or inaccurate predictions if they are trained on outdated medical knowledge. Therefore, models need to be adjusted to reflect the most recent advancements in medical procedures and standards.

(b) **Patient Demographics:** Patient demographics, which include age, gender, and ethnic composition, can change significantly over time within healthcare facilities. These demographic shifts may impact the characteristics and distribution of medical data. For federated learning models to provide current and accurate recommendations and forecasts, they must be adaptable to population changes.

(c) **Data Distribution Shifts:** Within healthcare facilities, data distributions fluctuate alongside patient demographics and medical practices. These shifts can alter the statistical characteristics of the data. Federated learning models must be flexible enough to adjust to these distribution changes without producing inaccurate or outdated predictions.

(d) **Model Drift:** Model drift refers to the phenomenon in which changes in incoming data or inputs lead to a decline in a machine learning model's performance over time. This can be especially problematic in healthcare, as it may result in inaccurate treatment recommendations or diagnoses. Federated learning models need to undergo constant tuning and refinement to minimize model drift.

(e) **Transfer Learning and Fine-Tuning:** Utilizing transfer learning and fine-tuning is one strategy to combat model drift. Pre-trained models can be reinforced using federated data from healthcare facilities, having already been trained on large and diverse datasets. Fine-tuning helps the model become more resilient to changes in data by maintaining the pre-training data while allowing the model to adapt to specific institutional adjustments.

(f) **Frequent Updates:** To incorporate new information, policies, and procedures, healthcare organizations must frequently update their federated learning models. This ensures that the model's knowledge remains current and applicable.

(g) **Feedback Loops and Monitoring:** The inclusion of feedback loops and monitoring in the federated learning system can facilitate the early identification of model drift. The model itself may initiate retraining if necessary. Institutions can also provide feedback on the model's performance.

(h) **Collaborative Information Sharing:** Institutions share information collaboratively using federated learning. This cooperative approach can facilitate the model's adaptation to changes by promoting the exchange of novel medical practices and knowledge.

2.6.9 Resource Constraints

Some healthcare facilities may find it difficult to engage in federated learning due to limited computational resources. These resource constraints, which are often caused by differences in technology infrastructure or financial limitations, can make it harder for them to participate effectively in collaborative machine-learning projects. To address this issue, several strategies and considerations need to be taken into account to ensure that participants with limited resources can still make meaningful contributions to federated learning projects.

(a) First and foremost, resource efficiency and scalability should be prioritized in the design of federated learning frameworks. This involves creating machine-learning models that are lightweight and effective on devices with constrained processing capabilities. By requiring less memory and complexity from the model, resource-constrained organizations can participate actively without incurring a substantial computational cost.

(b) Secondly, adaptive learning techniques should be integrated into federated algorithms. For organizations with limited resources, this means allowing them to update their models less frequently using smaller sample sizes of data. Adaptive techniques make federated learning accessible to those with limited computational abilities without overwhelming them.
(c) Implementing hierarchical structures could also benefit federated systems. In these cases, larger, more computationally powerful healthcare institutions can initiate more complex model training efforts, while smaller organizations can focus on local updates or simpler tasks according to their capacities. This hierarchical approach optimizes resource allocation within the federated network.
(d) Model quantization and compression techniques are particularly beneficial for federated systems. These methods minimize model size and the amount of data transmitted for updates, making them especially helpful for clients with limited bandwidth and storage.
(e) Institutions should be encouraged to collaborate and share resources. Participants with limited resources could utilize edge devices or cloud computing services provided by organizations with greater computational capacities. This collaborative strategy facilitates a more equitable distribution of the computing load and enables all institutions to participate, regardless of resource limitations.
(f) Lastly, healthcare facilities with limited resources should explore funding opportunities and financial support to acquire the infrastructure needed to participate in federated learning. Partnerships between public and private sectors can provide financial assistance as well as technical support to bridge the resource gap and enhance inclusion in collaborative machine-learning initiatives in healthcare.

2.6.10 Bias and Fairness

The quality of federated models can be significantly impacted by the inherent complexity and frequent presence of errors, hidden values, and discrepancies in the overall database related to healthcare. Issues such as patient record-keeping, errors in data entry, or the lack of certain medical procedures or tests can result in missing values in healthcare datasets.

These missing values can lead to incomplete local datasets when using federated learning, potentially hindering collaborating institutions' ability to actively participate in model training.

Human errors in data entry, variances in the methods used by healthcare practitioners for data input, and updates in medical language and coding standards over time can all lead to errors and discrepancies in healthcare data. These differences may compromise the integrity of the federated learning model by introducing noise into the data. Such data problems also adversely affect federated model training; the inability to aggregate local updates due to missing data may result in global models that are biased or incomplete. Errors and inconsistencies may lead models to produce inaccurate forecasts or overlook critical trends in the data, which can impact patient care.

To address these challenges, federated learning in the healthcare sector requires careful data preparation and cleaning.

Data quality control procedures should be established before or during model training to identify and correct errors, inconsistencies, and missing values. Collaborating partner institutions can also work together to identify and rectify data discrepancies, ultimately improving the overall quality of federated datasets. Federated learning systems should also incorporate resiliency to manage noisy data and handle missing values effectively. Robust model designs and imputation strategies for missing values are two approaches that can help mitigate the negative effects of data quality issues on the performance of the federated model.

2.6.11 Interoperability

The use of disparate electronic health record systems and data standards by different organizations presents significant challenges for healthcare organizations striving to ensure data harmonization and interoperability in federated learning. These differences may lead to data silos, complicating the smooth integration and analysis of healthcare data across various companies.

One of the main challenges is the lack of common terminology and data formats among different EHR systems. Compiling and comparing data from multiple sources can be difficult, as various institutions may use different coding schemes, clinical languages, and data formats. This variance in data format and semantics can result in discrepancies and misinterpretations during the federated model training process.

To address these issues, healthcare data standards and interoperability must be improved. Initiatives like Fast Healthcare Interoperability

Resources (FHIR) aim to enable the integration and sharing of EHR data through standardized data exchange protocols. Achieving widespread adoption of these standards across all healthcare facilities may take time, as it is an ongoing process. Effective handling of data heterogeneity requires the incorporation of data preprocessing and mapping algorithms into federated learning frameworks. This involves mapping regional data schemas to a common representation, harmonizing a collection of data formats, and converting different coding systems using consistent methodologies. These strategies ensure data consistency and comprehensibility throughout the network, allowing member institutions to contribute effectively to the federated learning model. Furthermore, partnerships and cooperation between regulatory agencies, industry players, and healthcare facilities can aid in the harmonization of data. These collaborations may support the creation and adoption of data standards, foster the exchange of best practices, and provide guidance on achieving interoperability while complying with security and privacy laws.

2.6.12 Engagement and Incentives Related to Patients

It can be quite challenging to encourage people to actively engage in healthcare-related data exchange and federated initiatives in education. To promote patient involvement and confidence in these projects, it is crucial to address patients' legitimate concerns about the security and privacy of their personal health data with incentives and clear communication strategies. Healthcare organizations and researchers must prioritize open, ethical communication with patients to meet this challenge. Patients need to understand the goals, benefits, and potential drawbacks of federated learning and data sharing. To alleviate privacy concerns, healthcare institutions should be transparent about how patient information is encrypted, anonymized, and safeguarded throughout the process.

Another crucial element is the development of incentives to encourage patient participation. If patients perceive immediate benefits, they may be more inclined to share their data. Incentives can include individualized treatment plans, access to state-of-the-art medical services, or participation in cutting-edge studies that could enhance patients' health outcomes. The importance of patient contributions to scientific discoveries and improved medical outcomes cannot be overstated. Furthermore, obtaining patients' informed consent should be the top priority for data-sharing programs. Patients should have options regarding the extent of data usage, and consent procedures should be straightforward and easy to understand.

Building trust requires honoring the patient's autonomy and wishes. To ensure that patients' interests are protected and represented in data sharing and the federated learning process, patient advocates or representatives can be incorporated into data governance systems. Patient involvement in the formulation of policies and decision-making processes can also enhance trust. Incentives that emphasize the greater social benefits of using data collectively through federated learning, rather than just personal ones, may be more appealing to patients. Highlighting how these initiatives can accelerate medical research, improve patient outcomes, and deepen our understanding of diseases could foster compassion and a commitment to contribute to the greater good.

Ultimately, trust and patient participation depend on ongoing communication and feedback systems. Hospitals should proactively address any concerns or inquiries that may arise, demonstrate to patients how their data is used responsibly, and provide regular updates on the status of programs.

2.6.13 Scalability

Federated learning in the healthcare sector often entails cooperation among a wide range of individuals and organizations. Maintaining the system's scalability as additional institutions join these projects becomes a vital logistical concern. To handle the increasing volume of data, maintain high standards of service delivery and information sharing, scalability is crucial.

The design of the federated learning system is a key factor to consider when discussing scalability. Careful planning and a scalable architecture are required to manage the increasing network traffic, processing loads, and participant growth. Distributed computing frameworks, edge computing, and cloud-based solutions can all be employed to meet the rising demands.

Another essential component of scalability is effective communication. The volume of data shared between institutions can grow exponentially with additional participants, potentially causing delays and network congestion. Techniques such as data compression, batch updates, and prioritizing critical information can help avoid bottlenecks and optimize communication. Scalability should also be considered when designing federated algorithms. These algorithms should efficiently manage large and dynamic federated networks. Methods such as load balancing, asynchronous updates, and federated averaging with hierarchical aggregation can help distribute computational efforts across users.

As the number of participants increases, data security and privacy must also scale. It becomes more challenging to ensure that data is protected and complies with regulations such as HIPAA and GDPR as the number of institutions involved grows. A scalable security and privacy framework must include strong encryption, access controls, and auditing procedures. Coordination and standardization efforts within institutions can facilitate the onboarding process for new members. Developing interoperability principles, data-sharing policies, and standardized data formats can simplify the process of merging data from various sources. Sustaining the system's scalability requires continuous monitoring, optimization, and performance assessment. Regular evaluations of resource usage, system performance, and communication effectiveness can help identify bottlenecks and potential areas for improvement as the federated learning network expands.

2.6.14 Considerations Based on Ethics

Patient data are dynamic and unique, which presents a number of issues. Patients at medical facilities provide a plethora of data, such as genetic information, diagnostic images, and medical records. In a federated learning scenario, it can be difficult to explain to patients how their data will be used, as this requires complex translating mechanisms and principles of data science into language that individuals with various levels of health-related knowledge can understand. Clear and open communication is necessary to obtain patients' informed consent for data utilization and sharing in federated learning. Patients need to be aware of the purpose of data sharing, as well as any potential benefits (such as improved treatments or advances in research) and risks.

This process involves creating consent forms and other materials that are understandable and accessible while also being compliant with legal standards. Furthermore, patient consent needs to be explicit, allowing individuals to decide which specific details of their data they are comfortable sharing and with whom. Consent procedures may become more complicated if patients wish to grant consent for some research initiatives but not others.

Obtaining and maintaining patient consent on a large scale can present logistical challenges. Healthcare facilities must establish effective procedures for obtaining and recording consent, which may include integrating consent management into electronic consent platforms or EHR systems. Revocation and amendment of consent policies are also necessary, as patients' priorities may shift over time.

Patients have a right to know that medical institutions are handling their data with care, security, privacy, and protection. Patients must have peace of mind knowing that their permissions will be respected and that their data will only be used for the purposes intended.

It is a logistically challenging yet crucial step to ensure that patients are properly informed about and have given their agreement for their data to be used in federated learning. Robust data management systems, user-friendly consent procedures, options for granular consent, and transparent communication are all essential. Adherence to legal and ethical standards while emphasizing and centering around patients is very important in navigating these hurdles and maintaining the integrity of patient records and healthcare.

A multidisciplinary approach combining expertise in cybersecurity, machine learning, data protection, and healthcare is required to overcome these challenges. Additionally, ongoing collaboration between academics, policymakers, medical practitioners, and technology experts is necessary to fully realize the potential for data security and privacy while addressing all the factors mentioned in the context of federated learning.

2.7 Healthcare Issues and Their Solutions Related to Federated Learning

Federated learning in the healthcare sector raises many challenges; however, there are various ways to effectively address these challenges and find solutions. Let us now discuss a few primary outcomes as solutions to important recurring issues encountered by the healthcare sector when using federated learning [9, 38].

(i) **Data Security and Privacy:** The key to the solution is the use of robust encryption techniques, including homomorphic encryption, federated learning with differential privacy, and secure multi-party computing (MPC). These techniques protect sensitive data privacy by encrypting patient data during model training and aggregation.

(ii) **Inversion and Attack Models:** Model inversion attacks can be prevented by employing advanced strategies like federated learning with differential privacy, which introduces noise into the model updates. Use secure federated learning protocols and monitor for malicious behaviors to guard against these risks.

(iii) **Exploratory Attacks and Evasion Attacks:** Techniques such as input preprocessing, model distillation, and adversarial training can help the model defend itself against evasion attempts. Provide tools for detecting threats so that suspicious activities can be identified.

(iv) **Robustness and Model Training Deficiencies:** Implement strict quality control and model validation procedures. Consult with medical experts and regularly audit and assess model performance to ensure that all models meet international best standards and practices.

(v) **Resource Crunch Approach:** Develop resource-efficient federated learning models by utilizing edge computing and model quantization. Collaborative optimization can help distribute computational demands across participants to balance resource restrictions.

(vi) **Data Quality Issues:** Address these issues by creating data preparation pipelines that handle errors, inconsistencies, and missing values in healthcare data. Standardize terminology and data formats to enhance data harmonization and quality.

(vii) **Harmonization of Data and Interoperability:** Encourage the use of Fast Healthcare Interoperability Resources (FHIR) and other healthcare data standards. Apply data mapping and transformation strategies to harmonize disparate EHR systems and data sources.

(viii) **Patient Consent and Trust:** Establish clear and comprehensible consent procedures and resources. Provide patients with precise control over the sharing of their data and maintain open lines of communication about the benefits and risks of participation. Uphold strict security and data protection protocols to build and maintain patient trust.

(ix) **Scalability:** Create scalable federated learning systems by utilizing distributed, cloud, and edge computing frameworks. As more participants join, implement communication optimization strategies to manage the increasing network traffic.

(x) **Consistent Updates and Flexibility:** Establish procedures for routinely updating the model and adjusting it to reflect changing patient demographics, medical recommendations, and practices.

(xi) **Cooperation and Standardization:** Promote collaboration between healthcare facilities, regulatory bodies, and industry participants to create standard data-sharing protocols, interoperability guidelines, and best practices. This will facilitate the integration of data from multiple sources.

(xii) **Incentives and Patient Engagement:** Develop clear communication strategies to help patients understand the benefits of participating. Offer incentives that cater to patients' needs, such as individualized care, access to improved healthcare facilities, or participation in studies aimed at enhancing patient outcomes.

By implementing these strategies and solutions, the healthcare sector can effectively tackle the challenges posed by federated learning while capitalizing on its potential to improve patient care, medical research, and data-driven healthcare applications, all while upholding ethical compliance, privacy, and security.

2.8 Directions for Future Use of Federated Learning in the Medical System

Federated learning has revolutionized the field of smart healthcare systems by prioritizing security and privacy and facilitating collaborative model training across several decentralized data sources. It is anticipated that federated learning for intelligent healthcare systems will take several important turns in the future. First, the development of more complex algorithms and frameworks that can manage a variety of data types, such as real-time sensor data, genetic data, medical imaging, and electronic health records, will likely receive greater attention. The expansion of data modalities will necessitate more sophisticated and specialized federated learning models to handle the complexity of healthcare data.

Additionally, advancements in edge computing and the integration of federated learning with edge devices will enable faster processing and real-time analysis at the point of care, facilitating timely decision-making and action. Furthermore, it will remain crucial to enhance privacy-preserving methods like secure aggregation and differential privacy to ensure compliance with healthcare data regulations and foster cooperation across various healthcare facilities. Ultimately, federated learning is expected to shape the future of smart healthcare and lead to more individualized, efficient, and secure healthcare solutions for individuals and communities when combined with other cutting-edge technologies like blockchain for secure data exchange and AI-powered predictive analytics.

2.9 Conclusion

Moreover, developments in edge computing and the integration of federated learning with edge devices will facilitate quicker attention for post-analysis and care, enabling prompt decision-making and action. Improving privacy-preserving methods like secure aggregation and differential privacy will continue to be a top priority to maintain compliance with healthcare data regulations while promoting cooperation among various healthcare organizations. Ultimately, federated learning is set to shape the future of smart healthcare and lead to more individualized, efficient, and secure healthcare solutions for individuals and communities when combined with other advanced technologies like blockchain for secure data exchange and AI-powered predictive analytics.

Despite FL's potential to address security concerns, heterogeneity remains a significant obstacle that needs to be overcome. One proposed solution is Healthcare 5.0, a paradigm shift focused on patient-centric ecosystems and customization, representing a disruptive approach to patient care and system efficiency in today's rapidly evolving healthcare landscape. FL technology built on blockchain has also been introduced to offer medical solutions, enabling the protection and facilitation of essential daily tasks such as voting and shopping. This technology has proven to be a valuable tool, as it can quickly access insurance and medical information on patients and assist hospitals in making improved decisions.

As this chapter concludes, it is clear that federated learning has the potential to greatly benefit the healthcare sector moving forward by streamlining processes and improving accessibility across all locations. However, it also presents serious concerns regarding data breaches and ethical dilemmas. Nevertheless, technological advancements have allowed us to achieve seemingly unattainable goals. Innovations such as "organ-on-a-chip" and "lab-on-a-chip" are key in transforming the healthcare industry. The goal for the upcoming century may be to maximize patient satisfaction with healthcare facilities and expedite standard response times through further research and advancements.

References

1. Aminoshariae, A., Kulild, J., Nagendrababu, V., Artificial Intelligence in Endodontics: Current Applications and Future Directions. *J. Endod., 47*, 9, 1352–1357, 2021, September, doi:10.1016/j.joen.2021.06.003.
2. Arasteh, H., Hosseinnezhad, V., Loia, V., Tommasetti, A., Troisi, O., Shafie-khah, M., Iot-based smart cities: A survey, in: *2016 IEEE 16th International Conference on Environment and Electrical Engineering (EEEIC)*, IEEE, Florence, Italy.
3. Beasley, R.A., Medical robots: Current systems and research directions. *J. Rob.*, 2012, 1–14, 2012, doi: 10.1155/2012/401613.
4. Bertino, E. and Islam, N., Botnets and internet of things security. *Computer*, 50, 2, 76–79, 2017, doi: 10.1109/MC.2017.62.
5. Bibi, N., Sikandar, M., Ud Din, I., Almogren, A., Ali, S., IoMT-Based Automated Detection and Classification of Leukemia Using Deep Learning. *J. Healthc. Eng.*, 2020, 1 6648574, 1–12, 2020, https://doi.org/10.1155/2020/6648574.
6. Cai, J., Martorella, M., Guo, J., Liu, Q., Ding, Z., Giusti, E., 3D ISAR imaging: Multi-view image fusion problem. *IET International Radar Conference (IET IRC 2020) Online Conference: Institution of Engineering and Technology*, pp. 1200–4, 2021.
7. Campanile, L., Marrone, S., Marulli, F., Verde, L., Challenges and Trends in Federated Learning for Well-being and Healthcare. *Procedia Comput. Sci.*, 207, 1144–1153, 2022, January 1, doi:10.1016/j. procs.2022.09.170.
8. Cheng, Y., Liu, Y., Chen, T., Yang, Q., Federated Learning for privacy-preserving AI. *Commun. ACM*, 63, 12, 33–36, 2020, doi: 10.1145/3387107.
9. Dasaradharami Reddy, K. and Gadekallu, T.R., A Comprehensive Survey on Federated Learning Techniques for Healthcare Informatics. *Comput. Intell. Neurosci.*, 1–19, 2023, March 1, doi:10.1155/2023/8393990.
10. Deshmukh, S., Artificial intelligence in dentistry. *J. Int. Clin. Dent. Res. Organ.*, 10, 2, 47, 2018, doi:10.4103/ jicdro.jicdro_17_18.
11. Drolet, B.C., Marwaha, J.S., Hyatt, B., Blazar, P.E., Lifchez, S.D., Electronic Communication of Protected Health Information: Privacy, Security, and HIPAA Compliance. *J. Hand Surg.*, 42, 6, 411–416, 2017, June, doi:10.1016/j. jhsa.2017.03.023.
12. Elayan, H., Aloqaily, M., Guizani, M., Sustainability of Healthcare Data Analysis IoT-Based Systems Using Deep Federated Learning. *IEEE Internet Things J.*, 9, 10, 7338–7346, 2022, May 15, doi: 10.1109/JIOT.2021.3103635.
13. Gostin, L.O., National health information privacy: Regulations under the health insurance portability and accountability act. *J. Am. Med. Assoc.*, 285, 23, 3015–3021, 2001, doi: 10.1001/jama.285.23.3015.
14. Granqvist, F., Seigel, M., van Dalen, R., Cahill, Shum, S., Paulik, M., Improving on-device speaker verification using federated learning with privacy. *INTERSPEECH 2020*, Shanghai, China, October 25–29, 2020, https://arxiv.org/abs/2008.02651.

15. Jie, Y., Pei, J.Y., Jun, L., Yun, G., Wei, X., Smart home system based on iot technologies. *2013 International Conference on Computational and Information Sciences*, pp. 1789–91, 2013, 10.1109/ICCIS.2013.468.
16. Joshi, M., Pal, A., Sankarasubbu, M., Federated learning for healthcare domain pipeline, applications, and challenges. *ACM Trans. Comput. Healthcare*, 3, 4, 1–36, 2022, November 3, doi: 10.1145/3533708.
17. Khanagar, S.B., Alkadi, L., Alghilan, M.A., Kalagi, S., Awawdeh, M., Bijai, L.K., Vishwanathaiah, S., Aldhebaib, A., Singh, O.G., Application and Performance of Artificial Intelligence (AI) in Oral Cancer Diagnosis and Prediction Using Histopathological Images: A Systematic Review. *Biomedicines*, 11, 6, 1612, 2023, June 1, doi:10.3390/biomedicines11061612.
18. Konečný, McMahan, Yu, Richt.rik, Suresh, Bacon, Federated learning: Strategies for improving communication efficiency. *Comput. Sci.*, 2016, 1–10, Published in arXiv.org 18 October 2016, https://arxiv.org/abs/1610.05492.
19. LeCun, Y., Bengio, Y., Hinton, G., Deep Learning. *Nature*, 521, 7553, 436–444, 2015, doi:10.1038/ nature14539.
20. Lei, X., Tu, G.-H., Li, C.-Y., Xie, T., Zhang, M., SecWIR: Securing smart home IoT communications via wi-fi routers with embedded intelligence. *Proceedings of the 18th International Conference on Mobile Systems, Applications, and Services*, pp. 260–72, 2020, 10.1145/3386901.3388941.
21. Li, T., Sahu, A.K., Talwalkar, A., Smith, V., Federated learning: Challenges, methods, and future directions. *IEEE Signal Process. Mag.*, 37, 3, 50–60, 2020, doi:10.1109/MSP.2020.2975749.
22. Liu, D., Miller, T., Sayeed, R., Mandl, K.D., *FADL:Federated-Autonomous Deep Learning for Distributed Electronic Health Record*, Computational Health Informatics Program Boston Children's Hospital and Harvard Medical School ,One Autumn Street Boston, MA USA, 2018, July 2024, DOI: 10.1201/9781032694870, ISBN:9781032694870, Lab: VRD Research Lab.
23. Loey, M., Smarandache, F., Khalifa, N.E.M., Within the lack of chest COVID-19 X-ray dataset: A novel detection model based on GAN and deep transfer learning. *Symmetry*, 12, 651, 2020, doi: 10.3390ym12040651.
24. Lv, Z., Qiao, L., Hossain, M.S., Choi, B.J., Analysis of Using Blockchain to Protect the Privacy of Drone Big Data. *IEEE Network*, 35, 1, 44–49, 2021, January, doi:10.1109/MNET.011.2000154.
25. Mansoor, I., The medical uses of internet and how to stay current with internet. *J. Fam. Community Med.*, 9, 1, 63, 2002, doi: 10.4103/2230-8229.98057 PMID:23008665.
26. Mohamed, K.S., The Era of Internet of Things: Towards a Smart World, Springer International Publishing, ISBN 978-3-030-18132-1 ISBN 978-3-030-18133-8 (eBook) © Springer Nature Switzerland AG 2019, https://doi.org/10.1007/978-3-030-18133-8.
27. Moradipari, A., Tucker, N., Zhang, T., Cezar, G., Alizadeh, M., Mobility-Aware Smart Charging of Electric Bus Fleets, in: *2020 IEEE Power &*

Energy Society General Meeting (PESGM), IEEE, 2020, doi:10.1109/PESGM41954.2020.9281897.

28. Rahman, A., Hossain, M.S., Muhammad, G., Kundu, D., Debnath, T., Rahman, M., Khan, M.S.I., Tiwari, P., Band, S.S., Federated learning-based AI approaches in smart healthcare: Concepts, taxonomies, challenges and open issues. *Cluster Comput.*, 26, 4, 2271–2311, 2023, August, doi:10.100710586-022- 03658-4.
29. Rajab, H. and Cinkelr, T., IoT based Smart Cities, in: *2018 International Symposium on Networks, Computers and Communications (ISNCC)*, IEEE, Rome, 2018.
30. Rani, S., Kataria, A., Kumar, S., Tiwari, P., Federated learning for secure IoMT applications in smart healthcare systems: A comprehensive review. *Knowledge-Based Syst.*, 274, 110658, 2023, August, doi: 10.1016/j.knosys.2023.110658.
31. Rey, V., SaÅLnchez, P.M.S., CeldraÅLn, A.H., Bovet, G., Jaggi, M., Federated learning for malware detection in IoT devices, 2021, arXiv preprint, arXiv:2104.09994v3 [cs.CR] 19 Nov 2021.
32. Rieke, N., Hancox, J., Li, W., Milletari, F., Roth, H.R., Albarqouni, S., Bakas, S., Galtier, M.N., Landman, B.A., Maier-Hein, K., Ourselin, S., Sheller, M., Summers, R.M., Trask, A., Xu, D., Baust, M., Cardoso, M.J., The future of digital health with federated learning. *NPJ Digital Med.*, 3, 1, 119, 2020, September 14, doi:10.103841746-020-00323-1.
33. Sharma, S., Xing, C., Liu, Y., Kang, Y., Secure and Efficient Federated Transfer Learning, in: *2019 IEEE International Conference on Big Data (Big Data)*, IEEE, Los Angeles, CA, USA, 2019, 10.1109/BigData47090.2019.9006280.
34. Shokri, R. and Shmatikov, V., Privacy-preserving deep learning. *Proceedings of the 22nd ACM SIGSAC Conference on Computer and Communications Security*, pp. 1310–21, 2015.
35. Srivastava, U.C., Singh, A., Kumar, D.K.S., Intracranial Haemorrhage Detection Using Neural Network Based Methods with Federated Learning, arXiv:2005.08644v3 [cs.CV] 17 Mar 2022, https://arxiv.org/pdf/2005.08644.2022, May 2020, DOI: 10.13140/RG.2.2.10157.31206, License: CC BY-SA 4.0, Lab: Next Tech Lab.
36. Syed, A.S., Sierra-Sosa, D., Kumar, A., Elmaghraby, A., IoT in Smart Cities: A Survey of Technologies, Practices and Challenges. *Smart Cities*, 4, 2, 429–475, 2021, March 30, doi:10.3390martcities4020024.
37. Warin, K., Limprasert, W., Suebnukarn, S., Jinaporntham, S., Jantana, P., Vicharueang, S., AI-based analysis of oral lesions using novel deep convolutional neural networks for early detection of oral cancer. *PLoS One*, 17, 8, 1–14, 2022.
38. Wen, J., Zhang, Z., Lan, Y., Cui, Z., Cai, J., Zhang, W., A survey on federated learning: Challenges and applications. *Int. J. Mach. Learn. Cybern.*, 14, 2, 513–535, 2023, February, doi:10.100713042-022-01647-y PMID:36407495.

39. Wu, Q., Chen, X., Zhou, Z., Zhang, J., Fedhome. Cloud-edge based personalized federated learning for in-home health monitoring. *IEEE Trans. Mob. Comput.*, 21, 8, 2818–32, n.d.
40. Xu, L.D., Xu, E.L., Li, L., Industry 4.0: State of the art and future trends. *Int. J. Prod. Res.*, 56, 8, 2941–2962, 2018, April 18, doi: 10.1080/00207543.2018.1444806.
41. Yan, B., Wang, J., Cheng, J., Zhou, Y., Zhang, Y., Yang, Y., Experiments of Federated Learning for COVID-19 Chest X-ray Images, in: *Advances in Artificial Intelligence and Security*, Springer International Publishing, Cham, 2021, doi:10.1007/978-3-030-78618-2_4.
42. Yang, S., Ren, B., Zhou, X., Liu, L., *Parallel Distributed Logistic Regression for Vertical Federated Learning without Third-Party Coordinator*, IJCAI-19 Workshop on Federated Machine Learning for User Privacy and Data Confidentiality (IJCAI (FML)) 2019, 22 November 2019, Published in arXiv.org, Computer Science.
43. Yaqoob, I., Ahmed, E., Hashem, I.A.T., Ahmed, A.I.A., Gani, A., Imran, M., Guizani, M., Internet of things architecture: Recent advances, taxonomy, requirements, and open challenges. *IEEE Wireless Commun.*, 24, 3, 10–16, 22 June 2017, Computer Science, Engineering, Environmental Science.
44. Yu, H., Liu, Z., Liu, Y., Chen, T., Cong, M., Weng, X., Niyato, D., Yang, Q., A fairness-aware incentive scheme for federated learning. *Proceedings of the AAAI/ACM Conference on AI, Ethics, and Society*, pp. 393–9, 2020, 10.1145/3375627.3375840.
45. Zhang, T., He, C., Ma, T., Gao, L., Ma, M., Avestimehr, S., Federated Learning for Internet of Things, in: *Proceedings of the 19th ACM Conference on Embedded Networked Sensor Systems*, ACM, Coimbra Portugal, 2021, 10.1145/3485730.3493444.
46. Zhang, W., Zhou, T., Lu, Q., Wang, X., Zhu, C., Sun, H., Wang, Z., Lo, S.K., Wang, F.-Y., Dynamic-fusion-based federated learning for COVID-19 detection. *IEEE Internet Things J.*, 8, 8, 15884–15891, 2021, doi:10.1109/JIOT.2021.3056185 PMID:35663640.
47. Zhao, Y., Li, M., Lai, L., Suda, N., Civin, D., Chandra, V., Federated Learning with Non-IID Data. *Neurocomputing*, 465, 4–2, 371–390, 2018, September 2021, DOI: 10.1016/j.neucom.2021.07.098.

3

Intelligent Fusion: Federated Learning and Blockchain in Sustainable Healthcare 5.0

Pankaj Kumar Jadwal and Hemant Kumar Saini*

Amity University Rajasthan, Jaipur, India

Abstract

The Internet of Healthcare Things (IoHT) has experienced rapid evolution in recent years, on a global scale. Because of the massive deployment and complexity of IoMT networks, security and privacy are major problems. The capabilities and amenities of healthcare 5.0 have been greatly improved by machine learning (ML) and blockchain (BC) technologies, giving rise to a new field called "Smart Healthcare." A smart healthcare system can help prevent long-term harm by detecting issues early on. Patients' quality of life will be improved, and stress and medical expenses will be decreased. Intelligent and interactive healthcare is one of the many information technology functionalities made possible by the Internet of Medical Things. To train a potent machine learning model, consolidating medical data into a single storage site, however, brings up more focused privacy, ownership, and regulatory issues. Federated learning (FL) uses a centralized aggregate server to spread a global learning model, which solves the above issues. The local participant maintains control over patient data while guaranteeing data security and confidentiality. The research on blockchain technology and federated learning in healthcare is thoroughly examined in this chapter. This chapter describes how to use medical sensors to monitor patients and use blockchain technology and the FL approach to forecast diseases and take appropriate action on a regular basis.

***Keywords*:** IOHT, sustainable healthcare, blockchain, federated learning, EHR, EMR, smart contracts

**Corresponding author*: hemantrhce@rediffmail.com

S. Rakesh Kumar, N. Gayathri and Seifedine Kadry (eds.) Federated Intelligent System for Healthcare: A Practical Guide, (61–80) © 2025 Scrivener Publishing LLC

3.1 Introduction

A major advancement in healthcare delivery, digital healthcare transformation is marked by cutting-edge technologies, individualized care, and a patient-centric mindset. Federated learning (FL) is a paradigm shift in learning that uses collective training of algorithms—without moving data itself—to address concerns about data privacy and governance. Despite being initially designed for use in a range of scenarios, including mobile and edge device use cases, it has recently acquired popularity in the healthcare sector [1]. A successful FL implementation could have a major impact on the ability to practice precision medicine on a large scale by producing models that respect governance and privacy issues, generate objective judgments, accurately represent an individual's physiology, and are sensitive to rare illnesses.

To ensure that the algorithm is operating as effectively as feasible without jeopardizing patient safety or privacy, FL still requires meticulous technical analysis. Nonetheless, it can get beyond the drawbacks of methods that depend on a single, centralized data source [2]. Numerous huge datasets have been collected from multiple organizations. Though these are large data lakes, they hold great potential for commercial purposes—as was the case with Merge Healthcare's acquisition of International Business Machines—or to use the data as a resource for advancements in science and business [3].

In the setting of electronic health records (EHR), FL can be used to identify and characterize clinically comparable patients as well as predict hospitalizations due to cardiac events, death, and length of ICU stay [4]. In the field of medical imaging, FL's value and advantages have also been demonstrated for both MRI whole-brain segmentation and the segmentation of brain tumors. MRI classifiers identify biomarkers using such methodology and have been introduced as a unique strategy in the context of COVID-19. Global FL establishment may guarantee clinical judgments of the highest caliber, independent of the patient's treatment site.

The ML-based prescriptions can be generated for rural patients where significantly high-quality data have been utilized. However, because health information is sensitive, security and privacy issues have become increasingly important in recent years, raising ethical and legal concerns [5]. The FL idea known as "collaborative learning" refers to the process of teaching algorithms using decentralized sample data among several servers or devices without requiring the sharing of actual data [6].

Compared to other widely used techniques, such as uploading samples to servers or storing data samples in a distributed architecture, this approach is very different. Stronger modeling developed from the other side without data sharing results in more secure solutions with greater data access rights [7]. FL is utilized in numerous IoT and digital education applications [8]. FL is quite dependable because of its application and the many experiments that have already been carried out [9]. Despite FL's great promise, there are still a number of unsolved technical questions about hardware, software, platforms, and a host of other subjects related to data security and access. The rapidly developing FL concept aims to improve data processing and privacy for a number of industries [10]. Collaboratively creating machine learning models with decentralized data are made feasible by a new method called federated learning. The Gboard query recommendation use case originated with Google [11], where the machine auto-learns the user's words through the history of local words that the users type, which is embedded in their own language design.

Local models were combined by a central coordinator to create a global model, which was then distributed to each participant for additional instruction or inference. Facilitating participant cooperation is the primary goal of FL, as it enables them to jointly construct a better model than they could individually. FL is currently in its early stages of development and is experiencing new hurdles in 6G situations, despite its enormous potential for AI-enabled 6G. Researchers face moral conundrums while handling medical records. It is true that patient information that could be dangerous to reveal is contained in medical records. Recently, due to breaches of private health records of patients, new vulnerabilities have emerged [12]. Medical facilities are reluctant to share medical records as a result [13].

Medical data set requests and use require time-consuming processes from researchers, frequently at the expense of effectively furthering their work. The dilemma is made worse for data scientists who work with huge, diverse data sets that are dispersed among various websites. Medical data processing has historically included anonymization techniques [14]. Patients should be aware of how and by whom their data are used, according to data transparency [15]. Additionally, usage permission grants data subjects the freedom to choose when and how their information is used [16]. Regrettably, when handling patient data, these issues are frequently overlooked, and if data sets are anonymized, consent may occasionally be taken for granted [17]. The big-data era has complicated matters further by dispersing and processing data sets by several, frequently non-communicating parties [18].

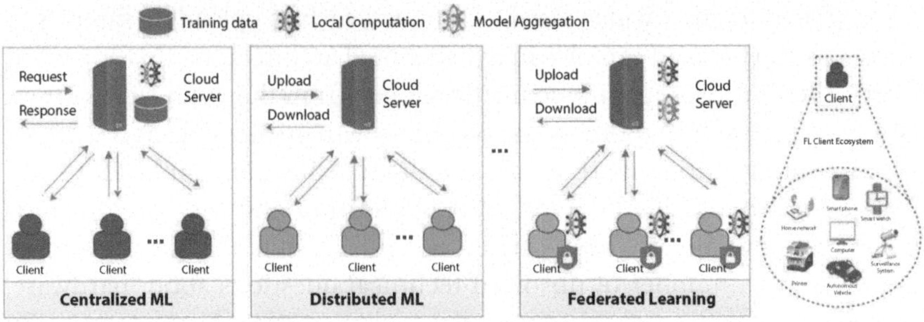

Figure 3.1 Types of learning paradigms in healthcare.

As a result, two technologies that address some of the aforementioned problems independently arose. A paradigm known as federated learning (FL) was developed to minimize the risk of exposing sensitive data when training machine learning (ML) models across decentralized devices [19]. In contrast, blockchain has emerged as a technology that provides previously unheard-of assurances of dependability and usage transparency in decentralized environments [20], as seen in Figure 3.1.

3.2 Distributed Data in Healthcare

Numerous opportunities exist for enhancing care quality and cutting expenses with medical data [21]. Conversely, healthcare units also have their data in an ambiguous and destructed form, which needs to be processed before training [21]. In response to these conditions, FL evolved, offering a means of minimizing data transfers while training ML models in heterogeneous and dispersed environments [13, 14, 20]. Due to the delicate nature of the data processed, it has been employed in healthcare settings [32].

Comparatively, because the blockchain offers guarantees of use (immutability and transparency), it is implemented in healthcare [7, 22]. Here the synergy of both the blockchain and FL motivates a new adaptive decision model where patients can receive treatment as early as possible.

3.2.1 FL Algorithms

FL includes a range of implementations suited to different conditions and situations. We examine the three main FL implementation types in more detail below: federated transfer learning, vertical FL, and horizontal FL.

Horizontal Federated Learning (HFL): HFL entails training models across several clients or devices with comparable data distributions that are not allowed to share raw data because of legal or privacy issues. With this method, every client uses its own data to train a local model, sharing with a central server only model updates, like gradients or model parameters [23]. After compiling these modifications, the server distributes a revised global model to clients for further improvement. This repeated process is carried out until convergence is attained. HFL is especially well-suited when data are dispersed among devices or clients with comparable features, such as mutual wisdom in IoT at the edges or electroencephalography [23, 24]. In order to achieve accurate results, horizontal federated learning frequently faces difficulties with model aggregation strategies, communication efficiency, and privacy-preserving procedures [25].

Vertical Federated Learning (VFL): VFL deals with situations in which data are dispersed across several parties with complementary characteristics but direct sharing is not possible due to proprietary or privacy issues. Vertical federated learning works with data that have distinct but complementary qualities, as opposed to horizontal federated learning, which concentrates on data with comparable distributions [26]. The objective of vertical federated learning is to mutually instruct raw data, with each participant holding a subset of features pertinent to the learning task. To facilitate calculation with cryptographic data, homomorphic encryption and secure multi-party computation (SMPC) algorithms are frequently used. By using such methods, parties compute the updates without revealing personal data. Some applications for vertical federated learning are seen in hospitals and labs where patient data need to be maintained in privacy [27].

Federated Relocate Learning (FRL): FRL is a learning paradigm in federated environments, where models are trained using information from similar tasks or domains across several decentralized datasets. Federated transfer learning includes collecting knowledge from several decentralized datasets with pre-trained models to outperform existing models. In FRL, a base model is initiated from scratch or with a pre-trained model, and it is then refined by aggregating model updates from decentralized clients. This methodology enables the utilization of insights from heterogeneous data sources while accounting for differences in data patterns and characteristics [28]. FRL is impactful in situations, such as ECG, where there are no chances of labeled data and where the data are often in ambiguous form [28].

3.2.2 Blockchain Approaches

In order to address the consensus issue in a decentralized, trustless network, blockchain was developed [29]. In other words, blockchain offers a mathematically sound means of confirming that the data we keep on our device matches the data that other peers hold, even in a distrusting peer network. Blockchain was initially created with financial applications in mind but has swiftly expanded to other fields [30].

The qualities of blockchain—decentralization, immutability, and transparency—have been particularly useful in the medical field, where it has been extensively used. The management of electronic health records (EHRs) is one such application that has been well investigated. Since stakeholders in EHR management are spread among patients, healthcare facilities, and occasionally governmental organizations, the system is inherently decentralized. Blockchain-based technologies ensure consent for usage (records access) and enable many stakeholders to manage EHRs transparently [31].

3.2.3 Fusion of BC and FL

We explored a reliable blockchain-based federated learning architecture. This enhances federated learning systems' transparency and equity. Blockchain guarantees data integrity because of its immutability. Because of the transparency of blockchain, every document stored on it may be audited by any authorized party. Additionally, smart contracts and blockchain's immutability encourage accountability. This makes it impossible for records to be altered after they are posted on the blockchain.

If data are stored in centralized systems, it may encounter its own issues. In order to mitigate these issues, researchers proposed the idea of decentralization, where data are managed and stored across various terminal nodes. Furthermore, security concerns arose, which gave birth to blockchain technology. Our FL architecture design (blockchain-based) attempts to attach at least one blockchain node to the dedicated server and every client, resulting in the establishment of the network. The complete transaction data are kept on the local node in the form of blockchains. Furthermore, smart contracts, where each participant is addressed through a particular blockchain address, are used for data provenance in blockchain. This helps in making federated learning more accountable. Off-chain databases save data locally, while on-chain hashed data are created and kept in a registry smart contract.

Real local and global models are kept on client devices and the primary server using conventional database systems. The blockchain only keeps the hashed versions. For tasks like uploading, aggregating, and downloading, the storage of the data is planned onto the exclusive blockchains since large data are processed through federated learning processes. Storing only the hashed versions on the blockchain ensures that the records of the models are immutable and transparent to stakeholders. To verify a model's origin, one can compare the hash value of an off-chain model to its corresponding on-chain record. This method enables the architecture to maintain model provenance by using an off-chain data storage design, which keeps the federated learning process viable and efficient. Thus, while the original models are kept in database systems, their hashed versions are securely stored on the blockchain.

3.2.4 Framework/Architecture

The smart healthcare system is primarily a combination of the edge node layer and user layer. Mobile terminals, wearable sensors, and MIoT devices make up the user layer. These instruments are employed to monitor patients' physiological states and gather clinical information. Moreover, FL models undergo local training. Base stations and edge computing servers are connected to edge nodes, which offer a robust computing and communication setup. This framework shows how to set up, save, and retrieve parameters for the blockchain as miners.

Furthermore, parameters are authenticated by consensus protocols. The complete training process is depicted below in Figure 3.2.

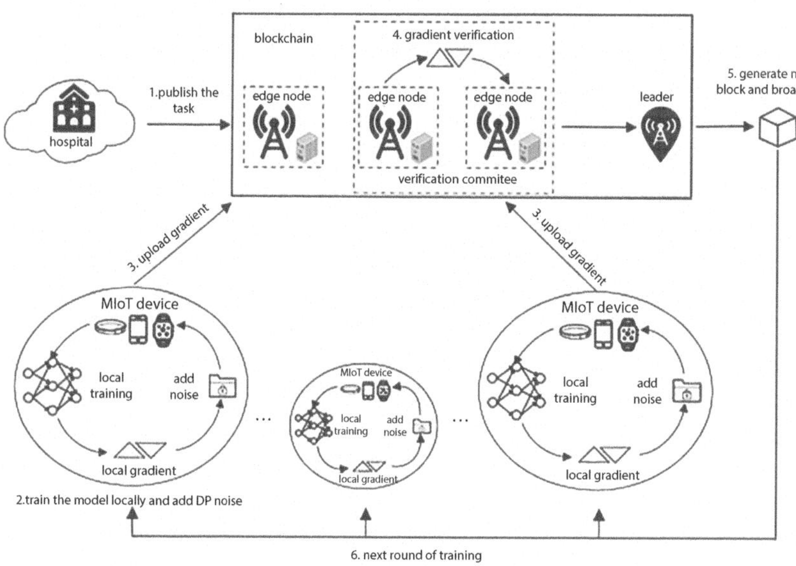

Figure 3.2 Architecture of training and verification of hospital data.

The following steps can be used to design a training procedure that lasts one round, as seen in Figure 3.2:

(1) Hospitals complete and submit the training work to the blockchain. Additionally, a genesis block is generated and dispersed throughout all edge nodes and MIoT devices. The result was the model initialization. The first model's parameters and the total number of training rounds are stored in this genesis block, along with the public keys connected to each participant who helped create the signature, initial reputation values of MIoT devices and edge nodes, and a function tracking the update of reputation.
(2) In addition to adding differential privacy noise to the local gradient, the MIoT device trains the model using locally gathered clinical data. This is done to address Threat 1.
(3) In terms of the transaction, the MIoT device uploads the noise gradient and the signature to its nearby edge node.
(4) Following the collection of data from devices inside the coverage area, the edge nodes first verify the signature's authenticity through cross-checking. Subsequently, the verification committee assesses the condition of the local gradients and verifies that there is no threat.
(5) In order to generate a new block, a leader is selected randomly. This block contains the essential model parameters to perform the training. Further, the verification committee comes into the picture. In order to synchronize the ledgers of all edge nodes and handle security threats, it checks and broadcasts the legitimate one.
(6) The MIoT device uses the global gradient that is stored in the block to modify its local model after retrieving the most recent block from its linked edge node. This is where the additional training session begins and continues until it reaches maximum rounds or convergence.

Due to the dispersed nature of MIoT on open networks, clinical data collection may encounter quality problems in addition to data poisoning. Consequently, local gradient training with such data will deviate from the general trend of convergence. To address the concerns presented, gradient verification is combined with a consensus protocol to create an edge node consensus mechanism. Malicious gradients uploaded by linked MIoT devices are identified and removed by each edge node. This will guarantee that the necessary gradients are present in order to produce a trustworthy FL and an optimized global model. This suggests an enhanced version of [32], in contrast to the proof of work (PoW) protocol, which uses up the majority of computational resources. In this version, a small number of miners are chosen to validate the new block by the Byzantine agreement protocol in each round. Additionally, there is less unnecessary communication among some miners. The appropriate information is as follows:

(1) Miners are selected from a pool of edge nodes with strong computational and communication capabilities. The block must be generated and verified by these miners. The gradient verification must also be carried out by these miners. We ensure that a minority (1/3) of miners can protect the network. Additionally, a reputation value is initialized for every miner. A miner's reputation value will drop by 1 if other miners discover that it has returned a bogus block or a distorted verification result.

(2) Gradient Verification: The miner first checks the digital signature to confirm the sender's legitimacy after gathering data from its linked MIoT devices. The miner combines the transaction pool and local gradient if the signature is authentic. A verification committee, consisting of a few miners, is also formed to detect and remove malicious gradients. In particular, it rehashes the first SHA-256 hash of the final block and then maps the hash ring result, given a hash ring whose space is allotted to miners. A member of the verification committee is chosen from among the miners connected to the area where the hash is located. Until committee M reaches its maximum size, this cycle is repeated. Figure 3.3 illustrates it. The basic operation of the suggested work is comparable to that of Algorand [33]. The likelihood of a party being chosen is correlated with its reputation.

    The verification committee accepts the top majority of the gradients in each training round after applying the multi-KRUM algorithm [34] to the gradients in the transaction pool.

(3) Verification of Candidate Block: First, we randomly pick a miner to lead this training session. The candidate miner is chosen by the verification committee. In the transaction pool, the leader collects qualified gradients and creates a new pool. The diagram indicates that the block includes the

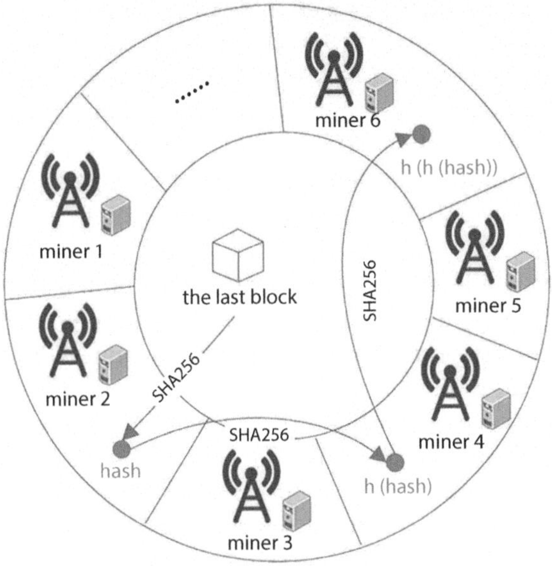

Figure 3.3 Hashing using SHA-256.

following data: qualified gradients, verification committee signatures, and a hash value that serves as a connection to the previous block. Additionally, the verification committee receives the new block along with the leader's signature to verify its legitimacy. If more than two-thirds of the verifiers provide a positive response for the block, the block is broadcasted and passed to reach consensus in the blockchain. An empty block is created if the verification phase is unsuccessful.

(4) Global Model Training: Every MIoT device tries to download the most recent block from the blockchain, computes the global gradient by taking the mean of all passed gradients that are stored in the block, and updates the local models that correspond with the global gradient. The next training round begins until the model converges or reaches the maximum number of rounds. The flagged MIoT device's reputation value increases by 1 during each training cycle. The local gradient of the flagged MIoT is identified and verified by the committee. If the MIoT device is not flagged, then its reputation value is decreased. The process continues until the reputation value reaches zero, at which point the

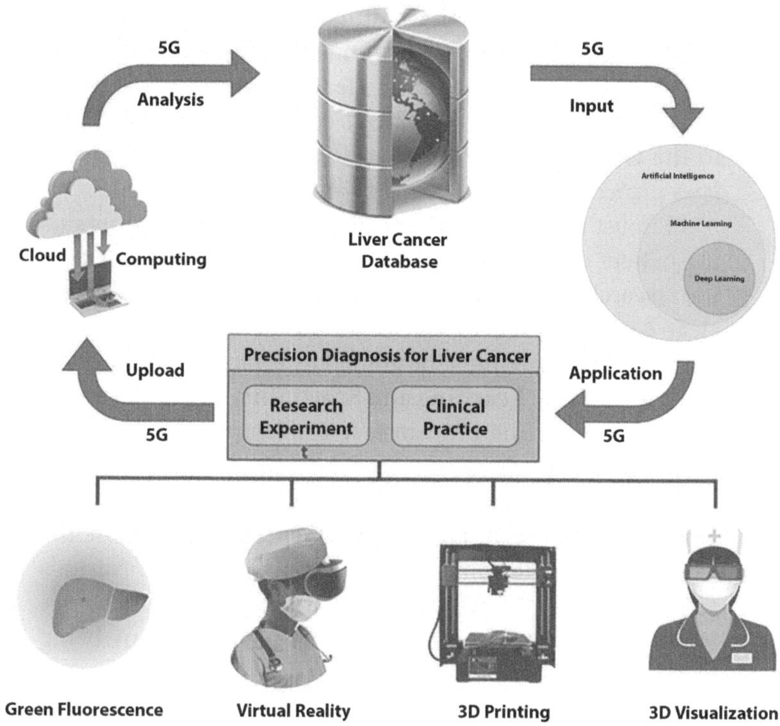

Figure 3.4 Diagnosis of any diseases with cloud and FL.

entity is flagged as blacklisted and restricted from participating in the consensus, as seen in Figure 3.4.

3.3 IoHT Applications and Their Wideband Challenges

FL plays a significant role in the healthcare domain, where the potentials of ML algorithms are utilized for collaborative development subjected to data privacy and minimal data transfer costs. However, there are certain barriers to utilizing the full potential of the FL. These challenges are depicted below.

1. **Technical and Computational Limitations:** FL requires technical expertise as well as highly computational devices, which is not feasible for all participating institutions. This results in computational discrepancies, which must be resolved in order to successfully apply FL.

2. **Regulatory and Ethical Compliance:** Federated Learning (FL) must follow various rules and ethical guidelines. In the US, FL must comply with the Health Insurance Portability and Accountability Act (HIPAA). In Europe, it must adhere to the General Data Protection Regulation (GDPR). These laws protect patient data privacy and security.

   FL must also consider ethical issues. This means obtaining patient consent to use their data. It also means ensuring the research benefits everyone fairly. To address these issues, clear data governance policies are needed. The application of FL in healthcare must be guided by ethical frameworks.
3. **Both Real-Time Learning and Scalability:** FL supports collaborative modeling but can face challenges with real-time monitoring and managing large datasets. The success of FL depends on effectively addressing these issues.
4. **Data Heterogeneity and Model Generalizability:** In the medical field, data comes from many sources and in various formats, making it heterogeneous. This heterogeneity causes issues in training the model and prevents it from being generalized.

3.3.1 In Medical Units

Electronic Health Records (EHRs) digitally store the medical background of patients, which helps in diagnosis. Medical images, like radiology images, are part of EHRs. They also include laboratory test results. EHRs serve as a blueprint of patient conditions that help in deciding the medicines and techniques for checkups. Examples of such EHRs include X-ray, Computed Tomography (CT) [35], Magnetic Resonance Imaging (MRI) [35], Ultrasound [36], Nuclear Medicine [36], Positron Emission Tomography (PET) [35], and Fluoroscopy [35], among others.

In clinical testing, medical imaging data aids in drug development and discovery. This imaging data can be analyzed by FL models, which assess the impact of novel medications or treatments on the course of illness. FL models can also identify potential drug targets. Additionally, they help optimize drug delivery methods.

3.3.2 Remote Healthcare from Homes

These data are retrieved from bed sensors and fall detectors. Fall detectors are extremely important for elderly individuals. Bed sensors monitor bed occupancy, sleep patterns, and several sleep-based parameters. ML sensor data are retrieved from multiple sources, including medical equipment, wearable devices, and other monitoring tools. This data are crucial for obtaining real-time insights into a person's activities and health. Based on the data, ML can contribute to prediction and classification, providing personalized insights. Some of these utilities include Vital Signs Monitoring, wearable devices for activity tracking, Blood Glucose and Continuous Glucose Monitoring (CGM) [37], Electrocardiogram (ECG) Monitoring [38], Sleep Monitoring [38], Environmental Sensors, Medication Adherence Monitoring [38], and Fall Detection and Activity Recognition [39].

3.3.3 Patient-Generated Data

Patient-generated data (PGD) are information provided by patients in healthcare ML. It is quite different from clinical records data. This information is retrieved directly from patients through mobile apps, wearables, and self-reported outcomes. PGD promotes a data-driven and patient-focused approach, making it easier to identify health problems early, provide individualized care, and improve communication between the patient and the healthcare system.

It is extremely important to adhere to data privacy policies. Ethical considerations must be upheld when developing and using ML models in healthcare. Along with sensor data, the use of PGD in healthcare ML includes various sources: social media and online communities, telehealth and virtual visits, sharing of genomic and genetic data, mobile health apps, and surveys [40].

3.4 Tools

Some of the tools based on different technologies include:

1. **Blockchain Platforms:**
   - **Ethereum:** A decentralized platform that facilitates the use of decentralized apps (DApps) and smart contracts.
   - **Hyperledger Fabric:** An enterprise-focused permissioned blockchain technology with a modular design and privacy features.
   - **Corda:** A blockchain platform designed for business applications, ensuring privacy and scalability.

2. **Federated Learning Tools:**
    - **TensorFlow Federated:** An open-source framework used for decentralized data processing, including machine learning.
    - **PySyft:** A Python library for secure and private deep learning, enabling FL and other privacy-preserving techniques.
    - **Flower:** A scalable framework for FL, supporting various machine learning frameworks and providing flexibility for different use cases.
3. **Integration Tools:**
    - **Smart Contract Development Tools:** Tools like Solidity for Ethereum and Chaincode for Hyperledger Fabric to develop and deploy smart contracts.
    - **Data Privacy Tools:** Libraries and frameworks for implementing differential privacy, homomorphic encryption, and secure multi-party computation (SMPC) in FL environments.

3.5 Case Studies

The synergy of Federated Learning (FL) and Blockchain (BC) offers a viable solution to the healthcare industry's continuous search for improved data privacy and security. This research explores how the merging of FL and BC facilitates collaborative healthcare analytics while protecting patient data privacy. The following are the study's main findings:

- **Decentralized Training:** FL enables local model training at different medical facilities, guaranteeing that private patient information stays on-site.
- **Security Enhancement:** Smart contracts and tamper-proof ledgers are two of the secure frameworks that blockchain offers for managing data and model integrity across institutions.
- **Scalability and Dependability:** By utilizing a customized architecture, the integration strikes a balance between decentralization, scalability, and dependability.
- **Applications:** The framework is intended to improve teamwork in fields, including drug discovery, medical image processing, and disease prediction.

This integration leads to improvements in privacy-preserving techniques and collaborative medical research, enhancing data security and potentially revolutionizing healthcare analytics.

FL has great potential in the healthcare industry since it allows different organizations, such as hospitals and research centers, to work together to construct robust ML models while protecting patient privacy. This strategy trains the local datasets and transfers only the differential results to the server in order to achieve high performance with fewer privacy issues and data transfer costs.

Compared to traditional centralized learning, FL in healthcare offers a number of benefits, such as improved privacy and the ability to use a variety of datasets without requiring centralization. Some of the FL-based applications include:

- **Multidisciplinary Cooperation in Illness Diagnosis:** Collaborative projects aimed at diagnosing diseases are among the most noteworthy achievements of FL in the healthcare field. For instance, FL was utilized by a group of global medical facilities to create models that forecast patient outcomes in critical care. High accuracy in predicting outcomes like length of hospital stay and mortality was achieved by these models through the utilization of data from varied populations while protecting data privacy.

  The Rhino Health Consortium, a global collaboration of esteemed institutions and specialists, is an example of a successful implementation. Assuta Medical Centres (Israel), Dasa S.A. (Brazil), National Taiwan University (Taiwan), Lahey Hospital and Medical Centre (U.S.), University of Cambridge School of Medicine (UK), and Seoul National University Hospital (South Korea) are among the organizations involved in this collaboration. These partnerships highlight the international endeavor to use FL to improve healthcare delivery and medical research while protecting data security and privacy.
- **Improving Medication Discovery and Development:** Predictive models for medication response and toxicity have been created in pharmaceutical research using FL. For example, various drug industries collaboratively predict the efficacy of medicinal molecules through computational models instead of relying solely on data, thereby expediting the drug discovery process and safeguarding confidential information [40].

3.6 Conclusion

The use of MIoT-based smart healthcare has expanded recently, allowing for the full utilization of clinical data to improve the precision of medical services and illness diagnosis. However, it still has to contend with issues like adversarial attacks and patient privacy breaches. In order to achieve this, FL is integrated into blockchain-based healthcare units. Specifically, we develop an adaptive differential privacy technique that meticulously modifies the noise applied to the gradient to achieve a compromise between accuracy deterioration and privacy budget. A consensus protocol based on verification oversees the FL process to guard against single points of failure and poisoning assaults. The experimental findings on a real-world diabetes dataset show that our technique can achieve a comparable degree of accuracy to the original FL within a reasonable running time.

We also demonstrate how resilient it is against poisoning assaults and how much less privacy budget it consumes. To further enhance intelligent healthcare, we will work with the public to investigate and develop our approach in the future.

We explored how FL supports several healthcare applications, such as drug development, medical image processing, and patient monitoring, with the FL approach replacing traditional centralized storing techniques. This transition addresses the problem of patient privacy. While FL creates vulnerabilities, it also provides privacy benefits. These issues are resolved by the tamper-proof nature of blockchain and smart contracts, which protect against hostile activity and guarantee data integrity.

This chapter provided an overview of how FL helps train smart hospitals using blockchain techniques while maintaining high performance and data privacy. Future research, cooperation, and creativity among the scientific community have great potential to realize FL's full capabilities. This cooperative endeavor will pave the way for a healthcare environment that is safer, more open, and more inclusive, ultimately resulting in better patient outcomes.

Future Directions

We propose the development of advanced privacy-preserving techniques and cutting-edge methods created for safeguarding privacy, such as homomorphic encryption and differential privacy, to improve data security in blockchain and FL settings. The integration of blockchain, FL, AI, and machine learning aims to create more intelligent and self-sufficient healthcare systems.

Real-time analytics and data processing tools are essential for facilitating prompt and informed healthcare decision-making but are still lacking. Another significant issue is the implementation of improved interoperability standards to enable seamless data transfer among various healthcare devices and systems. Furthermore, establishing international cooperation platforms that utilize FL and blockchain to facilitate data sharing and cross-border healthcare research is essential for furthering collaborative efforts in this field.

References

1. Schneble, C.O., Elger, B.S., Shaw, D.M., Google's project nightingale highlights the necessity of data science ethics review. *EMBO Mol. Med.*, 12, 3, e12053, 2020.
2. Mehta, N. and Pandit, A., Concurrence of big data analytics and healthcare: a systematic review. *Int. J. Med. Inf.*, 114, 57–65, 2018.
3. Mittelstadt, B.D. and Floridi, L., The ethics of big data: current and foreseeable issues in biomedical contexts. *Sci. Eng. Ethics*, 22, 2, 303–341, 2016.
4. Schneble, C.O., Elger, B.S., Shaw, D.M., Google's project nightingale highlight the necessity of data science ethics review. *EMBO Mol. Med.*, 12, 3, e12053, 2020.
5. Alsamhi, S.H. and Lee, B., Blockchain-empowered multi-robot collaboration to fight COVID-19 and future pandemics. *IEEE Access*, 9, 44173–44197, 2020.
6. Fikri, N., Rida, M., Abghour, N., Moussaid, K., El Omri, A., A blockchain-based decentralized microservices: Minimal architecture for accounting, in: *2022 7th international conference on big data analytics (ICBDA)*, IEEE, pp. 165–169, 2022, March.
7. Leonelli, S., Locating ethics in data science: responsibility and accountability in global and distributed knowledge production systems. *Philos. Trans. R. Soc. Math. Phys. Eng. Sci.*, 374, 2083, 20160122, 2016.
8. Korkmaz, C., Kocas, H.E., Uysal, A., Masry, A., Ozkasap, O., Akgun, B., Chain FL: decentralized federated machine learning via blockchain, in: *2020 Second International Conference on Blockchain Computing and Applications (BCCA)*, November, IEEE, pp. 140–146, 2020.
9. Ma, C., Li, J., Shi, L., Ding, M., Wang, T., Han, Z., Poor, H.V., When federated learning meets blockchain: a new distributed learning paradigm. *IEEE Comput. Intell. Mag.*, 17, 3, 26–33, 2022.
10. Segal, G., Segev, A., Brom, A., Lifshitz, Y., Wasserstrum, Y., Zimlichman, E., Reducing drug prescription errors and adverse drug events by application of a probabilistic, machine-learning based clinical decision support system in an inpatient setting. *J. Am. Med. Inf. Assoc.*, 26, 12, 1560–1565, 2019.

11. Verma, D., Bach, K., Mork, P.J., Application of machine learning methods on patient reported outcome measurements for predicting outcomes: a literature review. *Informatics*, 8, 3, 56, 2021.
12. Russell, S.J. and Norvig, P., *Artificial intelligence a modern approach*, London, England, 2010.
13. Weizenbaum, J., Eliza—a computer program for the study of natural language communication between man and machine. *Commun. ACM*, 9, 1, 36–45, 1966.
14. Shortliffe, E.H., Mycin: A rule-based computer program for advising physicians regarding antimicrobial therapy selection, 1974, Ph.D. dissertation, Stanford University Ph. D. dissertation.
15. Bishop, C., *Neural networks for pattern recognition*, vol. 2, pp. 223–228, Clarendon Press google schola, Central Oxford, England, 1995.
16. Lo, S.-C.B., Chan, H.-P., Lin, J.-S., Li, H., Freedman, M.T., Mun, S.K., Artificial convolution neural network for medical image pattern recognition. *Neural Netw.*, 8, 7–8, 1201–1214, 1995.
17. Iakovidis, I., Towards personal health record: current situation, obstacles and trends in implementation of electronic healthcare record in europe. *Int. J. Med. Inf.*, 52, 1–3, 105–115, 1998.
18. Duncan, J.S. and Ayache, N., Medical image analysis: Progress over two decades and the challenges ahead. *IEEE Trans. Pattern Anal. Mach. Intell.*, 22, 1, 85–106, 2000.
19. Demner-Fushman, D., Chapman, W.W., McDonald, C.J., What can natural language processing do for clinical decision support? *J. Biomed. Inf.*, 42, 5, 760–772, 2009.
20. Chen, Y., Argentinis, J.E., Weber, G., Ibm watson: how cognitive computing can be applied to big data challenges in life sciences research. *Clin. Ther.*, 38, 4, 688–701, 2016.
21. Younis, H.A., Eisa, T.A.E., Nasser, M., Sahib, T.M., Noor, A.A., Alyasiri, O.M., Salisu, S., Hayder, I.M., Younis, H.A., A systematic review and meta-analysis of artificial intelligence tools in medicine and healthcare: Applications, considerations, limitations, motivation and challenges. *Diagnostics*, 14, 1, 109, 2024.
22. Nuseir, M.T., Akour, I.A., Alzoubi, H.M., Al Kurdi, B., Alshurideh, M.T., AlHamad, A., Role of big data analytics to empower patient healthcare record management system, in: *Cyber Security Impact on Digitalization and Business Intelligence: Big Cyber Security for Information Management: Opportunities and Challenges*, pp. 39–52, Springer, Deutschland GmbH, 2024.
23. Gowda, D., Shashikala, S., Manu, Y., Kaur, M., Jha, S.K., Introduction to cloud computing and healthcare 5.0: Transforming the future of healthcare, in: *Federated Learning and AI for Healthcare 5.0*, pp. 26–45, IGI Global, Hershey, PA, 2024.
24. Chaddad, A., Peng, J., Xu, J., Bouridane, A., Survey of explainable ai techniques in healthcare. *Sensors*, 23, 2, 634, 2023.

25. Esteva, A., Robicquet, A., Ramsundar, B., Kuleshov, V., DePristo, M., Chou, K., Cui, C., Corrado, G., Thrun, S., Dean, J., A guide to deep learning in healthcare. *Nat. Med.*, 25, 1, 24–29, 2019.
26. Jaiswal, A.K., Tiwari, P., Kumar, S., Gupta, D., Khanna, A., Rodrigues, J.J., Identifying pneumonia in chest x-rays: A deep learning approach. *Measurement*, 145, 511–518, 2019.
27. Havaei, M., Davy, A., Warde-Farley, D., Biard, A., Courville, A., Bengio, Y., Pal, C., Jodoin, P.-M., Larochelle, H., Brain tumor segmentation with deep neural networks. *Med. Image Anal.*, 35, 18–31, 2017.
28. Setio, A.A.A., Traverso, A., De Bel, T., Berens, M.S., VanDen Bogaard, C., Cerello, P., Chen, H., Dou, Q., Fantacci, M.E., Geurts, B., *et al.*, Validation, comparison, and combination of algorithms for automatic detection of pulmonary nodules in computed tomography images: the luna16 challenge. *Med. Image Anal.*, 42, 1–13, 2017.
29. Zhavoronkov, A., Ivanenkov, Y.A., Aliper, A., Veselov, M.S., Aladinskiy, V.A., Aladinskaya, A.V., Terentiev, V.A., Polykovskiy, D.A., Kuznetsov, M.D., Asadulaev, A., *et al.*, Deep learning enables rapid identification of potent ddr1 kinase inhibitors. *Nat. Biotechnol.*, 37, 9, 1038–1040, 2019.
30. Chan, H.S., Shan, H., Dahoun, T., Vogel, H., Yuan, S., Advancing drug discovery via artificial intelligence. *Trends Pharmacol. Sci.*, 40, 8, 592–604, 2019.
31. Obermeyer, Z. and Emanuel, E.J., Predicting the future—big data, machine learning, and clinical medicine. *New Engl. J. Med.*, 375, 13, 1216, 2016.
32. Rajkomar, A., Oren, E., Chen, K., Dai, A.M., Hajaj, N., Hardt, M., Liu, P.J., Liu, X., Marcus, J., Sun, M., *et al.*, Scalable and accurate deep learning with electronic health records. *NPJ Digital Med.*, 1, 1, 18, 2018.
33. Gulshan, V., Peng, L., Coram, M., Stumpe, M.C., Wu, D., Narayanaswamy, A., Venugopalan, S., Widner, K., Madams, T., Cuadros, J., *et al.*, Development and validation of a deep learning algorithm for detection of diabetic retinopathy in retinal fundus photographs. *JAMA*, 316, 22, 2402–2410, 2016.
34. Futoma, J., Hariharan, S., Heller, K., Learning to detect sepsis with a multitask gaussian process rnn classifier, in: *International Conference on Machine Learning*, pp. 1174–1182, PMLR, Sydney, Australia, 2017.
35. Henry, K.E., Hager, D.N., Pronovost, P.J., Saria, S., A targeted real-time early warning score (trewscore) for septic shock. *Sci. Transl. Med.*, 7, 299, 299ra122–299ra122, 2015.
36. Kassahun, Y., Yu, B., Tibebu, A.T., Stoyanov, D., Giannarou, S., Metzen, J.H., Vander Poorten, E., Surgical robotics beyond enhanced dexterity instrumentation: a survey of machine learning techniques and their role in intelligent and autonomous surgical actions. *Int. J. Comput. Assisted Radiol. Surg.*, 11, 553–568, 2016.
37. Holzer, R., Bloch, W., Brinkmann, C., Continuous Glucose Monitoring in Healthy Adults—Possible Applications in Health Care, Wellness, and Sports. *Sensors*, 22, 5, 2030, 2022, https://doi.org/10.3390/s22052030.

38. Serhani, M.A., El Kassabi, H.T., Ismail, H., Nujum Navaz, A., ECG monitoring systems: Review, architecture, processes, and key challenges. *Sensors*, 20, 6, 1796, 2020.
39. Ramirez, H., Velastin, S.A., Meza, I., Fabregas, E., Makris, D., Farias, G., Fall detection and activity recognition using human skeleton features. *IEEE Access*, 9, 33532–33542, 2021.
40. Wosik, J., Fudim, M., Cameron, B., Gellad, Z.F., Cho, A., Phinney, D., Tcheng, J., Telehealth transformation: COVID-19 and the rise of virtual care. *J. Am. Med. Inf. Assoc.*, 27, 6, 957–962, 2020.

4

Foundations of Federated Intelligent Systems in Healthcare

Rachna Behl*, **Indu Kashyap and Neha Garg**

Department of CSE, Manav Rachna International Institute of Research and Studies, Faridabad, Haryana, India

Abstract

A new era in the healthcare industry has begun with the emergence of Artificial Intelligence (AI). AI plays a vital role by providing improved accuracy in diagnosis, operational efficiency, and personalized treatment. Traditionally, to perform predictions and calculations on patient data, the system works in a centralized manner. The system may face challenges and issues associated with the privacy and security of data with the constraints imposed by regularity bodies. Federated AI provides an innovative way of involving several users in a decentralized manner. This chapter discusses the concepts, including its training process, principles, and a comparison with conventional systems. It also highlights the utilization of Federated Learning (FL) in healthcare, the working of decentralized AI, the need and role of FL, data privacy, and security concerns. Practical aspects of FL in healthcare have been discussed through different case studies, such as a pilot study performed by Apple & Stanford medicine, brain imagining for Alzheimer's diagnosis, and mood detection have been discussed. The case studies highlight the impact of these frameworks on issues like privacy and security along with patient outcomes.

The chapter also focuses on challenges and ethical considerations associated with Federated AI, including data diversity, traceability and accountability, transparency, trust, data ownership, and the need for federated governance frameworks. The ethical consideration also involves compliances imposed by the global regulations for utilizing the health industry data. Federated AI provides a framework for the health industry to work on heterogeneous datasets while maintaining the privacy and security of the data. The present chapter also provides an overview of the present state of the art for Federated AI with prospects. The chapter aims

**Corresponding author*: rachnabehl@gmail.com

S. Rakesh Kumar, N. Gayathri and Seifedine Kadry (eds.) Federated Intelligent System for Healthcare: A Practical Guide, (81–100) © 2025 Scrivener Publishing LLC

to guide policymakers, practitioners, and researchers in understanding the role of Federated AI for improved health outcomes and medical advancements.

Keywords: Decentralized AI, federated learning, healthcare AI, privacy preservation

4.1 Introduction

In this era of big data, the Healthcare sector has undergone significant transformations due to frequently occurring technological advancements and data-driven analysis. Federated learning has evolved from these innovative amalgamations. This approach of federated learning makes use of machine learning and artificial intelligence to handle various security issues like confidentiality, integrity, availability, and durability. Federated Learning works on the principle of a decentralized architecture in comparison with traditional centralized architecture. This decentralized Federated Learning architecture principle enables individual users to train their models solely rather than depending on data sharing among various users [1]. This decentralized approach allows parameters to be passed on to trained models. FL server will further aggregate these parameters and communicate these revised parameter weights to the individual participants. All these participants can collectively collaborate to create a global model without disclosing their datasets. FL training promotes collaborative training on various decentralized Datasets. This process of collaborative training of FL ensures Patient Data privacy in the healthcare sector by avoiding the sharing of individual raw data.

FL is a novel technique used for healthcare analytics wherein data privacy is of utmost importance in the healthcare sector. Google and Stanford Medicine collaborated to create a precise prediction model for hospital readmissions. In this predictive model, patient data has been collected from various healthcare units/organizations that delivered tailored readmission risk estimations while protecting patient privacy.

Likewise, FL, by making use of this decentralized server and collaborative process, has been utilized in various healthcare applications, namely clinical decision support systems, large-scale clinical data mining, drug discovery, collaborative disease diagnosis, and population health management. Furthermore, in this chapter, practical cases of the healthcare industry and challenges are discussed in detail.

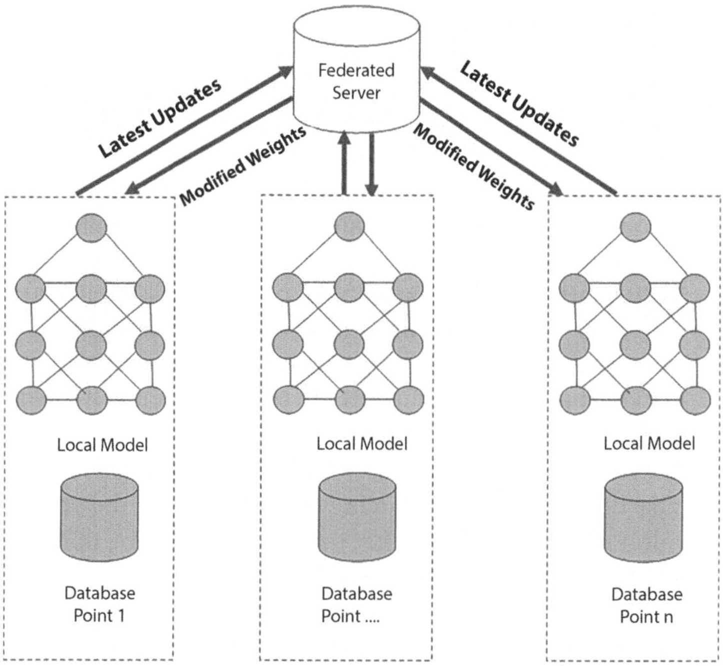

Figure 4.1 Architecture of federated learning.

4.2 Core Concepts of Federated Learning

Federated Learning is an ML algorithm that provides a way for collective learning of a distributed model while maintaining the privacy of the data stored on individual devices. It is a distributed ML process that runs across various heterogeneous clients. Each N clients $\{C_1, C_2, C_3, \ldots\ldots C_n)$, indexed by k, possesses its local dataset $\{LD_1, LD_2, LD_3 \ldots\ldots LD_n\}$, which remains on the client's device and is not shared with other clients or acquired by any third party. The process is usually coordinated by a central server that monitors the training for various clients. It allows ML models to be equipped with decentralized data while maintaining user confidentiality. The shared machine learning model is more often used in cases where information security is crucial. Figure 4.1 demonstrates the architecture of FL.

4.2.1 Federated Learning Training Process

In FL, data resides on client sides in a local manner and trains decentralized clients in a distributed manner. The local data is utilized to train clients, and afterwards system parameters are exchanged to the center server for creating a global model [30]. Additionally, users do not divulge their private data to other systems while utilizing Federated Learning. In practice, every user needs to effectively transfer their trained model to the server for efficient processing. The server combines local data received from various clients into a global network using iterative procedure. Figure 4.2 depicts the training steps of federated machine learning. This process comprises following steps:

1. **Initialization:** At the beginning of each communication cycle, the clients acquire the most recent global model (v_t) from the server in order to initialize their local models.
2. **Local Training:** Each client (C_k) conducts iteratively trains on their respective local dataset (LD_k) using the hyperparameter (η). The local model (v_k^t) is updated to (v_k^{t+1}) after a particular number of training epochs based on the update rule $v_k^{t+1} \leftarrow v_k^t(\eta, LD^k)$. After the above action, the updated local models are returned back to the server.
3. **Model Aggregation:** The server aggregates the received local models to update the global model using the following aggregation process: $v_{glob}^{t+1} = \text{Agg}(v_k^t; \text{k} \ \varepsilon \ [1, \text{N}])$. This aggregation procedure usually entails calculating a weighted average of the local model updates.

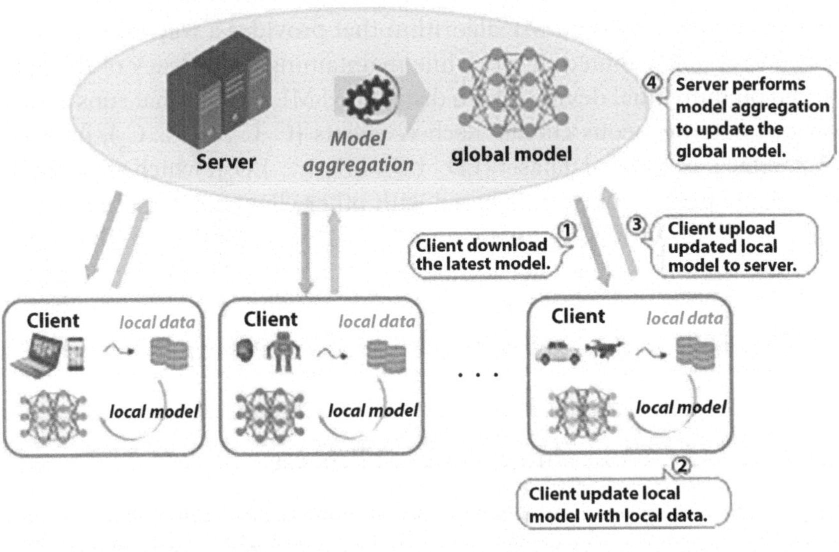

Figure 4.2 Federated learning training process (source: [20]).

Federated Learning is a distributed processing system based on the concepts of AI, ML, and Blockchain algorithms. Here the system receives trained sub-models from the participants, instead of raw data. Moreover, Federated Learning allows for asynchronous transmission, which results in reduction for communication requirements.

4.2.2 Key Principles of Federated Learning

Federated learning is a decentralized approach of machine learning that enables multiple parties to collectively train an integrated framework without sharing their data. Federated learning comprises important principles as mentioned below:

Data Locality: Federated learning makes sure that data remains distributed across clients' devices or within their respective institutions. This principle prevents sensitive data, such as personal health records, from leaving the local environment. Clients execute calculations and computations on their local datasets, to lower down the risks of data breaches and unauthorized access.

Privacy Preservation: FL prioritizes the privacy of clients' data by employing several techniques to secure individual data points during the training process. The privacy-preserving strategy comprises of:

- **Differential Privacy:** Integrating random noise to data or model updates to protect sensitive information during aggregation.
- **Secure Multiparty Computation (SMPC):** This facilitates multiple parties to compute a function with their respective local inputs.
- **Homomorphic Encryption** allows computations to be performed on encrypted data, permitting aggregation of model updates without decryption, thereby preserving data confidentiality.
- **Federated Averaging:** Averaging the updates from multiple clients to prevent the central server from accessing individual updates, further protecting privacy.

Evolutionary Learning: The training process in Federated learning is continuous improvement learning. The process involves multiple interactions between clients and server, and after each iteration the trained model is improved. The learning process constitutes the following phases:

1. During the first phase a model is configured by the server and is distributed to the clients. This is termed as the **Model Configuration** phase.
2. In the next phase each client trains the shared model on their local datasets. After **Local Training**, the clients update, summarize and encrypt the model configurations, and communicate the same to the server.
3. After the clients had sent local model updates to the cloud server, **Model Aggregation** is performed to update the global model.
4. After **Global Model Distribution**, this process is executed again. The entire training can have multiple iterations, till the model achieves the desire level of accuracy and performance.

Safe Interaction: In FL, the data should be transmitted securely between client and server. The safe transmission includes prevention from unauthorized access, confidentiality, integrity, and security of data, during communication between client and server. To ensure safe transmission various encryption techniques, such as Transport Layer Security (TLS) are used by different models.
Scalable Framework: Scalability is one of the key components of federated learning. This feature makes it perfect for a wide range of applications like mobile device networks or healthcare systems with limited hardware constraints. Robust machine learning solutions can be built ensuring scalability and flexibility.

4.2.3 Comparing Traditional and Federated Learning: Data Management, Privacy, Scalability, and Performance

To provide data-driven decision support and automation, Machine learning (ML) has a crucial role in many domains. The distinct challenges and benefits are associated with various approaches of ML and FL frameworks. The following section provides a comparative analysis between these two approaches based on the data management, the privacy and scalability handled, and the model performance.

A centralized repository is maintained to store data in traditional machine learning models. The homogeneous and high-quality data from several sources is employed for training purposes. Whereas, federated learning employs distributed data across multiple clients. Each client performs local training and only model updates are shared with the server. The training is performed at clients' locations on heterogeneous data, reflecting different distributions, qualities, and data types.

Traditional machine learning is prone to data breaches and significant privacy risks. It is challenging to adhere to data protection regulations. Nevertheless, federated learning deals with these issues by localizing data at local nodes and strict compliance with privacy regulations. Earlier Machine Learning algorithms were not as scalable as Federated Learning. This is because conventional machine learning relies on central processing power and storage. However, in FL, the processing is executed at multiple client sites in a distributive manner, hence it is highly scalable. Conventional learning achieves higher accuracy and improves model performance because of voluminous data at its discretion. Federated Learning, in contrast, may impact model performance due to data localization and variations. Additionally, utilizing aggregation techniques makes it challenging to ensure model consistency and performance. The key distinctions between federated and conventional machine learning are outlined in Table 4.1.

Table 4.1 Key differentiating factors of traditional ML and federated learning.

Key factors	Traditional ML	Federated learning
Data Management	Centralized	Distributed
Data Type	Homogeneous	Heterogeneous
Privacy Risk	Yes	No
Compliances Challenges (e.g., GDPR, HIPAA)	Yes	No
Scalability	Limited	Inherently Scalable
Data bottleneck	Yes	No
Training Data	Uniform	To maintain model consistency, it may face challenges.
Accuracy and Model Performance	high	Not consistent

4.2.4 Applications of Federated Learning

Federated Learning is an innovative technique that has inherent capabilities and advantages in securing data [3], handling data disparities and heterogeneity. It provides a distributed environment for model training to preserve data integrity. Here we will highlight applications built using FL framework:

Smartphone Applications
Federated learning has shown potential to capture user behavior and build models for face recognition, next word prediction, and voice detection. For example, Google's Voice Assistant has employed federated learning for enhancing machine learning models for voice recognition.

Self-Driving Vehicles
Federated learning has been promising in addressing issues such as real-time decision making, predicting steering angles and deviations based on real-time road conditions and significant improvement in autonomous driving.

Banking and Insurance industries
These industries are also taking advantage of federated learning framework to protect sensitive transactional data and build robust applications to safeguard user information.

4.3 FL in Healthcare

4.3.1 Need of FL in Healthcare

Federated learning is promising in the healthcare domain due to its data distribution technique. The following reasons present how federated learning is advantageous in healthcare:

1. The principle of collaboration for ML model training can be applied by healthcare businesses. The collaborative training and data decentralization preserves patients' privacy and disease-related information.
2. Federated Learning and Machine Learning enable personalized treatment recommendations to doctors and medical practitioners, thereby improving patient care. Doctors are also

abreast with technological advancement and latest information by utilizing FL techniques. As a result, diagnostic and treatment procedures are more accurate.
3. Utilizing FL in healthcare can help break data barriers and promote integration and interoperability of healthcare data for careful examination of the medical condition of a patient.
4. ML systems can detect early symptoms of a disease by evaluating large datasets resulting in less costs and better diagnosis.
5. Personal medical treatments are provided according to each patient's needs depending upon their genetic conditions thus achieving high success rates.
6. Machine learning and federated learning can predict disease outbreaks, equipment maintenance needs and patient admission requirements; hence, improve healthcare resources.
7. FL provides effective solutions through digital services and remote patient monitoring. This helps in improved follow up and remote healthcare delivery.

4.3.2 Types of FL for Healthcare

Based on the application of FL in the health sector, FL is categorized into three categories [18].

1. Horizontal Federated Learning (HFL)- HFL has a scenario where various clients may have different sample spaces with overlapping feature sets, as shown in Figure 4.3a. In this approach, local FL players may use the same ML model to train their datasets [18]. The server will then integrate the local changes supplied by local participants to create a global update, eliminating the necessity for direct access to local data [19]. For example- two or more hospitals can work together to make an FL model for the early prediction of diabetes. Here, in this scenario, each hospital has a different sample space but will have the same feature set.
2. Vertical Federated Learning (VFL)- In continuation to this, VFL involves a scenario where various clients may have overlapping sample space with different feature sets, as shown in Figure 4.3b. For example, in this scenario, a diabetes hospital, ENT hospital, eye clinic, and lung hospital can collaborate [21]. Here, these hospitals will have different

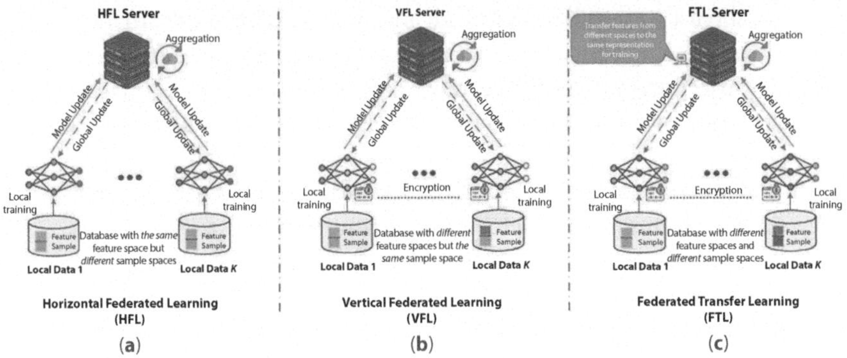

Figure 4.3 Types of FL [18].

feature sets but may have overlapping sample sets to determine the impact of diabetes on other body parts of a particular patient.

3. Federated Transfer Learning (FTL)- FTL is utilized when both sample sets and feature sets are different, as shown in Figure 4.3c. This scenario can be used to analyze the impact of drugs on the set of patients with common diseases. Here, the datasets of hospitals and pharmaceutical companies can be used, and both industries have different feature sets and sample sets. Still, some sets of data and features may overlap. [21].

4.3.3 Role of Federated Learning in Healthcare

The innovative process of machine learning utilized by Federated Learning has successfully resolved the problems related to data privacy in the healthcare sector. It allows Training across various devices or institutions without sharing raw data, thereby maintaining data confidentiality and privacy [4]. It facilitates multi-institutional collaborations with medical image analysis while preserving patient data [5, 6].

The main roles of FL are elucidated below:

1. **Preserving Data Privacy** - Amidst the dynamic nature of healthcare, Federated Learning has evolved as an effective approach to handling Patient privacy. While performing

data learning, its dependency on centralized servers has made healthcare systems vulnerable to data privacy. Federated learning trains a shared model by aggregating local updates from numerous client devices, eliminating the need to send actual patient data [7]. In addition to federated learning, differential privacy approaches further enhance data protection.

2. **Improving Model Performance** - FL can provide more robust and broadly applicable models than models trained on data from a single institution by combining insights from several datasets from several institutions.

   Federated Learning uses a central server to coordinate training across several clients, ensuring that data are stored locally on the devices [8]. During training, clients repeatedly enhance their local models using their datasets while exchanging privacy-preserving information with the central server, such as model parameters, synthetic data, or expertise.

3. **Enhancing Precision Medicine** - The application of a federated learning platform for patient similarity learning is also playing a vital role [9] by enabling the identification of similar patients across institutions without sharing individual-level data. These similar patients are called digital twins (DTs). Doctors use a wide range of data, including molecular, clinical, lifestyle (e.g., wearables), behavioral, and environmental data, to provide precision medicines to either a group of patients with similar characteristics (disease types) or a single patient based on biomarkers, mainly genetic or genomic markers [10]. Precision medicine powered by DTs can provide new insights into customized risk factors, medication interactions, procedure safety, and therapy alternatives [11].

4. **Supporting Remote and Rural Healthcare** - Hospitals and clinics in distant places can work with larger medical institutions to develop strong models. For example, a rural clinic could train a model using local data, which could then be combined with models from nearby clinics and institutions to create a complete model that helps all participants [12]. FL permits the creation of models that can make the most use of limited resources in rural settings [13]. For instance, better resource optimization is possible through predictive techniques. Additionally, patient flow management and

optimal decisions can be made to distribute medical supplies. Patients can seek the benefits of improved telemedicine and virtual care through precise and accurate personalized health information provided by federated learning [14].

5. **Enabling Real-Time and Continuous Learning** - Federated learning allows ML models to remain updated and perform effectively, especially in dynamic fields like healthcare, where streaming data occurs frequently. Models adapt to new data and emerging patterns. This continuous learning process is implemented in a distributed data environment to ensure privacy and compliance with data regulations. The model is flexible to new data and generates suitable predictions in real time. Healthcare applications for diabetes [15], COVID-19 diagnosis [16], and medical imaging [17] rely on federated learning for accurate predictions.

4.4 Federated Learning in Healthcare: Case Studies

Apple & Stanford Medicine collaborated on a pilot study "FLADS: Federated Learning with an Asynchronous Distributed System" [26]. The group trained a model on anonymized smartwatch data for identifying atrial fibrillation. They investigated how to combine asynchronous distributed systems and federated learning to build a fault-tolerant, privacy-preserving network for smart gadgets. Traditional smart devices collect data and run machine learning algorithms, often relying on centralized servers that raise privacy and dependency concerns. FLADS resolved these by enabling nodes (smart devices) to train models locally and share gradients rather than raw data, using a modified Zookeeper Atomic Broadcast (ZAB) protocol for consistency. The decentralized architecture protects privacy and prevents single points of failure because no device distributes its raw data. The authors implemented FLADS by following modular strategy, thus it is compatible with various gradient-based algorithms. The experiment was performed by authors using MNIST dataset, demonstrating high training throughput with and a marginal accuracy loss. Moreover, the researchers investigated the performance of proposed architecture on different data samples with skewed distributions, and the results indicated increase in accuracy. However, the system has communication overhead, which restricts the use of deep neural networks. FLADS effectively balances efficiency, privacy, and fault tolerance in distributed machine learning environments. Future research may focus on optimizing the communication cost and improving the system's leader election mechanism.

Federated Learning via Attentive Margin of Semantic Feature Representations (FedMargin) [27] is novel federated learning (FL) algorithm, designed by authors to optimize vision models in distributed IoT systems. Model optimization in FedMargin is performed by employing margins of feature representations. They utilized prototypical margins (PM) to calculate the confidence of local and aggregate models. Once computed, both local and aggregate prototype margins helped the method to effectively measure the deviation of prototypes before and after training. Margin based weight attention mechanism ultimately improved model aggregation. The experiments and simulations were conducted on various computer vision tasks, such as image classification and semantic segmentation. Four classification datasets were taken, and FedMargin was compared with baseline approaches such as FedAvg, FairAvg, FeSEM, etc. It was validated that the proposed approach surpassed the competitors in terms of accuracy and showed better convergence. It was effective in handling system and statistical heterogeneity within IoT environments.

An FL-based system has been developed by [28] that analyzed brain imaging data to improve Alzheimer's disease diagnosis. Researchers in [28] addressed the major hurdles and innovations in utilizing Electronic Health Records (EHR) for biomedical research. The authors proposed the SHIR method integrated with the DataSHIELD framework to analyze high dimensional data. The study examined how data heterogeneity affected the forecasting of the risk of acute kidney injury (AKI) and sepsis in an intensive care unit (ICU) by comparing local, pooled, and federated settings. Compared to existing approaches such as SMA and DebiasL&B, SHIR demonstrated superior performance making it appropriate for classifying various diseases in electronic health records. The technique is more effective at handling model heterogeneity and high dimensionality across distributed datasets because it maintains a balance between model complexity and loss using a generalized information criterion. SHIR has proven to improve the accuracy, paving the way for more effective translational biomedical research using EHR data.

The research study conducted by [1] explores the vulnerabilities and attacks as well as the defense mechanisms to be followed to ensure data privacy. Different sources of susceptibilities and challenges specifically, data poisoning, model inversion, and inference attacks, are discussed by the authors. Further, the authors highlighted multiple ways to mitigate these attacks. The authors did a comprehensive survey of different mitigation techniques that include secure multiparty computation, differential privacy, and homomorphic encryption.

The research work "FedMood: Federated Learning on Mobile Health Data for Mood Detection" by [2] explores the application of FL in diagnosing depression using data from mobile devices. In this work the authors captured different metadata through customized virtual keyboards configured on smartphones without disrupting the activities. The data included alphanumeric characters, special characters, and accelerometer values. The researchers implemented Deep Mood architecture to predict depression levels through the collected data. Additionally, federated learning has been applied by authors to protect patient privacy and enhance prediction accuracy. They executed models under IID and non-IID settings and demonstrated that federated learning surpasses local training methods. 85.13% accuracy was obtained under IID data distribution and 76.95% with non-IID settings. The results indicate that utilizing FL to diagnose mental health conditions, predict mood disorders, and recommend treatments accordingly is effective as compared to traditional machine learning.

4.5 Challenges and Ethical Consideration

Federated learning has proven to be beneficial in many applications, offering major advantages such as security, diversity, decentralization. However, for efficient training quality data, reduced bias and standardization are necessary for efficient model training. These challenges must be overcome through careful study design, consistent data collection processes, organized reporting, and sophisticated approaches for detecting bias and hidden stratification. In the upcoming section, we will explore the challenges that should be addressed during FL implementation for the healthcare sector.

Data Diversity

Medical data is diversified in varied features. These include data dimension, it's type, ways of data collection, quality and brand of medical device utilized, and many more. Building models on heterogeneous datasets is challenging, but FL can mitigate bias though. However, the uneven data distribution poses a challenge for these strategies, where the data is independently and identically distributed across all nodes [31]. Although the FL training process is feasible, in the above mentioned situations, FedAvg and other aggregation strategies have demonstrated poor success. To overcome these challenges FedProx or different data sharing strategies may be adopted. FL's data diversity may result in global optima, not suitable for individual participants, necessitating consensus on optimal model training definition before training begins.

Privacy and security

There is a requirement of privacy especially in healthcare domain to safeguard patient data. Ensuring data privacy is established by robust technologies such as federated learning due to its decentralized process. Methods such as differential privacy, secure multiparty computation, homomorphic encryption, federated averaging, secure communication protocols, trusted execution environments, and data anonymization play vital roles in ensuring that patient data remains secure and confidential [29]. Healthcare organizations can be benefited by collaborative model training to design effective and secure solutions.

Traceability and accountability

Reproducibility is a key component in federated learning for healthcare, involving multiple parties with different setups. It can be achieved

Table 4.2 Challenges in FL and ML.

Key factors	Federated learning	Machine learning
Data Privacy and Data Security [22]	Less Risk due to decentralized model training.	Implement encryption and other access controls to ensure data security.
Data Ownership [23]	Remains with local organization	May be shared with central entity.
Informed Consent [25]	Due to distributive nature, ensure clear communication and transparency about usage of data.	Develop explicit consent protocols and mechanisms to help patients understand and regulate data usage.
Regulatory Compliance [25]	Must manage various data ownership laws and standards challenges.	Must ensure strict compliance.
Equity and Accessibility [24]	Can serve small organizations to reduce bias and cost and enable global participation.	For small organizations, this may lead to bias.
Transparency and Trust [23]	requires sophisticated approaches to explain complex models and build trust	also struggles with model interpretability.

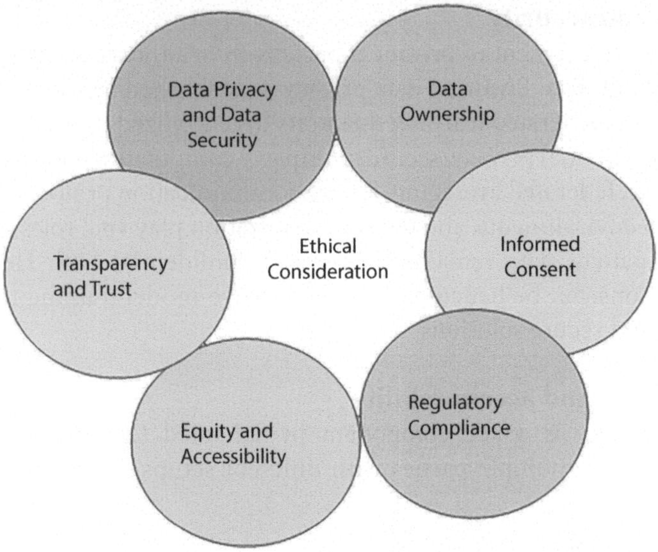

Figure 4.4 Ethical considerations of FL in healthcare.

by configuring training environments and hyperparameter tuning. Traceability and accountability are essential for integrity in non-trusted federations. They guarantee fair execution in FL system and maintain a log so that each participant contribution is evaluated. These processes ensure balancing computational powers of participants and establish an unbiased revenue-sharing agreement.

FL may generate unexpected results which are difficult to interpret by the researchers. Consequently, a balance between transparency and data protection has to be maintained which is achieved by employing secure view at each site. Different challenges associated with ML and Federated learning and overcoming these is shown in Table 4.2.

Figure 4.4, factors to be considered in developing applications using FL for Healthcare.

4.6 Conclusion and Future Scope

Federated learning is a decentralized paradigm where collaborative learning and model training occur on distributed data. FL has triggered and revolutionized the healthcare domain. Researchers' attention has recently been diverted from ML to FL for designing healthcare applications where patient privacy is of utmost importance. As federated learning adheres to data protection laws, it shows significant capabilities to overcome machine learning issues. The issues, for instance - privacy, single-point failure related to data centralization, etc., are addressed. Federated learning ensures that only essential attributes are shared enhancing data protection and reducing data leakages. Organizations can maintain trust among patients that their information is secured by established privacy mechanisms.

FL models capture voluminous heterogeneous data and act upon patients with varied demographics. It has a remarkable effect on digital health. Federated learning has a significant impact on many healthcare applications such as brain segmentation using MRI, identifying clinical similarities among patients, early detection of diabetes, and classifying Alzheimer's biomarkers. Other health projects, where federated learning has delivered sufficient improvement are personalized treatment plans for patients, clinical decision support systems, and drug prediction. However, adopting FL globally demands sophisticated mechanisms and resilient architecture for different healthcare organizations. This also requires maintaining harmony among stakeholders like regulatory bodies, healthcare facilities, and digital agencies. Federated learning brings a revolution in the healthcare industry. Unlocking FL's full potential to promote innovation and quality in healthcare requires ongoing developments and strategic collaborations.

References

1. Jeong, H. and Chung, T.M., Security and Privacy Issues and Solutions in Federated Learning for Digital Healthcare, in: *International Conference on Future Data and Security Engineering*, 2022, November, Springer Nature Singapore, Singapore, pp. 316–331.
2. Xu, X., Peng, H., Sun, L., Bhuiyan, M.Z.A., Liu, L., He, L., Fedmood: Federated learning on mobile health data for mood detection, 2021.
3. Bharati, S., Mondal, M., Podder, P., Prasath, V.B., Federated learning: Applications, challenges and future directions. *Int. J. Hybrid Intell. Syst.*, *18*, 1–2, 19–35, 2022, arXiv preprint arXiv:2102.09342.
4. Ali, M., Naeem, F., Tariq, M., Kaddoum, G., Federated learning for privacy preservation in smart healthcare systems: A comprehensive survey. *IEEE J. Biomed. Health Inf.*, *27*, 2, 778–789, 2022.
5. Díaz, J.S.P. and García, A.L., Study of the performance and scalability of federated learning for medical imaging with intermittent clients. *Neurocomputing*, *518*, 142–154, 2023.
6. Sheller, M.J., Edwards, B., Reina, G.A., Martin, J., Pati, S., Kotrotsou, A., Bakas, S., Federated learning in medicine: facilitating multi-institutional collaborations without sharing patient data. *Sci. Rep.*, *10*, 1, 12598, 2020.

7. Konečný, J., McMahan, H.B., Ramage, D., Richtárik, P., Federated optimization: Distributed machine learning for on-device intelligence, 2016, arXiv preprint arXiv:1610.02527.
8. Bhowmick, A., Duchi, J., Freudiger, J., Kapoor, G., Rogers, R., Protection against reconstruction and its applications in private federated learning, 2018, arXiv preprint arXiv:1812.00984.
9. Lee, J., Sun, J., Wang, F., Wang, S., Jun, C.H., Jiang, X., Privacy-preserving patient similarity learning in a federated environment: development and analysis. *JMIR Med. Inf.*, 6, 2, e7744, 2018.
10. Williams, J.R., Lorenzo, D., Salerno, J., Yeh, V.M., Mitrani, V.B., Kripalani, S., Current applications of precision medicine: a bibliometric analysis. *Pers. Med.*, *16*, 4, 351–359, 2019.
11. Nagaraj, D., Khandelwal, P., Steyaert, S., Gevaert, O., Augmenting digital twins with federated learning in medicine. *Lancet Digital Health*, *5*, 5, e251–e253, 2023.
12. Burdorf, B.T., Comparing magnetic resonance imaging and computed tomography machine accessibility among urban and rural county hospitals. *J. Public Health Res.*, *11*, 1, 45–54, 2022, jphr-2021.
13. Gupta, A., Misra, S., Pathak, N., Das, D., Fedcare: Federated learning for resource-constrained healthcare devices in iomt system. *IEEE Trans. Comput. Soc. Syst.*, *10*, 4, 1587–1596, 2023.
14. Guo, K., Chen, T., Ren, S., Li, N., Hu, M., Kang, J., Federated learning empowered real-time medical data processing method for smart healthcare. *IEEE/ACM Trans. Comput. Biol. Bioinf.*, 19, 6, 3685–3696, 2022.
15. Islam, H. and Mosa, A., A federated mining approach on predicting diabetes-related complications: Demonstration using real-world clinical data, in: *AMIA Annual Symposium Proceedings*, vol. 2021, American Medical Informatics Association, p. 556, 2021.
16. Qayyum, A., Ahmad, K., Ahsan, M.A., Al-Fuqaha, A., Qadir, J., Collaborative federated learning for healthcare: Multi-modal covid-19 diagnosis at the edge. *IEEE Open J. Comput. Soc.*, *3*, 172–184, 2022.
17. Ng, D., Lan, X., Yao, M.M.S., Chan, W.P., Feng, M., Federated learning: a collaborative effort to achieve better medical imaging models for individual sites that have small labelled datasets. *Quant. Imag. Med. Surg.*, *11*, 2, 852, 2021.
18. Nguyen, D.C., Pham, Q.V., Pathirana, P.N., Ding, M., Seneviratne, A., Lin, Z., Dobre, O., Hwang, W.J., Federated learning for smart healthcare: A survey. *ACM Comput. Surv. (Csur)*, *55*, 3, 1–37, 2022.
19. Cheng, Y., Liu, Y., Chen, T., Yang, Q., Federated learning for privacy-preserving AI. *Commun. ACM*, *63*, 12, 33–36, 2020.
20. Qi, P., Chiaro, D., Guzzo, A., Ianni, M., Fortino, G., Picciallli, F., Model aggregation techniques in federated learning: A comprehensive survey. *Future Gener. Comput. Syst.*, 144, 1, 256–275, 2023.

21. Narmadha, K. and Varalakshmi, P., Federated Learning in Healthcare: A Privacy Preserving Approach. *Stud. Health Technol. Inform., 294*, 194–198, 2022, https://doi.org/10.3233/SHTI220436.
22. Gupta, M., Kumar, M., Gupta, Y., A blockchain-empowered federated learning-based framework for data privacy in lung disease detection system. *Comput. Hum. Behav., 158*, 108302, 2024.
23. Rieke, N., Hancox, J., Li, W., Milletari, F., Roth, H.R., Albarqouni, S., Bakas, S., Galtier, M.N., Landman, B.A., Maier-Hein, K., Ourselin, S., The future of digital health with federated learning. *NPJ Digit. Med., 3*, 1, 1–7, 2020.
24. Topaloglu, M.Y., Morrell, E.M., Rajendran, S., Topaloglu, U., In the pursuit of privacy: the promises and predicaments of federated learning in healthcare. *Front. Artif. Intell., 4*, 746497, 2021.
25. Truong, N., Sun, K., Wang, S., Guitton, F., Guo, Y., Privacy preservation in federated learning: An insightful survey from the GDPR perspective. *Comput. Secur., 110*, 102402, 2021.
26. Bansal, A., Chandrasekar, A., Mudel, G., FLADS: Federated Learning with an Asynchronous Distributed System. *IEEE Transactions on Neural Networks and Learning Systems*, 33,10, 4960–4971, 2022
27. Michieli, U., Toldo, M., Ozay, M., Federated learning via attentive margin of semantic feature representations. *IEEE Internet Things J., 10*, 2, 1517–1535, 2022.
28. Liu, M., *Federated and Transfer Learning with Multi-site Electronic Health Record Data*, Harvard University, Cambridge, Massachusetts, 2022.
29. Gu, X., Sabrina, F., Fan, Z., Sohail, S., A review of privacy enhancement methods for federated learning in healthcare systems. *Int. J. Environ. Res. Public Health, 20*, 15, 6539, 2023.
30. Rahman, A., Hossain, M.S., Muhammad, G., Kundu, D., Debnath, T., Rahman, M., Khan, M.S.I., Tiwari, P., Band, S.S., Federated learning-based AI approaches in smart healthcare: concepts, taxonomies, challenges and open issues. *Cluster Comput., 26*, 4, 2271–2311, 2023.

5

Integrating Edge Devices and Internet of Medical Things in Modern Healthcare

Manoj Kumar Patra* **and Nandita Bhanja Chaudhuri**

GITAM University, Hyderabad, India

Abstract

The integration of Edge Devices and the Internet of Medical Things (IoMT) is revolutionizing modern healthcare by enhancing patient care, improving diagnostic accuracy, and optimizing resource utilization. This chapter comprehensively explores how these advanced technologies are transforming healthcare delivery. It begins with an introduction to edge devices and IoMT, highlighting their significance and historical evolution. This chapter delves into the types and roles of edge devices in healthcare, elucidating their functionalities and applications. The benefits of integrating edge devices with IoMT are discussed, including improved patient monitoring, real-time data collection, enhanced decision-making, and cost-effectiveness. Key enabling technologies like edge computing, data analytics, machine learning, and communication protocols are examined. The chapter also covers practical applications and use cases, from remote patient monitoring and telemedicine to smart hospitals and emergency response systems. Challenges such as data privacy, interoperability, scalability, and regulatory compliance are addressed, providing a balanced view of the current landscape. Future trends and innovations, including advances in edge computing, personalized medicine, and the potential role of blockchain, are explored. This chapter highlights the transformative potential of integrating edge devices and IoMT in modern healthcare, pointing towards a future of more efficient, accurate, and patient-centered medical services.

***Keywords*:** Edge computing, IoMT, healthcare, personalized medicine, blockchain, patient monitoring

**Corresponding author*: manojpatracs@gmail.com

S. Rakesh Kumar, N. Gayathri and Seifedine Kadry (eds.) Federated Intelligent System for Healthcare: A Practical Guide, (101–126) © 2025 Scrivener Publishing LLC

5.1 Introduction

The Internet of Medical Things (IoMT) and Edge Devices are two related technologies that help improve healthcare delivery through better connectivity, data collection, and intelligent processing. Wearables, medical sensors, and smart medical devices are among the types of edge devices found at the network's fringe. These gadgets gather real-time information from patients or medical environments and process it right there using local methodologies that leverage the powers of edge computing to bring down latency for faster decision making. Conversely, IoMT is the interlinked system in which these healthcare gadgets communicate with each other and transmit information automatically so as to offer immediate integrated patient management services [1]. The combination of IoMT and edge devices forms a platform for continuous patient management by facilitating monitoring, diagnosing, and treatment.

5.1.1 Importance and Impact on Modern Healthcare

Modern healthcare is transforming due to the integration of edge devices with IoMT. This integration optimizes resource usage, boosting diagnostic accuracy and enhancing patient care. With real-time patient monitoring, data can be collected continuously, and interventions can be made quickly, which is one of the main advantages. As an example, wearables have the ability to track critical health metrics like heart rate, blood pressure, and glucose levels and then send that information to doctors in real-time. Healthcare providers can save lives by responding quickly to abnormalities detected by this continuous data stream. Additionally, IoMT and edge devices improve diagnostic accuracy by giving complete and current patient information, enabling more informed clinical decisions [2]. Because treatments can be customized to meet the unique needs of individuals using accurate data, this results in improved patient outcomes.

The Internet of Medical Things (IoMT) and edge devices significantly influence healthcare operational efficiency. Healthcare providers are able to devote their time and energy to the most essential parts of patient care; thanks to these technologies, which automate mundane jobs like data entry and monitoring. Workflow efficiency and error prevention are both enhanced by this automation. Just as significant are the advantages for patients. Reducing healthcare expenditures, improving patients' quality of life, and remote monitoring of chronic disorders minimize the frequency of hospital visits [3]. In addition, patients are encouraged to take a more active role in their healthcare by receiving individualized and responsive care, made possible by IoMT, which promotes a more proactive approach to health management.

5.1.2 Historical Context and Evolution of Medical Technology

The current developments with IoMT and edge devices are set against the crucial background of medical technology's progress. Medical interventions were more limited in scope and accuracy when healthcare was primarily based on manual processes and primitive equipment. A major step in modernizing healthcare and better managing patient data was adopting electronic health records (EHRs), which brought the industry into the information age. The next step in this field's revolution was the introduction of telemedicine, which made healthcare more accessible to people in underdeveloped or far-flung locations by enabling consultations and treatment remotely [4].

Healthcare has entered a new era of precision medicine with the emergence of advanced medical equipment and data analytics. These developments have made it possible to conduct thorough data analyses, leading to more precise diagnoses and individualized treatment programs. The most recent development in this line of progression is the integration of IoT with medical technology, which has given rise to IoMT. By bringing data processing closer to its origin, edge computing has further improved this integration, lowering latency and making healthcare systems more responsive.

Improvements in healthcare that are more efficient, accurate, and focused on the patient have been a constant goal throughout history. Healthcare delivery is set to undergo further transformation with the integration of IoMT and edge devices. These innovations will improve patient outcomes and the quality of care provided, showcasing the industry's continuous growth. The future of healthcare will be increasingly influenced by these technologies as they progress, leading to greater interconnection, intelligence, and responsiveness to patients' demands.

5.2 Edge Devices in Healthcare

In healthcare, "edge devices" refer to a wide variety of peripheral technologies placed near the patients and the point of care on the network's edge. The wearables, medical sensors, and smart devices mentioned here are all vital to healthcare delivery in the current era. Smartwatches and fitness trackers are just a few examples of wearable tech that can keep tabs on your vitals.

People concerned about their health and those managing chronic ailments love these devices since they provide constant health data. Implanted or externally worn, medical sensors monitor vital signs like blood pressure, oxygen saturation, and glucose levels in people with diabetes. Smart medical devices, such as connected insulin pens, smart inhalers, and systems for remote patient monitoring, offer improved functionality [5]. Patients and doctors alike can benefit from the real-time health data made possible by these devices' integration with mobile apps and cloud platforms, allowing for improved health management and decision-making.

5.2.1 Functionalities of Edge Devices in Patient Monitoring

Continuous and real-time data gathering, processing, and analysis are made possible by edge devices, which play a crucial role in patient monitoring and treatment. These gadgets can continuously record patients' vital signs and other health indicators, giving us a good idea of how they're doing. One use case is the early detection of irregular cardiac rhythms using a wearable device, which can notify the patient and their healthcare professional. Patients with implanted medical sensors can keep tabs on vital signs like blood glucose levels and receive notifications if the readings go over the normal range. This helps to avoid any possible emergencies. By collecting detailed health data from patients in their homes, smart devices like RPM systems can cut down on unnecessary hospital trips and enable rapid actions informed by real-time data [6].

In addition, edge devices improve patient care by facilitating individualized treatment programs. Healthcare providers can personalize therapy for each patient by analyzing the data generated by these devices to find trends and patterns. Asthma patients can benefit from smart inhaler data by learning their triggers and making medication adjustments based on that knowledge. Improved response times and patient outcomes are achieved by the localized processing capability of edge devices, which guarantee the immediate processing and action of crucial health data. Patients are given more agency in their healthcare when these devices provide intuitive interfaces and notifications that allow them to self-manage their health.

5.2.2 Edge Device Applications in Healthcare

A huge number of healthcare applications are incorporating edge devices, attesting to their adaptability and efficacy in improving patient care. The use of CGMs, or continuous glucose monitors, is a well-known example of managing diabetes. These discreet sensors monitor blood sugar levels in real-time and send that information to a linked device so patients can be notified when they need to make adjustments. Patients benefit from improved glucose management and a decreased risk of complications thanks to this real-time monitoring [7]. Wearable electronic cardiac monitors (ECGs) are another example of this technology in action. Early alerts from these devices can avert major cardiovascular problems by detecting anomalies like atrial fibrillation.

The use of RPM systems has been highly beneficial in the field of chronic disease management. These networks gather information from various peripheral devices, including scales and blood pressure monitors, to monitor patients' health status in real time. This data can be accessed remotely by healthcare providers, allowing them to make well-informed decisions regarding treatment changes and interventions. For example, a real-time patient monitoring (RPM) system can help patients with heart failure identify the first symptoms of fluid accumulation, leading to fast medication modifications and avoiding hospitalizations. Patients with asthma can benefit from smart inhalers because they keep track of their drug usage and provide reminders, which helps them stick to their treatment programs and lessens the likelihood of asthma attacks. By providing novel approaches to patient health monitoring, management, and improvement, these instances demonstrate the revolutionary potential of edge devices in healthcare [8]. The capacity to offer proactive, individualized, and efficient patient care is anticipated to be progressively improved with the anticipated expansion of edge device integration in healthcare as technology progresses.

5.3 Internet of Medical Things (IoMT)

An ecosystem of networked software applications, health systems, and medical devices that gather, analyze, and send health data over the Internet is called the Internet of Medical Things (IoMT). Among the several parts that make up IoMT are healthcare apps, smart medical equipment, home monitoring systems, and wearable gadgets. The sensors built into these devices can record several vital signs, including heart rate, blood pressure, glucose levels, and others. For additional analysis and decision-making, the data acquired from these devices is typically processed locally utilizing edge computing technologies or sent to central databases. As a result of the integration of IoMT with cloud computing, healthcare professionals can gain real-time insights into patient health through scalable data storage and enhanced analytics [9]. To further facilitate the free flow of information between medical equipment and databases, IoMT frequently uses

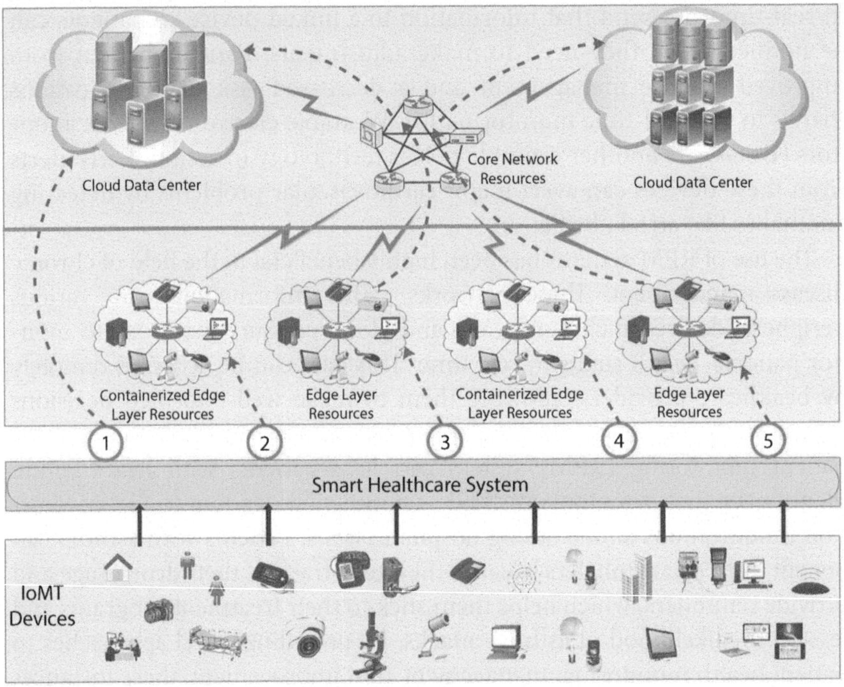

Figure 5.1 Edge device integrated internet of medical things.

industry-standard communication protocols and standards, including Bluetooth, Wi-Fi, and cellular networks. The architecture for edge device integrated IoMT is presented in Figure 5.1.

5.3.1 IoMT for Enhanced Healthcare Delivery

By facilitating early diagnosis, individualized treatment plans, and continuous real-time monitoring, IoMT significantly improves healthcare delivery and patient outcomes. The capacity to provide remote patient monitoring is one of the main advantages of IoMT. The continuous collection of health data via wearable devices and home monitoring systems enables healthcare providers to monitor patients' symptoms in real-time. By providing a steady flow of information, this system can better identify any health problems early on, allowing faster responses and less reliance on emergency rooms. Using a wearable electrocardiogram (ECG) monitor, the patient and the doctor can be notified of an abnormal cardiac rhythm, enabling prompt medical intervention. This proactive approach improves patient outcomes while reducing overall healthcare costs by reducing the number of in-person visits and preventing hospital stays [10].

On top of that, IoMT makes healthcare more personalized. More precise and tailored treatment programs are possible because of in-depth analysis of individual health patterns made possible by the massive amounts of data generated by IoMT devices. With this information, doctors may better meet the unique requirements of their patients and increase the efficacy of medical therapies. When it comes to managing diabetes, for example, continuous glucose monitors allow for improved glucose control and more accurate insulin doses by providing real-time data on blood sugar levels. Furthermore, by providing patients with access to their health data through linked apps and devices, IoMT enables enhanced patient engagement. Better treatment plan adherence and healthier lifestyle choices are the results of people becoming more involved in their own healthcare management [11].

5.3.2 Integration of IoMT with Existing Healthcare Systems

There are advantages and disadvantages to integrating IoMT with current healthcare systems. Improving EHRs with real-time data from IoMT devices is one of the leading prospects. Healthcare providers can now make better decisions for their patients; thanks to this integration, which gives them a complete picture of their health history and present status [12]. For instance, a continuous health timeline might be crucial in managing chronic diseases when data from wearable devices is integrated with EHRs. In addition, healthcare workers may devote more time to sophisticated patient care activities; thanks to the automation of mundane operations made possible by IoMT, which improves clinical workflows.

Nevertheless, several obstacles exist need to be overcome when integrating IoMT with preexisting systems. Data interoperability poses a substantial challenge due to the frequent differences in protocol and data format used by IoMT devices and healthcare systems. The key to successful integration is standardizing these protocols and guaranteeing smooth data transmission. Action must also be taken to address data security and privacy concerns. There has to be a system in place to prevent breaches and unauthorized access to the massive amounts of sensitive health data produced by IoMT devices. To protect patient information, stringent security measures, including healthcare legislation like HIPAA, must be implemented and followed. The last thing required to handle the deluge of data from IoMT devices is sufficient infrastructure and supporting systems. Healthcare organizations must invest money into scalable IT systems and learn how to handle and analyze data efficiently. By facilitating real-time monitoring, customized treatment, and improved patient interaction, IoMT can revolutionize healthcare delivery and boost patient outcomes [13]. The Internet of Medical Things (IoMT) has the potential to significantly improve healthcare by making it more efficient, linked, and patient-centered. However, there are several obstacles to overcome during the integration process. To effectively utilize the promise of IoMT in modern healthcare, it is essential to solve these problems as technology progresses.

5.4 Benefits of Integrating Edge Devices and IoMT

Patients can benefit significantly from real-time data collecting and monitoring when edge devices are integrated with the Internet of Medical Things (IoMT). Patient vitals like heart rate, blood pressure, glucose levels, and oxygen saturation are continuously collected by edge devices such as smart medical sensors and wearables. By continuously collecting data, healthcare providers may track their patients' vitals all day, allowing them to identify any changes or irregularities quickly. Because this data is updated in real-time, prompt action can be taken to avoid issues and save lives if needed. For instance, a smart ECG monitor can provide immediate alerts to patients with a history of cardiac difficulties if an irregular heartbeat is detected, enabling rapid medical intervention [14]. This continuous monitoring is especially effective for managing chronic illnesses and post-operative treatment, reducing the need for numerous in-person visits and hospitalizations.

5.4.1 Accuracy and Efficiency in Diagnostics and Treatment

The combination of IoMT with edge devices dramatically improves the precision and effectiveness of diagnosis and treatment. More accurate diagnoses are possible; thanks to the detailed and continuous data these devices provide, which illustrate a holistic picture of a patient's health.

To make sense of the massive volumes of data acquired, sophisticated analytics and machine learning algorithms can search for trends and anticipate serious health problems. These predictive capabilities make timely and focused treatment plans possible, leading to earlier and more accurate diagnoses. Also, by automating mundane operations like data collecting and monitoring, edge devices boost healthcare delivery efficiency, allowing doctors and nurses more time to concentrate on patients and important decisions [15]. For example, people with asthma can benefit from smart inhalers monitoring their medication use and environmental conditions. This allows for providing individualized insights and recommendations to prevent asthma episodes. Healthcare practitioners' workflow efficiency is improved, and patient outcomes are improved as a result.

5.4.2 Reduction in Latency and Faster Decision-Making

Two major benefits of combining IoMT with edge devices are lower latency and quicker decision-making. Instead of sending data to centralized cloud servers, edge computing enables processing to take place locally on edge devices or servers that are close by. Important medical records are always accessible because of this local processing capacity, which reduces the time it takes to analyze data and respond. For instance, when it comes to critical situations like identifying a sudden decrease in blood oxygen levels, quick data processing by edge devices might lead to quick medical intervention, which could prevent serious consequences [16]. Every second counts in acute care circumstances; thus, the ability to make quick decisions is vital. Patients and healthcare providers benefit from reduced latency because they can receive warnings and insights more quickly without the delays of cloud-based processing.

5.4.3 Cost-Effectiveness and Resource Optimization in Healthcare

Healthcare organizations may optimize resources and save money by integrating edge devices with IoMT. These technologies' automation and efficiency gains drastically cut down on the need for repeated jobs and heavy physical labor, resulting in substantial cost savings. The use of edge devices for remote patient monitoring reduces the number of hospital admissions and visits, which in turn reduces healthcare expenses for both patients and providers. Healthcare resource usage can be optimized with continuous data collecting and analysis capabilities [17]. For example, using real-time usage data to plan predictive maintenance, medical equipment might avoid unexpected problems and minimize downtime. In addition, edge devices and IoMT provide better resource allocation by giving healthcare workers access to accurate and timely data. This leads to more efficient medical staff, equipment, and facilities utilization. The operational costs are reduced, and the quality of care offered to patients is enhanced through this optimized management of resources. Improving patient monitoring and real-time data collection, reducing latency for faster decision-making, increasing accuracy and efficiency in diagnostics and treatment, and significantly optimizing resources and costs are just a few of the many advantages that can be gained by integrating edge devices with IoMT in healthcare. More responsive, efficient, and patient-centered healthcare is emerging due to these innovations. The Internet of Medical Things (IoMT) and edge devices have enormous untapped potential for enhancing healthcare delivery in the future, with the promise of even more significant advantages as technology advances [10].

5.5 Key Technologies Enabling Integration

A number of cutting-edge technologies allow for the integration of edge devices with the IoMT in healthcare. The delivery of healthcare is being revolutionized by these technologies, which cooperate to guarantee smooth data gathering, processing, and transmission. Some essential technologies include cloud computing, data analytics, machine learning, communication protocols, and standards [18]. These technologies are essential to put IoMT and edge devices to good use in healthcare environments.

5.5.1 Edge Computing

An essential component of IoMT, edge computing displaces data processing from distant cloud nodes and brings it closer to its point of origin. This targeted processing is necessary for reducing latency for life-or-death situations involving real-time medical applications. Edge devices, such as wearable cardiac monitors, can process data locally, immediately detecting arrhythmias and alerting patients and healthcare personnel, facilitating prompt intervention. When dealing with medical crises, such as monitoring patients with chronic heart diseases or managing acute incidents, the processing and response of data must be done immediately [19].

The scalability and dependability of IoMT systems are both improved by edge computing. Processing more data without putting too much strain on the system's central servers is possible by spreading the computing out to numerous edge devices. Even if some network portions have connectivity problems, healthcare services will continue functioning; thanks to this decentralized method. For instance, even in places with spotty internet coverage, edge devices can keep ticking and provide vital health monitoring services. Further, by lowering the amount of sensitive health data sent across public networks, edge computing enhances data privacy and security, making it easier to comply with strict health data standards and less likely that data breaches will occur.

5.5.2 Data Analytics and Machine Learning for Healthcare Insights

Technologies such as data analytics and ML are crucial for turning the health data gathered by IoMT devices into valuable insights. Machine learning algorithms can sift through mountains of data, searching for trends, correlations, and outliers that would otherwise go unnoticed by more conventional statistical approaches. Predicting patient outcomes, customizing treatment approaches, and enhancing overall care quality are greatly enhanced by these insights in healthcare. For instance, by using predictive analytics, we can foresee how chronic illness patients' conditions would worsen over time, which allows us to take preventative measures that lessen the likelihood of problems and hospitalizations.

The massive amounts, diverse types, and rapid speeds of data produced by IoMT devices are best handled by ML models. They improve their accuracy and usefulness by constantly learning from fresh data [20]. Patients with diabetes, for instance, can benefit from individualized insulin dosage recommendations generated by an ML algorithm coupled with a continuous glucose monitoring system. By keeping an eye on blood sugar levels in real time, this analysis helps lower the risk of diabetes-related problems. Data analytics can also help healthcare institutions maximize their operational efficiencies by examining trends in patient admissions, treatment efficacy, and resource use. This analysis leads to better management of hospital resources and better patient care.

5.5.3 Communication Protocols and Standards

The efficient transfer of health data and the seamless integration of IoMT devices depend on robust communication protocols and standards. Connectivity standards such as 5G, Bluetooth, and Wi-Fi allow for real-time data transfer between peripheral devices and main healthcare databases. Because it can handle the massive amounts of data produced by all those linked devices and make possible uses like remote surgery and real-time telemedicine, 5G is revolutionizing IoMT. For example, 5G can enable healthcare providers to transmit patient data in real time and conduct high-definition video consultations, allowing for precise remote diagnosis and treatment [21].

Bluetooth and Wi-Fi are crucial for connecting various medical devices in local environments, like homes or hospitals. Patients can easily track their vitals with the help of Bluetooth, which allows for short-range communication between wearables and cell phones. Wi-Fi enables more extensive connectivity, enabling several devices to link to a single network and send data to servers in the cloud for processing and storage. To construct cohesive and effective healthcare networks, it is crucial to standardize communication protocols so that various IoMT devices and systems may communicate with one another [22]. The ability to share and understand health information across multiple platforms and devices is crucial for improving the quality and continuity of patient care. Protocols like Fast Healthcare Interoperability Resources (FHIR) and Health Level Seven (HL7) make this possible through standardized data exchange.

5.5.4 Cloud Computing for Data Storage and Processing

Because of its scalable data storage and powerful processing capabilities, cloud computing is essential for IoMT integration. Robust storage systems are necessary to manage the volume, diversity, and velocity of health data, which is produced in large quantities by IoMT devices. The vast amounts of patient data and sensor readings can be safely stored in the cloud because of the platform's limitless storage capacity. Research and advanced healthcare applications rely on this centralized storage because it allows for thorough data analysis, comparisons with historical data, and tracking of long-term health trends. The cloud not only offers storage but also robust processing capabilities for data [23]. Advanced analytics and machine learning models housed on cloud platforms can handle and analyze massive datasets to facilitate clinical decision-making, producing valuable insights. Personalized treatment plans, early illness indicators, and patient outcomes can all be anticipated with the help of cloud-based AI algorithms. Additionally, healthcare providers can work together in real time; thanks to the cloud's secure data sharing and anytime, anywhere access. When working on complicated situations as a multidisciplinary team, all members must have access to the most up-to-date patient records and analytical findings.

Also, using cloud computing, additional digital health technologies like telehealth platforms and electronic health records (EHRs) can be easily integrated with IoMT. Data from IoMT devices can be easily integrated with existing health IT systems by utilizing cloud infrastructure, which improves healthcare system interoperability. Due to the integration, healthcare practitioners can access real-time data from IoMT devices and complete patient health information, improving the continuity of care [24]. To further guarantee the protection of sensitive health data throughout its lifetime, cloud-based solutions include increased data security features, such as encryption, access restrictions, and compliance with health standards like HIPAA.

In summary, healthcare IoMT integration and edge devices rely on cloud computing, data analytics, machine learning, communication protocols, and edge computing. The integration of these technologies is revolutionizing healthcare by making it more efficient, patient-centered, and linked. It allows real-time patient monitoring, improves diagnostic accuracy, decreases decision-making latency, and optimizes healthcare resources. Together, these technologies can radically alter healthcare delivery and the results patients get as they advance.

5.6 Applications and Use Cases of Edge Devices and IoMT

Patient care, results, and healthcare delivery have all been greatly improved; thanks to the many new applications and use cases made possible by combining edge devices with the IoMT in healthcare. Telemedicine and remote patient monitoring, chronic illness management, critical care and emergency response systems, and smart hospitals and healthcare facilities are some essential areas these technologies significantly influence.

5.6.1 Remote Patient Monitoring and Telemedicine

The most notable uses of edge devices and the Internet of Medical Things (IoMT) are telemedicine and remote patient monitoring (RPM), both revolutionizing healthcare delivery. To continuously gather health data from patients outside of conventional clinical settings, RPM employs a variety of wearable gadgets, smart sensors, and home monitoring systems. Edge devices subsequently process the data, enabling healthcare providers to monitor patients in real-time [12]. People who suffer from hypertension, for instance, can benefit from smart blood pressure monitors that notify their doctors at regular intervals. Medicine changes or lifestyle suggestions may be necessary in the event of a sudden and substantial rise or fall in blood pressure.

Patients can consult with healthcare specialists remotely using telemedicine, which is made possible by high-speed internet and IoMT. People in underserved or far-flung locations, who might not have easy access to healthcare institutions, would greatly benefit from this [25]. Thanks to video conferencing, patients don't even have to leave their homes to get a diagnosis, treatment plan, and follow-up care. During the COVID-19 pandemic, for example, telemedicine's ability to provide ongoing care while reducing the danger of virus transmission was crucial. Health outcomes and patient satisfaction are greatly enhanced when RPM and telemedicine are integrated, as patients are guaranteed comprehensive and continuous care.

5.6.2 Chronic Disease Management

Edge devices and IoMT are essential in managing long-term health conditions, including diabetes and heart disease. These conditions must be monitored constantly and treated promptly to avoid complications. One example of an edge device that provides real-time data on blood glucose levels is a continuous glucose monitor (CGM) used for diabetes management [26]. Continuous glucose monitors notify patients and medical professionals when glucose levels rise to risky level or fall too low. To avoid serious problems like hypoglycemia or hyperglycemia, this enables prompt remedial measures like changing insulin dosages or food consumption.

The Internet of Medical Things (IoMT) helps manage cardiovascular illness because of wearable electrocardiogram (ECG) monitors and smartwatches that can monitor heart rhythms and identify abnormalities. These gadgets can notify doctors and patients of possible problems like atrial fibrillation, so treatment can begin sooner rather than later. The patient's cardiovascular health can be better understood with the help of edge devices because they can also track additional vital signs like blood pressure and oxygen saturation [27]. The Internet of Medical Things (IoMT) dramatically enhances the management of chronic diseases, decreasing hospital admissions and enhancing patients' quality of life by enabling continuous monitoring and early detection of any problems.

5.6.3 Emergency Response Systems and Critical Care

When used in conjunction with IoMT, edge devices have the potential to save lives in critical care and emergency response systems. Critical in times of crisis, these technologies allow for quickly gathering and analyzing data. An example would be the ability of ambulances with Internet of Medical Things (IoMT) devices to track a patient's vitals on the way to the hospital and send that information to the emergency room in real-time [28]. The medical staff can start treatment regimens as soon as the patient arrives, saving valuable time.

Similarly, IoMT can be used by critical care units to keep tabs on patients around the clock. Several indicators, including heart rate, breathing rate, and body movements, can be monitored via smart beds fitted with sensors. Edge devices analyze this data for indications of distress or worsening, which then triggers rapid intervention by the medical team. Integrating IoMT with automated external defibrillators (AEDs) allows the patient's condition to be monitored in real-time, allowing for faster response times in the event of a cardiac arrest. IoMT's real-time capabilities guarantee that patients get interventions that improve their survival rates and outcomes when used in emergency and critical care situations.

5.6.4 Smart Hospitals and Healthcare Facilities

Smart hospitals and healthcare facilities utilize IoMT and edge devices to improve operational efficiency and patient care. From patient admission to discharge, these institutions use interconnected devices to simplify numerous processes. For instance, medical equipment can have its whereabouts and status tracked by asset tracking systems enabled by the Internet of Medical Things (IoMT), guaranteeing that crucial instruments are never out of commission. As a result, there is less downtime and more efficient use of resources.

Smart hospitals also use electronic health records (EHRs) connected with IoMT to improve patient management. Data from different edge devices can be updated automatically in patients' electronic health records. The data stored in EHR gives healthcare practitioners a complete and current picture of their patients' health. This integration improves care coordination because everyone on the healthcare team has access to the same information. Smart rooms with Internet of Medical Things (IoMT) devices can also continually monitor patients' vital signs and tailor environmental controls like lighting and temperature to each patient's preferences and needs, making them more comfortable and facilitating recovery. In addition, IoMT can aid in the predictive maintenance of medical equipment. IoMT constantly monitors equipment like MRI machines and ventilators to determine when maintenance is necessary. This prevents unexpected breakdowns and ensures the equipment is always in the best possible condition [29]. Healthcare facilities can save a lot of money; thanks to this preventative measure, which increases the durability and dependability of medical instruments.

In summary, there are many use cases and applications for edge devices and IoMT integration in healthcare that optimize healthcare delivery, improve results, and enrich patient care. These technologies, from telemedicine and remote patient monitoring to smart hospitals and emergency response systems, are making healthcare more efficient, connected, and patient-centered. The Internet of Medical Things (IoMT) and edge computing can significantly improve healthcare delivery and patient outcomes, and this promise will only grow as these technologies advance.

5.7 Challenges and Considerations

Assuring data privacy and security, achieving interoperability with existing healthcare systems, and maintaining scalability and network stability are key challenges and considerations when integrating IoMT and edge devices in healthcare. Since these technologies need to follow strict healthcare standards such as HIPAA and GDPR, it is also essential to address compliance and regulatory concerns. Full realization of the benefits of IoMT and edge computing in healthcare requires a complete approach that leverages improved security mechanisms, established protocols, and resilient infrastructure. This will help overcome these problems.

5.7.1 Data Privacy and Security Concerns in IoMT and Edge Devices

Integrating IoMT and edge devices into healthcare raises serious data security and privacy concerns. Because of the large volumes of sensitive health data, these devices transmit and gather; thus, they are easy targets for cybercriminals. It is essential to secure this data to keep patient information private and prevent data breaches. Because IoMT devices are dispersed, there is a larger potential attack surface, making it harder to secure all endpoints adequately. All devices must adhere to established security procedures, firewalls, and encryption standards [30]. However, these safeguards might not be enough because many edge devices are underpowered and need more resources to handle complex security tasks. Security at the device, network, and cloud levels are all necessary for healthcare providers to safeguard data at every stage of its lifetime.

In addition, there are data privacy problems related to meeting the requirements of strict laws like the EU's General Data Protection Regulation (GDPR) and the US's Health Insurance Portability and Accountability Act (HIPAA). Collecting, storing, and sharing health data is subject to stringent limits imposed by this legislation. Dealing with cross-border data transfers and varied local legislation can make ensuring that IoMT and edge devices comply with these regulations much more challenging. To protect their patients' personal information, healthcare organizations should anonymize data whenever possible, strictly enforce access rules, and do audits and evaluations regularly. Ensuring strong security measures are not at the expense of the easy access and interchange of data necessary to improve patient care.

5.7.2 Interoperability and Integration with Existing Healthcare Infrastructure

The successful deployment of IoMT and edge devices requires interoperability and integration with existing healthcare infrastructure [31]. These gadgets produce interoperable datasets with preexisting healthcare IT systems, such as EHRs and HIS. Data silos, caused by a lack of standards, prevent patients' vital health records from being shared across various systems and devices, which in turn limits their access to holistic treatment. Adopting industry standards like HL7, FHIR, and DICOM is essential for healthcare providers to achieve genuine interoperability. All necessary patient information may be quickly and easily accessed by healthcare providers; thanks to these standards, which allow for the smooth transfer of health data between different systems.

Still, getting everything to work together is no picnic. Due to their disparate origins and potential usage of proprietary formats and protocols, many healthcare systems need help to integrate. It may be necessary to upgrade or replace legacy systems entirely if they do not support current interoperability standards. Also, you may need to put a lot of time, money, and technical know-how into the integration process. Notwithstanding these obstacles, interoperability offers substantial advantages, including better care coordination, better clinical decision-making, and fewer administrative constraints. To ensure smooth data flow throughout the healthcare ecosystem, providers should prioritize interoperability efforts and collaborate closely with technology vendors, standards groups, and regulatory agencies to create and execute solutions.

5.7.3 Scalability and Network Reliability

For IoMT and edge devices to be widely used in healthcare, scalability, and network dependability are crucial factors to address. Healthcare providers must ensure their IT system can handle the increasing amount of data and the number of linked devices. Being able to handle the growing network complexity is just as important as adding more devices and processing more enormous datasets when it comes to scalability. By spreading the processing burden among numerous devices, edge computing improves system performance while decreasing the need for centralized cloud resources. However, healthcare providers must be cautious when designing their edge computing architecture to ensure it can grow well without sacrificing performance or dependability.

Because healthcare applications frequently necessitate the transmission and analysis of data in real-time or near-real-time, network reliability is of similar importance. In urgent and emergencies, any interruptions in network connectivity can have a major impact on patient care. Healthcare providers should prioritize the development of a robust network infrastructure. This includes reliable internet connections, backup paths, and cutting-edge technologies for managing and optimizing network performance [32]. The increasing needs of the Internet of Things (IoT) and edge devices can be met with the help of technologies like 5G, which provide potential solutions in the form of low latency and high bandwidth. While 5G is still in the works for broad implementation, healthcare providers may provide reliable network connectivity by combining existing technology.

5.7.4 Regulatory and Compliance Issues

Healthcare providers need help integrating IoMT and edge devices to navigate complex regulatory and compliance challenges. These devices must follow medical device, data privacy, and cybersecurity regulations. Internet of Medical Things (IoMT) devices are subject to regulation and clearance by the US Food and Drug Administration (FDA). To guarantee the safety and effectiveness of the equipment, the approval procedure can be long and rigorous, necessitating considerable testing and validation. Similarly, medical device development and deployment in Europe are subject to stringent regulations known as the Medical Device Regulation (MDR). If we want to sell IoMT devices and earn the confidence of doctors and patients, we must comply with these rules [32].

Compliance with data protection rules, such as GDPR and HIPAA, further complicates matters. Strict controls over the collection, storage, processing, and sharing of health data are mandated under this legislation. Ensuring compliance requires healthcare providers to establish robust data governance frameworks. These frameworks should include policies about data access, data sharing, and incident response. Legal responsibilities, reputational harm, and heavy fines await those who fail to comply. As the Internet of Things (IoT) and edge devices continue to develop, existing regulatory frameworks must change to accommodate these developments.

To stay up with technological innovations while protecting patient privacy and safety, legislation must be continuously updated through collaboration between healthcare providers, tech developers, regulatory agencies, and lawmakers.

Overall, healthcare has many advantages from incorporating IoMT and edge devices, but there are also many things to think about and handle. These technologies' successful adoption and deployment depend on resolving data privacy and security concerns, achieving interoperability, guaranteeing scalability and network stability, and overcoming regulatory and compliance difficulties. To overcome these limitations and fully realize the potential of IoMT and edge devices in improving patient care and outcomes, healthcare providers must adopt a comprehensive and proactive approach, employing the newest technology and best practices.

5.8 Future Trends and Innovations

The Internet of Medical Things (IoMT), edge computing, AI, predictive analytics, and blockchain are poised to revolutionize healthcare in the future. These developments allow data to be processed and analyzed in real time, leading to better diagnoses and faster actions. IoMT's capacity to collect extensive patient data will benefit personalized medicine, enabling specific treatment approaches. Disease management and prevention will be improved using AI and predictive analytics, which will also optimize the allocation of resources and lead to better patient outcomes. Blockchain technology will provide strong data security and integrity to facilitate safe data sharing and conformity with regulatory requirements. An improved, more efficient healthcare system, linked and focused on the patient, is within reach.

5.8.1 Advances in Edge Computing Technologies and Their Potential Impact

New developments in edge computing will speed up, improve efficiency, and make IoMT systems much more scalable, all of which will profoundly impact the healthcare system. With each new iteration, edge computing technology gains processing capacity and can process more complicated computations locally at the source of data generation. This change allows for the processing and analysis of data in real time while reducing the dependence on centralized cloud servers, which minimizes latency. For example, enhanced processors and machine learning capabilities allow newer edge devices to conduct complex analytics locally [33]. Applications like automated medical interventions, real-time patient monitoring, and emergency notifications rely on this power to respond instantly.

Such innovations might have far-reaching consequences. Quicker and more precise diagnoses, better patient outcomes due to prompt interventions, and a more pleasant patient experience are all possible thanks to edge computing in healthcare. In addition to reducing operational expenses, bandwidth constraints, and data volume transferred via networks, edge computing helps with these by processing data locally. As a result, healthcare providers can save money and use their resources better, while patients enjoy better care and shorter wait times. Healthcare operations will be even more streamlined, large-scale IoMT deployments will be easier to manage, and the continuous development and integration of edge computing technologies will support the demand for personalized and precision medicine.

5.8.2 Emerging Applications of IoMT in Personalized Medicine

Personalized medicine is a relatively new area of study that relies heavily on IoMT to further customize medical care to each patient based on their unique circumstances. Internet of Medical Things (IoMT) devices provide a holistic picture of a patient's health by collecting massive volumes of data on their physiological indicators, lifestyle choices, and environmental exposures. This information is priceless for creating tailored treatment regimens that outperform generic, generalized methods. One example is the development of personalized wellness and fitness regimens made possible by wearable gadgets that track vital signs, including heart rate, exercise, and sleep. Similarly, sophisticated insulin pumps and continuous glucose monitors allow for precise and dynamic diabetes treatment by altering insulin supply according to glucose levels in real-time [34].

In addition, IoMT makes it easier to incorporate omics data, including genomes, into therapeutic practice. Healthcare professionals can better anticipate illness risk, personalize preventive actions, and select the most effective therapies by integrating genetic information with real-time health data. To detect and treat diseases early, IoMT devices will regularly monitor patients with a family history of cardiovascular disease or cancer, for example. Health outcomes, patient involvement, and treatment plan adherence are all improved by this proactive strategy. New opportunities for precision healthcare and tailored patient care strategies will arise due to the growing number of uses for IoMT technology in customized medicine.

5.8.3 Integration with Artificial Intelligence and Predictive Analytics

More precise diagnoses, improved patient outcomes, and optimal care delivery are all possible results of integrating IoMT with AI and predictive analytics, which has the potential to revolutionize healthcare. Artificial intelligence systems can sift through the mountains of data produced by IoMT devices in search of trends, outliers, and health crises to come. One use case is the analysis of continuous data streams from wearable heart monitors by machine learning models. These models can then predict the likelihood of cardiac events, enabling timely prophylactic treatments. Similarly, AI can streamline clinical procedures and deliver individualized treatment suggestions by processing data from various sources, such as medical records and IoMT devices [35].

Areas like illness prevention, chronic condition management, and hospital resource optimization stand to benefit significantly from predictive analytics driven by AI. Disease outbreaks, patient admissions, and high-complication risk patients can be identified using prediction models that use historical data and real-time inputs from IoMT devices. These capabilities allow improved patient care, lower costs, and more efficient resource allocation. For instance, by using predictive analytics, hospital bed occupancy rates can be better managed, guaranteeing that resources are always available. Healthcare will significantly improve, becoming more proactive, individualized, and efficient by integrating AI and predictive analytics with IoMT.

5.8.4 Potential for Blockchain in Securing IoMT Data

One potential way to improve the safety and authenticity of IoMT data is with blockchain technology. It is critical to guarantee data privacy and security because of the delicate nature of health data and the growing number of cyberattacks. An appropriate solution for protecting IoMT data would be blockchain, which offers a distributed and immutable record of transactions [36]. It is challenging, if possible, to tamper with the data entered into an immutable chain of connected encrypted transactions. This function safeguards sensitive health information by preventing accidental or malicious changes or disclosure.

Blockchain technology has a wide range of possible uses in the IoMT. By limiting access to sensitive information to authorized users, blockchain technology can make it easier for healthcare providers, patients, and other stakeholders to share data securely. For instance, a blockchain network enables the safe transfer of patient health data acquired by IoMT devices to various healthcare providers while preserving the confidentiality and authenticity of the data. It is now much easier to trace the origin and transit of data thanks to blockchain technology, which also improves the accountability and traceability of data transactions [37]. This skill is vital to stay in line with regulations and keep patients' trust. In addition, smart contracts in healthcare are just one of the advanced applications blockchain can allow. Smart contracts are agreements whose terms are encoded into code and can execute themselves. Insurance claims processing, clinical trial administration, and patient consent management are just a few of the operations that can be automated to improve efficiency and alleviate administrative costs. Integrating blockchain with IoMT will create robust security frameworks as the technology develops, allowing for the secure and efficient use of health data in contemporary healthcare systems.

5.9 Conclusion

An enormous step forward in contemporary healthcare is the combination of edge devices with the Internet of Medical Things (IoMT), which opens up a world of possibilities for enhanced operational efficiency and better patient care. Remote patient monitoring, chronic disease management, emergency response, and smart healthcare facilities are just a few areas that have benefited from the integration discussed in this chapter. Other areas include the kinds and functions of edge devices, the significance of collecting and processing data in real time, and the applications. Data analytics, cloud computing, communication protocols, data privacy, interoperability, and regulatory compliance were some important topics covered, along with the critical technologies that make this integration possible, such as edge computing, cloud computing, data analytics, machine learning, and communication protocols.

Integrating edge devices with IoMT has enormous potential to revolutionize modern healthcare. These innovations pave the way for early diagnosis of health problems, prompt treatments, and individualized treatment programs by allowing continuous and real-time patient monitoring. By avoiding problems and hospitalizations, this preventative method improves patient outcomes and lessens the strain on healthcare systems. By improving clinical decision-making, maximizing resource usage, and offering actionable insights from massive amounts of health data, AI and predictive analytics significantly expand the capabilities of IoMT. In addition, using blockchain technology to safeguard IoMT data solves important problems with data privacy and security problems, making it possible to transmit sensitive health information to authorized parties safely. Other areas require additional research and development in the future to harness the power of edge devices and IoMT entirely in healthcare. One crucial area is the development of edge computing technology, which will allow for more advanced data processing and analytics capabilities at the edge. To guarantee smooth integration and data sharing, it is essential to research improving the interoperability of IoMT devices with current healthcare IT systems. Much of our efforts will also investigate how cutting-edge AI and ML models may improve the prediction and management of health issues. Another crucial issue is creating strong regulatory frameworks that guarantee data security and patient safety while keeping up with technological advances. In conclusion, if we want to see these technologies adopted widely in various healthcare contexts, from large urban hospitals to small rural clinics, we need to solve the problems of scalability and network reliability.

In conclusion, healthcare is on the brink of a revolution due to the potential for edge device integration with IoMT to bring about more connected, efficient, and patient-centered care. We may look forward to a future where healthcare is more accessible, preventative, and individualized; thanks to the persistent progress in associated technology and proactive measures to tackle present obstacles. Unleashing the full potential of IoMT and edge computing to change healthcare delivery and experiences worldwide will require ongoing research and innovation in this field.

References

1. Putra, K.T., *et al.*, A Review on the Application of Internet of Medical Things in Wearable Personal Health Monitoring: A Cloud-Edge Artificial Intelligence Approach, in: *IEEE Access*, vol. 12, pp. 21437–21452, 2024, doi: 10.1109/ACCESS.2024.3358827.
2. Pradyumna, G. R., Hegde R. B., Bommegowda, K. B., Jan, T. and Naik, G.R., Empowering Healthcare With IoMT: Evolution, Machine Learning Integration, Security, and Interoperability Challenges, in: *IEEE Access*, vol. 12, pp. 20603–20623, 2024, doi: 10.1109/ACCESS.2024.3362239.
3. El-Saleh, A.A., Sheikh, A.M., Albreem, M.A.M., *et al.*, The Internet of Medical Things (IoMT): opportunities and challenges. *Wireless Netw.*, 2024, https://doi.org/10.1007/s11276-024-03764-8.
4. Sharma, D., Singh Aujla, G., Bajaj, R., Evolution from ancient medication to human-centered Healthcare 4.0: A review on health care recommender systems. *Int. J. Commun. Syst.*, *36*, 12, e4058, 2023.

5. Hartmann, M., Hashmi, U.S., Imran, A., Edge computing in smart health care systems: Review, challenges, and research directions. *Trans. Emerging Telecommun. Technol.*, *33*, 3, e3710, 2022.
6. Pathinarupothi, R.K., Durga, P., Rangan, E.S., IoT-based smart edge for global health: Remote monitoring with severity detection and alerts transmission. *IEEE Internet Things J.*, *6*, 2, 2449–2462, 2018.
7. Ray, P.P., Dash, D., De, D., Edge computing for Internet of Things: A survey, e-healthcare case study and future direction. *J. Netw. Comput. Appl.*, *140*, 1–22, 2019.
8. Greco, L., Percannella, G., Ritrovato, P., Tortorella, F., Vento, M., Trends in IoT based solutions for health care: Moving AI to the edge. *Pattern Recognit. Lett.*, *135*, 346–353, 2020.
9. Patra, M.K., Kumari, A., Sahoo, B., Turuk, A.K., Smart healthcare system using cloud-integrated internet of medical things, in: *Exploring the Convergence of Computer and Medical Science Through Cloud Healthcare*, pp. 60–83, IGI Global, United States of America, 2023.
10. Ahmed, S.F., Alam, M.S.B., Afrin, S., Rafa, S.J., Rafa, N., Gandomi, A.H., Insights into Internet of Medical Things (IoMT): Data fusion, security issues and potential solutions. *Inf. Fusion*, *102*, 102060, 2024.
11. Arthi, K. and Chidhambararajan, B., Advanced Enabling Technologies of IoMT in Personalized Healthcare, in: *Technological Advancement in Internet of Medical Things and Blockchain for Personalized Healthcare*, pp. 1–15, CRC Press, Boca Raton, USA, 2024.
12. Sharma, N., Tiwari, S., Ilyas, M., Raghuvanshi, R., Verma, A., IoMT Implementation: Technological Overview for Healthcare Systems, in: *Federated Learning for Internet of Medical Things*, pp. 65–83, 2023.
13. Awotunde, J.B., Chakraborty, C., AbdulRaheem, M., Jimoh, R.G., Oladipo, I.D., Bhoi, A.K., Internet of medical things for enhanced smart healthcare systems, in: *Implementation of smart healthcare systems using AI, IoT, and blockchain*, pp. 1–28, Academic Press, Cambridge, Massachusetts, 2023.
14. Sharmila, E.M.N., Rama Krishna, K., Prasad, G.N.R., Anand, B., Kwatra, C.V., Kapila, D., IoMT—Applications, Benefits, and Future Challenges in the Healthcare Domain, in: *Advances in Fuzzy-Based Internet of Medical Things (IoMT)*, pp. 1–23, 2024.
15. Izhar, M., Naqvi, S.A.A., Ahmed, A., Abdullah, S., Alturki, N., Jamel, L., Enhancing Healthcare Efficacy Through IoT-Edge Fusion: A Novel Approach for Smart Health Monitoring and Diagnosis. *IEEE Access*, *11*, 136456–136467, 2023.
16. Kumar R.H. and Rajaram B., Design and Simulation of an Edge Compute Architecture for IoT-Based Clinical Decision Support System, in: *IEEE Access*, vol. 12, pp. 45456–45474, 2024, doi: 10.1109/ACCESS.2024.3380906.
17. Wen, B., Li, S. and Motevalli, H., Exploitation of healthcare IoT–fog-based smart e-health gateways: a resource optimization approach, *Cluster Comput.*, 27, 10733–10755, 2024, https://doi.org/10.1007/s10586-024-04502-7.

18. Verma, H., Chauhan, N., Awasthi, L.K., A Comprehensive review of 'Internet of Healthcare Things': Networking aspects, technologies, services, applications, challenges, and security concerns. *Comput. Sci. Rev.*, *50*, 100591, 2023.
19. Singh, A. and Chatterjee, K., Edge computing based secure health monitoring framework for electronic healthcare system. *Cluster Comput.*, *26*, 2, 1205–1220, 2023.
20. Sinha, A., Garcia, D.W., Kumar, B., Banerjee, P., Application of big data analytics and Internet of Medical Things (IoMT) in healthcare with view of explainable artificial intelligence: A survey, in: *Interpretable Cognitive Internet of Things for Healthcare*, pp. 129–163, Springer International Publishing, Cham, 2023.
21. Osama, M., Ateya, A.A., Sayed, M.S., Hammad, M., Pławiak, P., Abd El-Latif, A.A., Elsayed, R.A., Internet of medical things and healthcare 4.0: Trends, requirements, challenges, and research directions. *Sensors*, *23*, 17, 7435, 2023.
22. Kotha, A., Manohar, K., U, V., IaaSI: A device based interoperability as a service for IoMT devices. *J. Ambient Intell. Hum. Comput.*, *14*, 10, 14321–14332, 2023.
23. Patra, M.K., Sahoo, B., Turuk, A.K., Smart healthcare system using containerized internet of medical things, in: *Handbook of Research on Mathematical Modeling for Smart Healthcare Systems*, pp. 261–278, IGI Global, Hershey, Pennsylvania, 2022.
24. Inkollu, P., Besta, V.C., Krishna, Y.R., Vemula, K., Secure Efficient and Cloud-Centric Smart Healthcare System with Public Verifiability and Internet of Medical Things (IoMT), in: *Disruptive technologies in Computing and Communication Systems*, pp. 153–156, CRC Press, Abingdon, England, 2024.
25. Srivastava, M., Siddiqui, A.T., Srivastava, V., Application of Artificial Intelligence of Medical Things in Remote Healthcare Delivery, in: *Handbook of Security and Privacy of AI-Enabled Healthcare Systems and Internet of Medical Things*, pp. 169–190, CRC Press, Boca Raton, USA, 2024.
26. Wang, X. and Song, Y., Edge-assisted IoMT-based smart-home monitoring system for the elderly with chronic diseases. *IEEE Sens. Lett.*, *7*, 2, 1–4, 2023.
27. Nigar, N., Jaleel, A., Islam, S., Shahzad, M.K., Affum, E.A., IoMT meets machine learning: From edge to cloud chronic diseases diagnosis system. *J. Healthcare Eng.*, *2023*, 1, 9995292, 2023.
28. Shafiq, M., Choi, J.G., Cheikhrouhou, O., Hamam, H., Advances in IoMT for Healthcare Systems. *Sensors*, *24*, 1, 10, 2023.
29. Ramakrishnan, S., Jijitha, S., Amudha, T., Roadmap of AI and IoMT in smart healthcare: Current applications and future perspectives, in: *Internet of Medical Things in Smart Healthcare*, pp. 137–161, 2024.
30. Nair, A.K., Sahoo, J., Raj, E.D., Privacy preserving Federated Learning framework for IoMT based big data analysis using edge computing. *Comput. Stand. Interfaces*, *86*, 103720, 2023.

31. Subramaniam, E.V.D., Srinivasan, K., Qaisar, S.M., Pławiak, P., Interoperable IoMT approach for remote diagnosis with privacy-preservation perspective in edge systems. *Sensors, 23*, 17, 7474, 2023.
32. Meng, L. and Li, D., Novel Edge Computing-Based Privacy-Preserving Approach for Smart Healthcare Systems in the Internet of Medical Things. *J. Grid Comput., 21*, 4, 66, 2023.
33. Dilibal, C., Development of edge-IoMT computing architecture for smart healthcare monitoring platform, in: *2020 4th International Symposium on Multidisciplinary Studies and Innovative Technologies (ISMSIT)*, 2020, October, IEEE, pp. 1–4.
34. Gupta, S., Shabaz, M., Gupta, A., Alqahtani, A., Alsubai, S., Ofori, I., Personal HealthCare of Things: A novel paradigm and futuristic approach. *CAAI Transactions on Intelligence Technology*, https://doi.org/10.1049/cit2.12220.
35. Awotunde, J.B., Folorunso, S.O., Ajagbe, S.A., Garg, J., Ajamu, G.J., AiIoMT: IoMT-based system-enabled artificial intelligence for enhanced smart healthcare systems, in: *Machine learning for critical Internet of Medical Things: applications and use cases*, pp. 229–254, 2022.
36. Nie, X., Zhang, A., Chen, J., Qu, Y., Yu, S., Blockchain-empowered secure and privacy-preserving health data sharing in edge-based IoMT. *Secur. Commun. Netw., 2022*, 1, 8293716, 2022.
37. Arul, R., Al-Otaibi, Y. D., Alnumay, W. S., Tariq, U., Shoaib, U. and Piran, M.D.J., Multi-modal secure healthcare data dissemination framework using blockchain in IoMT, *Pers. Ubiquitous Comput.*, 28, 1, 3–15, 2024, https://doi.org/10.1007/s00779-021-01527-2.

6

Cloud Infrastructure and Federated Learning

Kanishka Gupta[1*], Amit Aylani[1], Prakash Parmar[1] and Deepak Hajoary[2]

[1]Vidyalankar Institute of Technology, Mumbai, India
[2]Bodoland University, Assam, India

Abstract

The arena of Artificial intelligence has been boosted by the advent of cloud computing along with machine learning techniques. Cloud computing is an affordable and scalable service that has completely transformed the IT environment. It offers on-demand services and can be accessed over the Internet. With these solutions, it is possible to provide technologically advanced services that are restricted only to large corporations, offering IT capabilities in a more democratic way. At its core, cloud computing employs a particular hardware and software infrastructure that enables virtualized resources, which in turn drive cost-effectiveness and allow for dynamic scaling.

Decentralized training methodology, encourages the security and privacy of federated learning and sets new standards for the machine learning style. Certain assumptions of privacy are tied to the classical methods, but FL allows for multiple devices to train a model together without exchanging raw data. The combination of federated learning with cloud infrastructure allows for the efficient handling of model updates from multiple edge devices, guaranteeing scalability and stability.

The cloud facilitates continuous learning from distributed data sources, enhancing model accuracy and generalizability. This synergy is particularly transformative in fields such as healthcare, where FL allows for the training of predictive models on patient data from multiple hospitals without compromising privacy.

In this chapter, the major principles of cloud infrastructure and federated learning, the technological components, and various use cases are examined. It still covers issues related to security, privacy, scalability, and legal issues in big data processing. The topics are well supported by case studies, demonstrating the integration's effects on service individualization, health care, intelligent manufacturing, and other fields,

**Corresponding author*: kanishkagupta8866@gmail.com

S. Rakesh Kumar, N. Gayathri and Seifedine Kadry (eds.) Federated Intelligent System for Healthcare: A Practical Guide, (127–152) © 2025 Scrivener Publishing LLC

which give direction to the future development of intelligent computing and data-driven decisions.

Keywords: Cloud infrastructure, federated learning, distributed computing, intelligent computing, centralized training, machine learning

6.1 Foundations of the Future: Cloud Infrastructure Meets Federated Learning

The advent of cloud computing has dramatically reshaped the IT landscape, providing unprecedented access to scalable, cost-effective services. This revolution has played a crucial role in the proliferation of Software as a Service (SaaS), which has redefined the development and procurement of IT hardware and software. By leveraging cloud technology, users can access a wide range of services over the internet, paying only for what they use. This pay-as-you-go model has made advanced IT capabilities accessible to businesses of all sizes, driving innovation and efficiency across various sectors.

At the very center of cloud computing lies an advanced infrastructure of hardware and software components of the resource pool that is to be used in rendering services to consumers. These would range from servers to networking equipment and data storage devices managed by a hardware abstraction layer that enables the virtualization of resources. This layer then allows two significant benefits for cloud computing: cost-effectiveness and dynamic scalability.

At the heart of the cloud computing concept is a model wherein different clients can access IT capabilities as services through the Internet [1]. These services include commercial applications, processing power, storage capacity, and more. The main goal is to offer network-enabled services that are scaled, reliable, and flexible enough to be used by as large a user base as possible. This model includes private, public, communal, and hybrid cloud installations; all of these offer special advantages suited to diverse requirements. Moreover, the three main cloud computing service models have their different benefits and drawbacks: Platform as a Service, Infrastructure as a Service, and Software as a Service.

Federated Learning is a very new approach to machine learning, putting the security of the data and privacy at the core of the training of models [2]. Unlike traditional techniques that require data to be centrally pooled, FL can train a model on several devices/nodes without actually exchanging the raw data. This decentralized approach satisfies the strictest data protection laws, such as GDPR or HIPAA, but more importantly, solves important privacy concerns [3].

Using sophisticated networking, scalable storage, and processing capacity in the cloud, FL integration goes a long way in enhancing this procedure. Such synergy ensures that there is scalable and reliable performance, since model updates from several edge devices are efficiently managed. The cloud infrastructure improves the precision and applicability of the models by ensuring continuous learning from dispersed data sources. For example, FL enables training predictive models on multisite patient data without loss of privacy, which the global architecture of the cloud harnesses to coordinate seamlessly.

Modern IT ecosystems have complex needs that organizations can meet by leveraging the privacy-preserving benefits of federated learning with the flexibility and scalability afforded by cloud computing. This strong combination can deliver strong performance, higher security, and cost-effective solutions for firms to thrive in the digital age. The technologies will continue to evolve, unlocking even more powerful capabilities that will reshape competitive strategies and organizational processes in light of a changing world market at large.

It is where the combination of cloud computing and federated learning makes a difference in the inclusion of improvement in scalability, data privacy, and collaborative learning. This integration solves the disadvantages of traditional centralized machine learning; and hence, opens the doors to more efficient and secure AI applications in many industries. Continuous development allows great potential for advanced services and opens the gates for innovation. Cloud and federated learning technologies stimulate this by providing remarkable competitive advantages in the digitalization era.

6.1.1 Types of Cloud Deployments

Cloud infrastructure will be utilized in several ways, each with distinct advantages. More than one type of cloud deployment has more relevance in most organizations to meet their expectations.

A. Public Cloud

Public clouds refer to computing that enables businesses to use computing resources like servers, storage, and applications via the Internet. That will mean providers, including AWS and Microsoft Azure, are the ones maintaining and handling all the required hardware and software infrastructure. This model is fine for companies seeking adaptable and extensible computing solutions but who would not like to have the headache of owning and managing their physical infrastructure.

B. Private Cloud

Consequently, a private cloud is a computing resource belonging to one organization. The resources can be located at the organization's on-site data center or hosted by a cloud provider. Private clouds offer better security and privacy by resources not shared with other customers [5]. This model offers the primary benefits of the public cloud, such as self-service, the ability to grow and shrink, and elasticity, but with greater control and customization. The use of private networks also boosts security and privacy by ensuring access to only authorized users.

C. Hybrid Cloud

Hybrid clouds combine the features of both private and public clouds, interrelated through the technology that enables data and applications to work seamlessly across these environments [4]. This model allows sensitive services and applications to host the secure private cloud while public-facing services can be managed in the public cloud. Hybrid clouds give companies and businesses the flexibility to deploy particular infrastructure requirements tailored to their applications. Major cloud providers support hybrid cloud models, enabling organizations to optimize their infrastructure deployment to meet various operational needs [4].

The different types of cloud deployments provide a lot of options for businesses to choose from, depending on their specific requirements for security, control, flexibility, and cost efficiency. Organizations can also enhance their operational capabilities by understanding these models.

6.1.2 Services of Cloud Computing

Cloud computing has become a widely recognized term and a key infrastructure for delivering services, offering significant advantages over traditional service providers. These advantages include high fault tolerance, availability, reduced investment, scalability, and performance. Consequently, cloud computing is widely adopted by leading IT companies such as Google, Microsoft, Salesforce, and Amazon. Governments and companies use cloud computing services to meet a variety of application and infrastructure needs, including database management, CRM, data storage, and computational tasks. Common attributes of cloud computing services include multi-tenancy, elasticity, network access, on-demand availability, virtualization, and metering/chargeback.

Major companies like Microsoft, Google, and Amazon are at the forefront of developing and offering cloud services. The most common cloud computing services, offered either internally or by third-party providers, fall into three primary categories: Software as a Service (SaaS), Platform as a Service (PaaS), and Infrastructure as a Service (IaaS).

A. Software-as-a-Service (SaaS)

Software as a Service (SaaS) refers to software that is deployed over the internet. In this model, a provider licenses an application to customers as a service on demand, through a subscription, charged per usage, or at no cost when other revenue streams, such as advertisements or user data sales, are viable. SaaS minimizes support and maintenance costs and is becoming ubiquitous in organizations. Key characteristics of SaaS include:

- Software delivered in a "one to many" model
- No requirement for users to handle software upgrades
- Web access to commercial software
- Centralized management of software
- APIs for integration between different software applications

B. Platform-as-a-Service (PaaS)

Platform as a Service (PaaS) offers a cloud-based framework that enables developers to create, test, and deploy web applications without the hassle of managing the underlying infrastructure like servers, storage, and networking [6]. This service model allows developers to concentrate on coding and improving application features. Unlike Software as a Service (SaaS), which delivers fully developed software solutions, PaaS supplies the infrastructure and tools essential for software development. PaaS environments typically include operating systems, databases, web servers, and integrated development tools. Platforms like Google App Engine and Microsoft Azure are examples of PaaS, offering support throughout the entire application lifecycle, from development to deployment. PaaS is distinguished by features such as automated scaling, efficient workflows, and support for multiple programming languages, making it an excellent choice for contemporary web development.

- Built-in scalability of deployed software, including load balancing and failover.
- Web-based user interface creation tools for developing, testing, and deploying different UI scenarios.

- Integration with web services and databases via common standards.
- Support for collaborative development teams.

C. Infrastructure-as-a-Service (IaaS)

Infrastructure as a Service (IaaS) involves distributing cloud computing infrastructure—servers, storage, networks, and operating systems—as an on-demand service. Clients can purchase these resources as a fully outsourced service instead of investing in physical servers, software, data centers, or network equipment. Defined by the Internet Engineering Task Force (IETF), IaaS is considered the most basic service model [7], involving virtual machines and access to virtualized infrastructures. The line between PaaS and IaaS is becoming blurred as vendors introduce tools within IaaS to facilitate deployment, including multi-cloud environments. Key characteristics of IaaS include:

- Resources distributed as a service.
- Multiple users sharing single hardware resources.
- Variable cost utility pricing model.
- Support for dynamic scaling.

Figure 6.1 illustrates the different types of cloud computing services, including SaaS, PaaS, and IaaS. These services are crucial for organizations, offering scalable, on-demand access to computing resources without the need for local installation or maintenance.

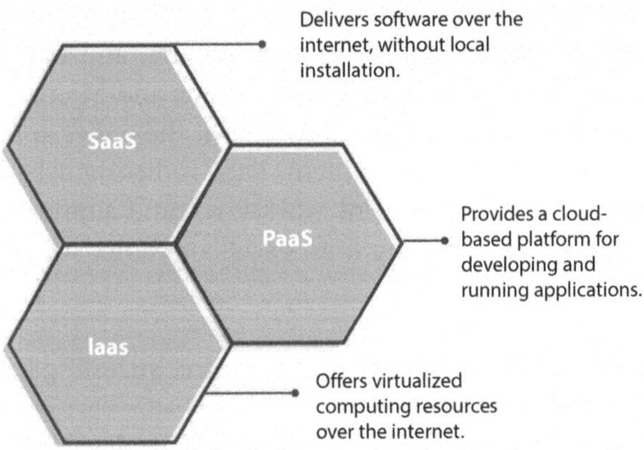

Figure 6.1 Types of cloud computing services.

6.2 What is Federated Learning?

Federated Learning (FL) is a cutting-edge machine learning technique that makes it easier to train AI models without requiring centralized data collecting, and protecting sensitive information. FL operates in a decentralized manner; instead of utilizing a central server; model training occurs directly on a variety of edge devices, such as laptops, cellphones, or Internet of Things sensors.

In Federated Learning, each device, or client, obtains the latest global model and trains it using its local data. This process keeps raw data on the device, addressing privacy issues. Once local training is complete, clients send model updates, usually in the form of gradients or model parameters, to a central server. These updates are much smaller in size than raw data, making the process bandwidth-efficient.

The central server combines the updates it receives from all clients by utilizing techniques such as Federated Averaging (FedAvg). This process melds the knowledge from various local models to enhance the global model's effectiveness. The aggregated global model is then re-partitioned to the clients. This loop of local training, update transmission, and aggregation continues iteratively until the required accuracy is achieved for a model [8].

Federated Learning is a decentralized data processing methodology where the training data sits on standalone edge devices. Data Privacy - As the raw data is not shared or centralized, this method helps to keep our privacy intact. FL, in contrast, enables training on many devices without the latter ever handling sensitive datasets. Each device offers updates of a model using its local data which produces an aggregate global model.

At its core, Federated Learning is a way to keep user data on client devices. In cases where the data is sensitive (using a personal health record or having an interaction with another user), you will need this information. Decentralized model training technology, including federated learning (FL), involves not only training models locally on edge devices but also securing the transport of model updates and combining these updates at a central server.

In mobile and edge computing environments Federated Learning becomes even more significant. Before federated learning, the standard centralized approach was expensive in terms of data transfer (having all images sent somewhere) hash and may hamper privacy. However, Fl requires only the transmission of the model updates, which saves the bandwidth and also enhances the data security. FL also uses strong cryptographic techniques such as advanced homomorphic encryption and differential privacy to guarantee the local data on every device is securely protected, even during updates. This application is mainly suited to conditions with high safety and privacy requirements - healthcare, finance or personal services [7].

6.2.1 Mechanics of Federated Learning

Federated Learning is a form of distributed machine learning system where training data does not leave the device that generates it and wherein collaborative model updates are trained between multiple edge devices. The process of FL involves multiple steps which enables the model to be trained on data that is distributed instead of centrally keeping all raw data. Read on to learn more about each of them. Figure 6.2 presents the core concept of federated learning, where multiple clients collaborate by sharing model updates without transferring raw data, maintaining data privacy while improving the global model.

A. Local Model Training

It is initiated by all devices, which want to learn such a model known as a client - they download the most recent version of a global model from the central server. Each client in this system then, uses the aggregate model information to train its local machine-learning models [9]. By doing this, we guarantee that all user data is only processed on the phone - no sensitive information leaves your device. Local training starts with traditional machine learning algorithms, where device updates its model parameters based on its own data to minimize a given loss function.

B. Model Update Transmission

Each of the generated updates (gradients/new parameters) is then sent back to the model, which aggregates these separated gradients into a single one before pushing an update. The client sends these new parameters to

Figure 6.2 Presentation of federated learning.

the central server, instead of sending raw data. They are more nimble than raw data, which makes this approach bandwidth-friendly. FL could significantly reduce the network latency by only transmitting the important model updates between client and server, instead of purely sending all data.

C. Global Model Aggregation

Hence, when the central server gets model updates from all active clients, it aggregates them to improve the global model. The most common technique is Federated Averaging (FedAvg), which aggregates updates from different clients to improve the parameters of a global model. It is executed in a way that leverages the knowledge present across data samples for all the clients without any raw access or moving of this private information to global space. This is a very necessary step for utilizing collective learning from numerous decentralized sources.

D. Iterative Optimization

Federated Learning works in rounds. When the central server aggregates all model updates, it returns the larger global model which is iteratively sent back and communicated with other clients for additional local training. This process of training on-site, sending out the updates, and averaging it goes on until the model converges to some target accuracy. That repeated process helps the model to evolve and get better by training on a rich and diverse set of data that is prevalent across all participating devices [8].

E. Decentralized Data Handling

One of the main attributes that Federated Learning is known for, actually stems from its distribution of how data will be managed. Instead of storing data on a central, fearsome server as is the norm with other methods, FL processes all its data locally at the client devices. This solution preserves user data privacy and security by storing raw data only on the device part. Finally, it solves the problems of data privacy protection and meets requirements like GDPR/HIPAA by allowing data to be processed on multiple devices.

F. Collaborative Model Training

Client devices are bigger than aggregation but equal to federated learning. Every device may train the model using their local data and supply these updates back to the central server. This effort is global and combines the computational properties and novel datasets of multiple devices to form a powerful model. The collaborative nature of FL ensures the global model benefits from a wide variety of data inputs, making it adaptable and highly effective in real-world scenarios.

G. Infrastructure and Security

Federated Learning requires a strong setup and infrastructure to manage the entire training process. This setup includes secure ways to send model updates, good methods for combining updates at the central server, and systems to manage the changing number of client devices. Advanced security techniques and encryption measures are often employed to ensure that even the transmitted model updates do not compromise the privacy of the local data. This setup helps train models efficiently and securely across many devices, making Federated Learning a good choice for applications needing high data security and privacy.

6.3 The Essence of Collaboration: Federated Learning Unveiled

6.3.1 Concept and Working of Federated Learning

Federated Learning (FL) Federated learning is a technique to de-centralize machine-learning processes, and focuses on keeping the data private pouring into cloud environments. FL emulates a distributed system where multiple devices or nodes can collaborate to train models by not sending raw data back to one common, central place where the processor resides. They also address critical data privacy, security, and compliance issues such as GDPR and HIPAA [10].

Federated Learning, is where only the training task is distributed to different devices (smartphones devices etc.). These devices are referred to as clients, and they train the model on their local data. This process begins with a central server - which creates the global model and sends it to all participating clients.

This is followed by each of the clients training the global model on its local dataset. To minimize the loss function concerning this model, we take a derivative of the loss function and apply that as an update step for parameters in the local training process. This allows the device to retain all raw data, securing privacy.

Clients produce updates to the model (typically new parameters) in a process known as federated on-device training, which transfers their learning without full data disclosure. These updates are significantly smaller than the raw data size, which results in efficient communication.

Every client sends its model updates to the central server. The server collects updates from every client and performs the aggregation efficiently [11]. Federated Averaging (FedAvg) assigns clients to improve the parameters of a global model by aggregating updates fed back and forth between several clients. The server aggregates them after taking updates from each client.

The updated global model is then sent back to the clients for further training. In such a manner, local training, update transmission, and global aggregation keep happening until the model converges to the desired accuracy. Repeating this process of FL ensures continuous model improvement by incorporating new data and learning from all the distributed datasets across participating devices.

Probably one of the greatest advantages of Federated Learning is decentralized management. Traditional machine learning requires a centralizing process for data accumulation and storage, which poses some risks related to breaches and unauthorized access. Unlike that, FL preserves data on the clients, reducing the likelihood of exposure and complying with the strictest data protection laws.

Another important aspect of Federated Learning is multi-client collaboration. Every client is engaged in the training process through the return of model updates from its local data. Herein, it exploits computational horsepower and variety in datasets across many devices for a robust and generalized global model. This will enable the global model to learn from the unique distributions in the data across different clients, hence being more generalizable and practical.

Federated learning pays attention and a highly reliable infrastructure to manage its complexity. This involves secure, two way communication channels that allow the central server to receive model updates from all the participating devices, effective methods to combine model updates at the central server, and mechanisms to handle the dynamic nature of the client devices participating. Even the transmitter model updates are ensured through advance end-to-end security techniques and differential privacy measures, ensuring that local data privacy remains uncompromised. This infrastructure supports efficient and secure model training across a distributed network, making FL particularly well-suited for applications where data security and privacy are of utmost importance.

Federated Learning finds applications in mobile and edge computing. The traditional centralized training model requires the transfer of enormous data to a central server, which can be extremely resource-intensive and may pose a privacy hazard. On the other hand, FL requires only network transmission of model updates between the parties, which saves bandwidth and improves the security of the data. This makes FL all the more valuable when the bandwidth is limited or when data privacy is imperative [12].

6.3.2 Types of Federated Learning

There are three main types depending on how data and model updates are handled: Horizontal Federated Learning (HFL), Vertical Federated Learning (VFL), and Federated Transfer Learning (FTL). Each type deals with specific data structures and collaborative scenarios, providing tailored solutions to the challenges of distributed machine learning. Figure 6.3 shows the types of federated learning and their data alignment across clients.

A. Horizontal Federated Learning (HFL)

The latter, referred to as Horizontal Federated Learning or Sample-based FL occurs when different organizations or devices have datasets with the same feature attributes, but they stand for distinct samples. Note: This FL type is appropriate when the datasets across different clients have similar feature types, but are of records for disparate entities. Here is an example: Many hospitals could have patient records that are similar in age, blood pressure, and diagnosis for different patients.

Initially, during the HFL process, an initial global model is provided by a central server to all decentralized clients. Each client then trains this model locally with their data. The local training process involves the modification of the model's parameters to minimize a loss function specific to the local dataset [13]. This strategy is safer and more private as it restricts the computations of raw data on local devices.

After each round of local training, the clients produce an update to the model (usually in terms of gradients or new parameters). These updates hide the raw data but encapsulate what we have learned. The model updates from the clients are then received by a central server. A central server will collect updates using algorithms such as FedAvg (which merges the partial update from multiple clients to adjust the global model). Clients then receive an updated copy of the global model for further training. This iterative process continues until the model reaches the desired level of accuracy.

Several financial institutions contribute to training a fraud detection model. There are different examples of transactions between customers but

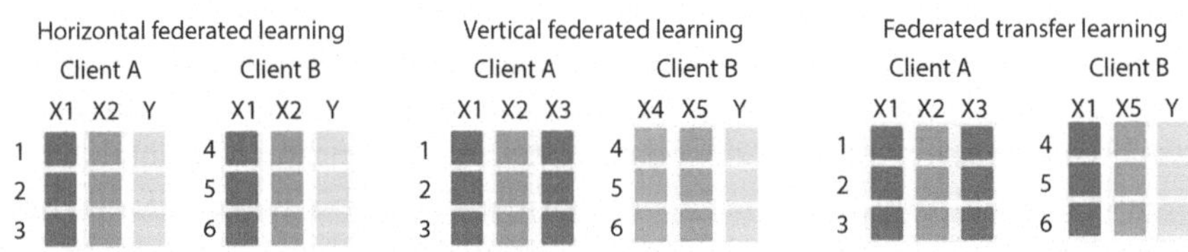

Figure 6.3 Types of federated learning.

the features (such as transaction amount, location and time) will surely be consistent across all institutions. With HFL, they can enhance the fraud detection model while ensuring that sensitive customer data remains secure and protected from exposure.

B. Vertical Federated Learning (VFL)

When separate organizations or devices hold similar samples (a.k.a. vertical partition) but have different features, i.e., a smartphone collects images while the doctor's office takes input directly. Vertical Federated Learning, also called feature-based FL can be applied. This form of FL can be used in a situation where there are different entities each having some complementary information about individuals. One might have had demographic data while the other might only have behavioral data.

Training is also different: in VFL, datasets are aligned over entity identities. A bank and an e-commerce company may choose to collaborate in this way, so that they can generate a more complete customer portrait. In this case, one of the two contributes financial data (the bank), while the other reels in past purchasing history through e-commerce. This way they can construct a strong model without commitment to share their actual data, by federating the datasets. It follows a similar iterative process of HFL for model training in VFL. During FedAvg the central server sends an initial global model to all users, and mobile devices, in this case, our clients and each client train that local copy of the global model using only its specific features [14]. The global model gets improved with these local updates from the central server. The above criterion starts recursively and keeps doing so, unless the model has an accuracy of around where we want to stop.

For example, a healthcare provider and an insurance company could team up to create a model that predicts how patients will fare. The healthcare provider refers to clinical data and the insurance company references claims data related to identical patients. With VFL, they can collaboratively build a more effective predictive model by exploiting the data resources of each other.

C. Federated Transfer Learning (FTL)

Federated Transfer Learning: it applies when the datasets are comprised of samples and feature spaces that may differ according to different organizations or devices, In FTL transfer techniques are used to allow knowledge from one domain to be adapted in another [14]. A different type of FL can be useful when a provider is holding one large labeled set, and another has created an attendant smaller yet related dataset.

In FTL, we want to enhance the model performance on the smaller dataset by transferring knowledge from a larger one. This is a 2-step process, first, we train on the bigger dataset. This pre-trained model is trained further, with a smaller set of related data. This fine-tuning adjusts the model parameters to better reflect the specific characteristics of our smaller dataset. This allows for creating strong models on little data due to the knowledge that it can obtain from its larger dataset.

For example, a big technology company with enormous labeled image data works together with another smaller company that only has small-scale images like medical scans as well. FTL allows the smaller company to use a pre-trained model from the larger company's dataset and unspin it to perform better on their specialized application [12].

6.4 Harmonizing Cloud and Edge: The Integration Paradigm

6.4.1 Leveraging Cloud Resources for Federated Learning

Federated Learning (FL) is a state-of-the-art machine learning procedure that distributes training and emphasizes data security and privacy. The idea is that many different devices or nodes can be used collaboratively without raw data leaving the physical control of wherever it was stored in the first place, which solves a bunch of problems asserting around sensitive information and being regulatory compliant.

Although it retains its unique merits, the decentralized nature of FL also brings some new challenges e.g., efficient coordination is needed; massive computational resources are required as well as scalable storage solutions. Leveraging cloud resources with federated learning provides complete challenges and results in better efficiency, scalability, and security overhead for the FL process [13].

Cloud platforms offer a flexible, reliable infrastructure that can satisfy the diverse requirements for federated learning. Organizations can leverage the computing power and storage capabilities provided by clouds to manage complex operations such as FL. The advantages of cloud platforms include on-demand access to large resources, which allows making the federated learning process scalable as more devices join and data size increases. So, this integration is an improved way of deploying FL to make it more natively run resilient, and scalable in the face of demand changes.

Cloud infrastructure must be used to secure federated learning. Advanced security features offered by cloud platforms, including encryption [16], access controls ensuring strictly limited visibility to the client side, and compliance with data protection laws. These guardrails combine to protect your sensitive data throughout the full federated learning lifecycle - from initial training on the device, through model update aggregations in the cloud. Combining cloud computing security features with federated learning, organizations can develop AI models that are much more protective of data privacy and also adhere to very strict security standards.

A. How Cloud Resources Are Leveraged for Federated Learning

1. **Centralized Coordination and Aggregation:**
   - **Setup:** Central server, cloud-based setup. Server- This server handles the federated learning by initiating the release of a global model and sends to all participating edge devices (clients).
   - **Aggregation:** This is the process after every client trains a model locally on data, and all updates (gradients or parameters) are sent back to cloud server. The server then combines it with the model.
   - **Iteration:** A never-ending cycle of improvement is created when the clients receive the improved global model back for additional local training.
2. **Scalable Storage Solutions:**
   - Cloud platforms offer scalable and secure storage options essential for managing the significant volumes of data generated and processed in federated learning. Data from various clients can be securely stored in distributed cloud storage services like Amazon S3, Google Cloud Storage, or Azure Blob Storage.
3. **Computational Resources:**
   - The cloud offers on-demand access to vast computational resources required for the aggregation and training processes. High-performance computing instances, such as those provided by AWS EC2, Google Cloud Compute Engine, or Azure Virtual Machines, ensure that the central server can handle the computational load efficiently.
4. **Networking and Communication:**
   - Efficient data transmission between the central server and edge devices is critical [18]. Cloud platforms provide optimized networking services, including content delivery networks (CDNs) and edge computing solutions

to minimize latency and improve data transfer speeds. Secure Communication channels, such as encrypted data links prevent adversaries from eavesdropping or altering model updates.

B. Why Cloud Resources Are Leveraged for Federated Learning

Cloud resources go hand-to-hand with federated learning, resulting in a vast range of benefits and hence, become imperative for current FL systems:

1. **Scalability:**
   - Cloud infrastructure allows being as elastic to scale the resources up or down upon workload fluctuations. This is essential for federated learning because the number of devices and amount of data varies dramatically.
2. **Cost Efficiency:**
   - Organizations no longer have to pay for the expensive capital costs of building out their data center solution if they choose an available cloud service. The idea is they don't have to buy a bunch of license capacity upfront, but rather can use what AWS calls the pay-as-you-go model which helps optimize costs and resource utilization.
3. **Data Security and Privacy:**
   - Advanced security capabilities, including encryption, IAM & regulatory standards are enforced at the cloud platforms offering these services. These are steps to protect the privacy of raw data during a federated learning process.
4. **Resource Optimization:**
   - Cloud resources make it easier to manage computational and storage resources. The federated learning system can handle large-scale training tasks with no bottlenecks via high-performance instances and scalable storage solutions.
5. **High Availability and Reliability:**
   - Cloud providers promise service resilience by ensuring high availability and reliability with redundant infrastructure, as well as modern fault-tolerance mechanisms. It allows federated learning to continue functioning even in the event of hardware failure.

C. When Cloud Resources Are Leveraged for Federated Learning

There are several end-use cases where the use of cloud resources for federated learning is considered, especially if:

1. **Large-Scale Collaborations:**
   - When working with many organizations or at times with devices to collaborate for training a machine learning model, allows cloud resources that will handle the task effectively and efficiently.
2. **Data Sensitivity:**
   - Federated learning provides a mechanism for large numbers of organizations to collaboratively build powerful ML models without sharing data, and is particularly favorably used in industries such as healthcare, finance, and government where the sensitive nature of some forms of personal or organizational information can prevent access to other traditional techniques.
3. **Resource Constraints:**
   - This responsibility also extends to model aggregation and storage, with the cloud handling these tasks, which increases the burden on devices participating in federated learning by reducing the strain on their limited computing power and storage capacity.
4. **Dynamic Workloads:**
   - Cloud based resources are flexible, thus in real-time analytics/IoT, the cloud can increase its capacity when there is high demand and reduce it during quieter time. This also helps the system to use just the right amount of resource needed and avoids wasting them when they're not, keeping costs and energy use low.

D. By What Means Cloud Resources Are Leveraged for Federated Learning

There are several technological measures to integrate cloud resources into federated learning:

1. **Cloud Platforms and Services:**
   - All of the major cloud providers such as Amazon Web Services (AWS), Google CloudPlatform (GCP), and Microsoft Azure provide extensive services that empower federated learning. Scalable compute instances, secure

storage solutions, and advanced networking capabilities are key services these distinct workloads will rely on [14]. Figure 6.4 demonstrates the integration of cloud infrastructure with edge devices, enabling decentralized model training and updates.

2. **Federated Learning Frameworks:**
   - Open-source platforms for federated learning like TensorFlow Federated (TFF) and PySyft offer an array of utilities that we can utilize in our attempt to decentralize the implementation of distributed machine-learning products. They provide out-of-the-box support for cloud integration with many, use using their included frameworks to easily leverage additional resources with just a few lines of code [7].
3. **Containerization and Orchestration:**
   - Docker and Kubernetes can help federated learning components to be deployed as containers making them more scalable and portable across different cloud environments [10]. In the case of Kubernetes, it provides strong orchestration functionalities to control the deployment, scaling, and operation of containerized applications.

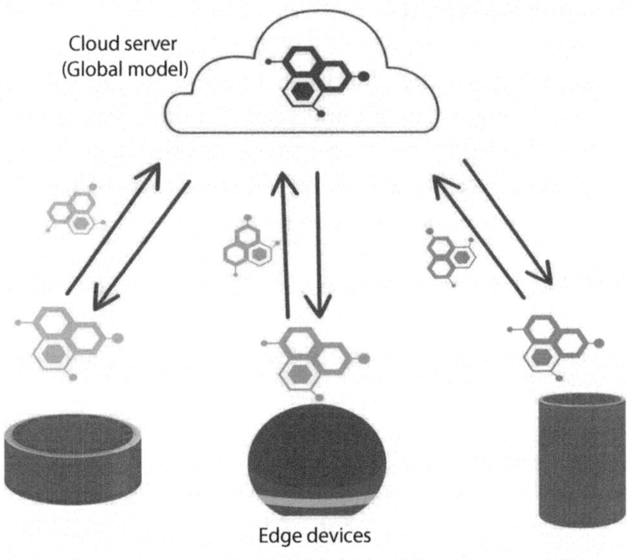

Figure 6.4 Integration of edge computing and federated learning.

4. **Security Protocols:**
   - Secure: Model updates are transmitted and aggregated using advanced security protocols based on Secure Multi-Party Computation (SMPC) and homomorphic Encryption to guarantee data privacy, and integrity. Such protocols are often used as part of federated learning frameworks, to improve security.
5. **Data Integration Tools:**
   - Cloud-native data extraction and ETL: Data integration tools and services that cloud platforms provide such as AWS Glue, Google Cloud Dataflow or Azure Data Factory pave the way to pre-process various types of raw datasets. These utilities will make sure that your data is prepared correctly in a format necessary for federated learning.

6.4.2 Deployment of Federated Learning Models on the Cloud

Traditional centralized ML algorithms often aggregate data from multiple sources onto a single server, which raises significant concerns about data privacy and security. On the other hand, FL distributes a training process that enables several devices or nodes to jointly train on the model without giving away raw data.

With more scrutiny on data privacy from the public and governments, the demand for FL has risen. Regulations like the Health Insurance Portability and Accountability Act (HIPAA) in the US or the European General Data Protection Regulation (GDPR) severely restrict how personal data can be collected, and stored, and used [11]. By reducing the risk of exposure and ensuring that sensitive data is kept on local devices, FL's decentralized approach satisfies such regulatory standards.

Federated learning must inherently deal with challenges. Integrating cloud resources to complement federated learning is vital in managing those challenges of FL. They offer the infrastructure for your application, including powerful computational power, sufficient storage resources, and high-quality network bandwidth. OSs such as AWS, GCP, and Azure are capable of providing scalable solutions for the dynamic nature of FL.

Similarly, continual learning is so important in FL that the model needs to be improved all the time with new data - which cannot be implemented without cloud infrastructure. Especially in rapidly mutating, high-throughput environments like IoT deployments (Edge and cloud), healthcare monitoring applications, real-time Big Data, or AI-powered financial analytics. The scalability of cloud platforms provides the necessary infrastructure to allow for an efficient and responsive federated learning process, as seen by its modeling referencing changing sizes in Input data sets [10].

Also, training federated learning models on the cloud enables global-spanning collaborations. Any organization in the world can join up the FL process and provide their local data for building a powerful global model. This federated learning approach enables the model to learn on a large and diverse set of data sources without sharing sensitive user-specific information. The universal backbone and networking assets that cloud platforms give allow all these international activities to be efficiently orchestrated, modeled updates, and aggregations.

As federated learning, the cloud infrastructure not only delivers scalability and allows global collaboration but also features important security and privacy tools. These tools cover encrypting data in motion and at rest, role-based access control to keep a tight leash on who gets the keys to your kingdom, and compliance with global security standards. These features allow organizations to ensure data protection at scale for the entire federated learning workflow - from protecting raw training datasets to building secure computation models and deploying them onto edge devices.

6.4.3 How Federated Learning Models are Deployed on the Cloud

Running federated learning models on the cloud requires a well-orchestrated system to enable effective, scalable, and confidential training. The following are the step-by-step guidelines to migrate your bot through this deployment process:

Step 1: Setting Up the Central Server

1. **Pick a Cloud Platform:** Select a cloud provider (AWS, GCP, or Azure) that provides the necessary infrastructure and services.
2. **Central Server:** VM/Container to act as the central server is created and configured. Make sure that enough computational power and data storage are available for it.
3. **Further Program:** Federated learning frameworks (Tensor Flow Federated, PySyft) and other dependencies needed for model training and aggregation need to be installed in this step.

Step 2: Initializing the Global Model

1. **Create the Machine Learning Model:** Define how to structure the global model based on your use case (neural networks, logistic regression...).
2. **Upload the Model to the Central Server:** Define a global model that sets its parameters in the initial phase.

Step 3: Distributing the Global Model to Clients

1. **Identify Participating Clients:** Define which edge devices (smartphones, IoT devices) would be part of the federated learning process.
2. **Deploy Client Software:** Have client software installed on every device for the global model consumption, local training, and sending updates back to a central server.
3. **Distribute the Global Model:** This will initially send the global model to all participating clients from a central server. Secure communication protocols to be used for this process to prevent data tampering.

Step 4: Local Model Training on Clients

1. **Prepare Local Data:** Clients prepare their local dataset for training and this data remains in the client-hosted device - never sent to a central server.
2. **Train Locally:** Instructions are sent to all clients where each client uses their local data and trains a global model by updating its parameters so it suffers less from the loss function of interest.

Step 5: Sending Model Updates to the Central Server

1. **Generate Model Update:** After training, on local data, clients generate updates (e.g., gradients or new model parameters) that summarize the learned information [15].
2. **Model Updates:** Model updates are encrypted and sent securely over to the central server, thus preventing sensitive data from being sent in plain text.

Step 6: Aggregating Model Updates on the Central Server

1. **Ask Clients to Send their Updates:** Every contribution will send the model updates of the clients back to a central server.
2. **Aggregating Updates:** The server adjusts the parameters of a global model by aggregating these updates using methods such as FederatedAveraging (FedAvg) - in this way, privacy ensures you maintain absolute control over your sensitive training data.

Step 7: Redistributing the Updated Global Model

1. **Update the Global Model:** The central server receives model name updates from all workers and aggregates them to improve the global model.
2. **Redistribute the Model:** The updated global model is shared with all clients for additional local training. The model is trained and re-tuned to achieve the desired accuracy, and this iterative loop continues.

Step 8: Ensuring Security and Privacy

1. **Implement Advanced Security Measures:** Use end-to-end encryption, secure multi-party computation (SMPC), and other advanced security protocols to ensure model updates are accurate and private.
2. **Regulatory Compliance:** Ensure that the entire process adheres to applicable data protection regulations (e.g., GDPR, HIPAA) in order not to compromise any privacy or security of your/most sensitive assets!

Step 9: Monitoring and Managing the Process

1. **Continuous Monitoring:** Implement cloud-based monitoring tools for continuous assessment of the performance and health checkup on the federated learning process.
2. **Resource Management:** Adjust cloud resources on the fly (compute, storage, and networking) to support current workload necessities for efficient operation [16].

3. **Troubleshooting and Optimization:** Identify problems in the training process and tune up with changing needs to enhance model performance.

6.5 Real-World Applications of Federated Learning

A. Mobile Applications:

Federated learning is a new approach to machine learning that enables the deployment of secure, private, and collaborative models across many mobile devices. It is built on a decentralized learning structure, which signifies a model can be trained with the accumulative measurement of user activity statistics from all smartphones without giving up personal records. In turn, this will significantly enhance consumer enjoyment and capability in a variety of cellular programs consisting of next-word prediction, face detection, voice reputation, etc. [17] An example that combines both edge and cloud - Google has deployed federated learning to upgrade on-device models like "Hey, Google" in Google Assistant by allowing users to issue any voice commands without a hitch [19].

B. Healthcare:

The need to protect this type of sensitive data at the source is, in large part, why Federated Learning is uniquely positioned to have a significant impact on healthcare and health insurance. Federated learning models might be the best solution for healthcare professionals seeking a wider data diversity harvest, considering that they pool together reports and facts from localities such as hospitals and electronic health record databases. This pooled information is incredibly valuable in the diagnosis of rare diseases and can serve to enhance patient care along with the efficiency of healthcare delivery. One of the most recent publications, "The Future of Digital Health with Federated Learning", highlights how federated learning can help solve issues around privacy and governance related to data ownership, while creating more robust models for system-level-observational studies in healthcare [18].

C. Autonomous Vehicles:

Federated learning is an extremely exciting opportunity to evolve strictly while ensuring higher and more secure self-use of automobile studies. Autonomous vehicles require real-time statistics and predictions, so that they can travel effectively from a certain place to another and adapt according to the dynamic nature of the road. Federated learning facilitates this by providing:

1. With up-to-date traffic and road conditions, cars can determine the best route much more efficiently than humans.
2. Instant decision-making ability: This enables vehicles to react timely on spontaneous scenarios and hazards of the road.
3. Yet the federated learning models can improve iteratively through inputs from many, which should lead to better performance and reliability.

In an experiment, federated learning was shown to significantly reduce the time of training for wheel steering angle prediction in self-driving cars and improve its safety from a driving resource-consumption perspective. [19].

6.6 Conclusion and Future Directions

In conclusion, the integration of federated and exponential learning has enabled rapid access to AI driven solutions in real-time healthcare crisis decision-making, thereby opening new horizons. This is the Federated learning that has been designed as an alternative to all, in which both data decentralization and privacy are important components for other methods. This approach aligns with the sensitivity of health data, ensuring patient privacy while complying with regulatory standards. Learning at this scale, building on computational power and data sales as discussed prior in conjunction with Community Learning of this nature has underscored the importance of exponential learning being a heavy-hitter within healthcare innovation.

For a complex health dataset, these exponential learning components of neural networks and their recently developed deep learning techniques, reinforcement (self-learning), transfer, and meta-learning strategies represent the strong foundation block to extract useful inferences from huge multi-variable health datasets.

The words evoke the modeling of learning, reconsideration, and renewal of decision-making leading to real improvements in patient outcomes and efficiency. Exponential learning workflow entails data processing, pre-processing, model training, and validation followed by deployment. These steps all lead to better analytics and decision support in healthcare. Techniques including federated learning and secure aggregation will be critical to preserve the privacy of health data, making them applicable for joint analysis of personalized medicine [19].

In conclusion, exponential healthcare learning has the potential to usher in a new era of individualized treatment, enhance patient outcomes, and lead toward catalyzing quality-improvement activities for increased effectiveness and efficiency in healthcare. By incorporating these advanced algorithms and leveraging their artificial intelligence-powered technologies, healthcare organizations are well-equipped to function in today's ever-complex world of health delivery which eventually paves the way for an integrated approach and leads to an efficient patient-centered medical system equipped with data-driven capabilities [20].

References

1. Haynie, M., Enterprise Cloud Services: Deriving Business Value from Cloud Computing, 2009, Microfocus, Tech. Report.
2. Wang, L., Tao, J., Kunze, M., Castellanos, A.C., Kramer, D., Karl, W., Scientific Cloud Computing: Early Definition and Experience. *2008 10th IEEE International Conference on High Performance Computing and Communications*, 2008.
3. Data Analytics as a Service: Unleashing the Power of Cloud and Big Data. Ascent White Paper, March 2013.
4. Market sand Markets, Cloud Database as a Service (DBaaS) Market - Global Forecast to 2023, http://www.marketsandmarkets.com/PressReleases/cloud-database-asa-service-dbaas.asp (accessed in December 2015).
5. Aslett, M., DBaaS Poised to Drive Next-Generation Database Growth. 451 Research, August 2013.
6. Linthicum, D.S., *Cloud Computing and SOA Convergence in Your Enterprise: A Step-by-Step Guide*. Addison-Wesley Information Technology Series, India, First Edition, 2010.
7. McMahan, B., Moore, E., Ramage, D., Hampson, S., y Arcas, B.A., Communication-efficient learning of deep networks from decentralized data, in: *Artificial intelligence and statistics*, pp. 1273–1282, PMLR, 2017, April.
8. Konečný, J., McMahan, H.B., Yu, F.X., Richtárik, P., Suresh, A.T., Bacon, D., Federated learning: Strategies for improving communication efficiency. arXiv preprint arXiv:1610.05492, 2016.
9. Bonawitz, K., Eichner, H., Grieskamp, W., Huba, D., Ingerman, A., Ivanov, V., Roselander, J., Towards federated learning at scale: System design. *Proc. Mach. Learn. Syst.*, *1*, 374–388, 2019.
10. Yang, Q., Liu, Y., Chen, T., Tong, Y., Federated machine learning: Concept and applications. *ACM Trans. Intell. Syst. Technol. (TIST)*, *10*, 2, 1–19, 2019.

11. Hard, A., Rao, K., Mathews, R., Ramaswamy, S., Beaufays, F., Augenstein, S., Ramage, D., Federated learning for mobile keyboard prediction. arXiv preprint arXiv:1811.03604, 2018.
12. Li, T., Sahu, A.K., Zaheer, M., Sanjabi, M., Talwalkar, A., Smith, V., Federated optimization in heterogeneous networks. *Proc. Mach. Learn. Syst.*, *2*, 429–450, 2020.
13. Lim, W.Y.B., Luong, N.C., Hoang, D.T., Jiao, Y., Liang, Y.C., Yang, Q., Miao, C., Federated learning in mobile edge networks: A comprehensive survey. *IEEE Commun. Surv. Tutor.*, *22*, 3, 2031–2063, 2020.
14. Geyer, R.C., Klein, T., Nabi, M., Differentially private federated learning: A client level perspective, *Comput. Sci.*, arXiv:1712.07557, 2017.
15. Shi, W., Cao, J., Zhang, Q., Li, Y., Xu, L., Edge computing: Vision and challenges. *IEEE Internet Things J.*, *3*, 5, 637–646, 2016.
16. Abadi, M., Chu, A., Goodfellow, I., McMahan, H.B., Mironov, I., Talwar, K., Zhang, L., Deep learning with differential privacy, in: *Proceedings of the 2016 ACM SIGSAC conference on computer and communications security*, pp. 308–318, 2016, October.
17. Kairouz, P., McMahan, H.B., Avent, B., Bellet, A., Bennis, M., Bhagoji, A.N., Zhao, S., Advances and open problems in federated learning. *Found. Trends® Mach. Learn.*, *14*, 1–2, 1–210, 2021.
18. Mamatha, S.M., Experiential Learning in Higher Education. *Int. J. Adv. Res. Innov.*, 9, 3, 214–218, 2021, ISSN 2347 - 3258.
19. Nguyen, D.C., Pham, Q.V., Ding, M., Seneviratne, A., Lin, Z., Dobre, O.A., Hwang, W., Federated Learning for Smart Healthcare: A Survey. *ACM Comput. Surv.*, 55, 3, Article No.: 60.
20. Wang, W., Li, X., Qiu, X., Zhang, X., Brusic, V., Zhao, J., A Privacy-Preserving Framework for Federated Learning in Smart Healthcare Systems. *Inf. Process. Manage.*, 60, 1, 103167, January 2023.

7

Machine Learning and Artificial Intelligence Fundamentals for Federated Systems

N. Vinaya Kumari[1], G. S. Pradeep Ghantasala[2*], Pellakuri Vidyullatha[3] and Rajesh Sharma R.[2]

[1]*Department of Computer Science and Engineering, Malla Reddy Engineering College for Women, Hyderabad, India*
[2]*Department of Computer Science and Engineering, Alliance College of Engineering and Design, Alliance University, Bengaluru, India*
[3]*Department of Computer Science and Engineering, KoneruLakshmaiah Education Foundation, Vaddeswaram, Guntur, Andhra Pradesh, India*

Abstract

Federated learning (FL) is a notable tool for a reading paradigm designed to train models collaboratively through decentralized devices or servers holding a network of information samples without changing them. This approach addresses key challenges in data privacy, security, and utilization. Unlike traditional centralized tool learning, where data is aggregated into a central server, FL allows model training on network data, thereby mitigating privacy risks and reducing latency and bandwidth consumption. This explores critical concepts of tool learning and artificial intelligence as applied to federated systems. It delves into the architectural framework of federated learning, highlighting its core components, including the network training process, aggregation algorithms, and communication protocols. It also covers several types of federated learning, which encompass horizontal FL, vertical FL, and federated transfer learning, emphasizing their applicability based on the nature of data distribution across clients. Furthermore, the discussion extends to the key challenges faced by federated systems, such as dealing with non-independent and identically distributed (IID) statistics, ensuring model robustness against adverse attacks, and maintaining efficient data communication. Solutions to these challenges, including federated averaging, differential privacy, and secure multi-party

**Corresponding author*: ggspradeep@gmail.com

S. Rakesh Kumar, N. Gayathri and Seifedine Kadry (eds.) Federated Intelligent System for Healthcare: A Practical Guide, (153–170) © 2025 Scrivener Publishing LLC

computation, are also reviewed. This offers a comprehensive assessment of how tool learning and AI principles underpin the federated learning framework, fostering advancements in efficient, privacy-preserving, and collaborative learning systems. Through this examination, the potential of federated learning to revolutionize industries reliant on extensive, distributed datasets is underscored, paving the way for innovative applications in healthcare, finance, and beyond.

Keywords: Federated learning, machine learning, artificial intelligence, independent and identically distributed, principles

7.1 Overview of Machine Learning and Artificial Intelligence

7.1.1 Definition of Machine Learning

Machine learning (ML) is a specialized area within artificial intelligence focused on creating algorithms that allow computer systems to learn from data and make predictions or decisions without being explicitly programmed. Unlike conventional programming, where explicit rules are provided, ML algorithms detect patterns in data and use those patterns to make decisions [1, 3]. The essential categories of ML include the following:

Supervised Learning: This involves training an algorithm on a categorized dataset, meaning the input data are paired with the ideal output. The algorithm learns to map inputs to outputs, making predictions on new, unseen data. Examples include Decision Trees, Linear Regression, and Support Vector Machines (SVM).

Unsupervised Learning: In this category, algorithms work on data without labeled responses. The intention is to discover hidden patterns or intrinsic structures within the data. Examples include Principal Component Analysis (PCA), K-Means Clustering, and Hierarchical Clustering.

Reinforcement Learning: Here, algorithms learn by interacting with an environment, receiving rewards or penalties based on actions taken. The aim is to maximize cumulative rewards. This approach is common in areas such as robotics, gaming, and autonomous navigation [2, 4].

7.1.2 Definition of Artificial Intelligence

Artificial intelligence (AI) is the overarching field concerning the creation of systems capable of performing tasks that typically require human intelligence. AI encompasses ML and focuses on building machines that can reason, learn, and act autonomously or semi-autonomously. There are two primary types of AI:

Narrow AI: These are AI systems designed to handle a specific task, such as voice recognition or image classification. These systems are highly specialized and operate within a limited scope [5].
General AI: This type refers to a more advanced AI that can understand, learn, and apply intelligence across a broad range of tasks, similar to human cognitive abilities. General AI remains a theoretical concept at this stage.

7.1.3 Importance of ML and AI in Modern Technology

ML and AI are revolutionizing various industries by providing advanced solutions to complex problems. Their significance is reflected in multiple applications:

Healthcare: AI technologies assist in diagnosing diseases, tailoring treatment plans, and managing patient care efficiently. For example, diagnostic systems can analyze medical images, and predictive models can anticipate disease outbreaks [6].
Finance: In the financial sector, AI models are employed for detecting fraud, managing risks, executing algorithmic trading, and providing personalized banking services. These models can analyze vast datasets to identify patterns and anomalies that may be difficult for humans to discern [7].
Retail: AI enhances personalized recommendations, inventory management, and demand forecasting. Retailers leverage machine learning algorithms to analyze consumer data and improve shopping experience.
Transportation: AI is essential for self-driving cars, traffic management systems, and predictive maintenance of vehicles, improving safety and efficiency. Autonomous driving technologies utilize reinforcement learning and computer vision to navigate roads [8].

7.2 Key Concepts in Machine Learning

7.2.1 Data and Features

Types of Data: Structured vs. Unstructured

Structured Data: This type of data is organized and formatted in a way that is easily searchable in databases. It is typically stored in tabular formats with rows and columns, such as spreadsheets or SQL databases. Examples include numerical data, dates, and categorical data [9].

Unstructured Data: Unstructured data lack a predefined format or organization, making it more complex to analyze. This includes text documents, images, audio files, and videos. Techniques such as natural language processing (NLP) and computer vision are often required to process unstructured data.

Feature Engineering and Selection

Feature Engineering: This is the process of using domain knowledge to create new features or variables that help machine learning algorithms perform better. It involves transforming raw data into a suitable format for model building, which can significantly enhance the overall performance of machine learning models [10].

Feature Selection: This involves choosing the most relevant features from the dataset that contribute the most to the predictive variable or output. It helps reduce the dimensionality of the data, which can improve model performance and reduce overfitting. Techniques include removing correlated features, using algorithms like Random Forest, and statistical tests like Chi-square.

7.2.2 Algorithms and Models

Common Algorithms

Linear Regression: A statistical approach that models the relationship between a dependent variable and one or more independent variables using a linear equation. It is used for predictive analysis and understanding the relationship between variables.

Decision Trees: A tree-like model used for classification and regression tasks. It splits the data into subsets based on the value of input features, creating a branching structure that results in a decision outcome.

Neural Networks: Computational models inspired by the human brain, consisting of interconnected layers of nodes (neurons). Neural networks can capture complex patterns and are applied in several tasks such as image recognition and language processing [10].

Model Evaluation Metrics and Techniques

Metrics: Different metrics are used to evaluate the performance of machine learning models depending on the type of problem (classification, regression, etc.) [11]. Common metrics include accuracy, precision, recall, F1

score for classification, and Mean Absolute Error (MAE), Mean Squared Error (MSE), and R-squared for regression.
Techniques: Model evaluation techniques include splitting the data into training and testing sets, using cross-validation methods, and assessing the model's performance on unseen data. Techniques like confusion matrix, ROC curves, and precision–recall curves are also used to evaluate classification models.

7.2.3 Training and Testing

Overfitting and Underfitting
Overfitting: This occurs when a model learns the training data too well, including the noise and outliers. It results in high accuracy on training data but poor generalization to new, unseen data. Overfitting can be mitigated by using techniques such as cross-validation, pruning in decision trees, and regularization in regression models.

7.3 Fundamentals of Artificial Intelligence

7.3.1 Neural Networks

Neural networks are constructed from interconnected layers of nodes, including an input layer, one or more hidden layers, and an output layer. Each node processes input data using an activation function such as sigmoid, tanh, or ReLU, introducing non-linearity and allowing the network to learn complex patterns. Training involves backpropagation, which adjusts weights by propagating errors backward through the network, and gradient descent, an optimization method that iteratively reduces the loss function by updating weights in the direction of the steepest descent [12].

7.3.2 Deep Learning

Deep learning uses advanced neural network architectures to tackle complex tasks. Convolutional Neural Networks (CNNs) are powerful for image and video analysis, using convolutional layers to detect spatial hierarchies. Recurrent Neural Networks (RNNs) are effective for sequential data, retaining a hidden state to remember previous information, with Long Short-Term Memory (LSTM) and Gated Recurrent Unit (GRU) networks enhancing long-term dependency handling. Generative Adversarial

Networks (GANs) comprise two neural networks, a generator and a discriminator, that are trained together in an adversarial manner to create realistic synthetic data, useful in applications like image generation [13].

7.3.3 Natural Language Processing (NLP)

Natural language processing (NLP) encompasses techniques for understanding and processing human language. Tokenization breaks text into manageable units such as words or subwords, facilitating further analysis. Embeddings transform words or phrases into continuous vector spaces, capturing semantic meanings and relationships, with popular techniques including Word2Vec, GloVe, BERT, and GPT. Sequence models, including RNNs, LSTMs, and Transformers, are pivotal for tasks like language translation, text generation, and sentiment analysis, with Transformers particularly notable for their ability to handle long-range dependencies in text using self-attention mechanisms [14].

7.3.4 Reinforcement Learning

Reinforcement learning focuses on agents that learn to achieve goals through interaction with an environment. The agent makes decisions based on a policy, which maps states to actions. The environment provides feedback in the form of rewards or penalties, guiding the agent toward optimal behavior. The primary goal is to maximize cumulative rewards over time by refining the policy. Core principles include agents, environments, rewards, and policies, with the objective being to identify the optimal strategy that yields the highest expected cumulative reward [15].

7.4 Federated Learning

7.4.1 Definition and Importance

Federated learning is a revolutionary approach to machine learning in which a global model is trained across multiple decentralized devices or servers, each holding local data samples, without changing the data itself. This decentralized approach allows for the training of machine learning models on data that remain on local devices, thereby preserving privacy and data security. Federated learning contrasts with conventional centralized machine learning, where data are typically aggregated and processed in a central location.

Privacy and Data Security: By keeping raw data on local devices and only sharing model updates (such as gradients), federated learning minimizes the risk of data breaches and enhances privacy. This approach is particularly valuable in sensitive domains like healthcare and finance, where data privacy is paramount. Federated learning enables organizations to comply with data protection regulations such as GDPR, HIPAA, and CCPA, which impose strict requirements on data handling and sharing.
Bandwidth Efficiency: Since only model updates are communicated between clients and the central server, as opposed to entire datasets, federated learning can be more bandwidth-efficient than centralized approaches.
Inclusivity: Federated learning can leverage data from diverse sources and devices, potentially leading to more robust and generalizable models [16].

7.4.2 Architecture of Federated Learning Systems

Federated learning systems consist of several core components that work together to train a global model:

Clients: These are the local devices or nodes (e.g., smartphones, IoT devices, or edge servers) that retain the data and perform local computations. Each client independently trains a local model using its own data and periodically sends updates (such as model parameters or gradients) to the central server.
Server: The central server (or aggregator) is responsible for coordinating the training process [17]. It collects updates from the clients, aggregates them (often through averaging), and updates the global model. The updated global model is then sent back to the clients for further local training.
Communication Protocols: Effective and secure communication protocols are crucial for federated learning. These protocols manage the exchange of model updates between clients and the server, ensuring minimal bandwidth usage while protecting the integrity and confidentiality of the data. Techniques such as secure aggregation, differential privacy, and homomorphic encryption may be employed to enhance security and privacy [18].

7.4.3 Applications of Federated Learning

Federated learning has significant applications across various industries, driven by the need for data privacy and collaborative model training:

Healthcare: Hospitals and medical institutions can collaboratively train machine learning models on patient data to enhance diagnostics, treatment plans, and predictive analytics without compromising patient privacy. For example, federated learning can be used to develop models for detecting diseases like cancer from medical images [19].

Finance: Financial institutions can collaborate to develop fraud detection models or credit scoring systems while maintaining the confidentiality of client data. By employing federated learning, banks and financial services can improve the accuracy of their predictive models without sharing sensitive information (Table 7.1).

Smart Devices and IoT: In the realm of the Internet of Things (IoT), federated learning facilitates the development of models based on data from multiple smart devices, including smartphones, wearable devices, and home automation systems, without transmitting individual data to a central server. This can enhance user experiences through personalized services while preserving privacy [20].

Telecommunications: Mobile network operators can utilize federated learning to optimize network performance and improve service quality by analyzing data from multiple users without compromising user privacy. This can lead to better resource allocation, network management, and customer satisfaction [21].

Autonomous Vehicles: Manufacturers of autonomous vehicles can use federated learning to enhance vehicle safety and performance by sharing driving data insights across a fleet of cars. Each vehicle learns from its own driving experiences and contributes to a collective model that improves navigation, obstacle detection, and decision-making capabilities.

Table 7.1 Applications of federated learning.

Industry/Application	Use case
Healthcare	Collaborative training of medical models across hospitals while preserving patient privacy.
Finance	Fraud detection and risk assessment models trained across financial institutions' data.
Internet of Things (IoT)	Edge devices sharing insights while protecting user data, enhancing smart city infrastructure.
Telecommunications	Network optimization and predictive maintenance without compromising customer data.

Retail and E-commerce: Retailers can use federated learning to improve recommendation systems, demand forecasting, and inventory management by leveraging customer data from different stores or online platforms while ensuring data privacy [22].

7.5 Challenges in Federated Learning

7.5.1 Data Heterogeneity

Data heterogeneity refers to the variability in data distributions across different clients or devices participating in federated learning. Key challenges include:

Non-IID Data Distributions: In federated learning, data on different devices may not follow identical and independently distributed (IID) patterns. This divergence can arise due to variations in user behavior, device capabilities, or geographic factors. Non-IID data can negatively impact model convergence and performance since the global model may struggle to generalize across disparate data distributions [23].

7.5.2 Communication Efficiency

Effective communication between clients and the central server is crucial in federated learning. Challenges in communication efficiency include:

Bandwidth Limitations: Clients often have limited bandwidth for transmitting model updates to the central server. This constraint can lead to delays in model aggregation and synchronization, negatively affecting the overall training performance.
Optimization Techniques: Techniques such as quantization (reducing the precision of model updates), compression (reducing the size of transmitted data), and differential privacy (including noise to model updates) are employed to optimize communication and reduce bandwidth usage while maintaining model accuracy.

7.5.3 Privacy and Security

Preserving data privacy and ensuring security are paramount in federated learning due to the decentralized nature of data processing. Challenges include:

- Data Privacy: Federated learning aims to train models without sharing raw data. Techniques like federated averaging (aggregating model updates instead of data), secure aggregation (encrypting model updates during transmission), and differential privacy (including noise to data or model updates) are used to protect sensitive information.
  Model Inversion Attacks: Adversaries may attempt to reverse-engineer sensitive information about clients from model updates. Techniques like federated learning with differential privacy and secure aggregation help mitigate these risks by adding noise to model updates and ensuring that individual client data remain confidential [24].

7.5.4 System and Computational Constraints

Federated learning must address diverse computational environments and resource limitations across client devices. Challenges include:

Device Variability: Clients may vary in computational power, storage capacity, and network connectivity. Managing these disparities is crucial to ensure fair participation and effective model training across all devices [25].
Resource Constraints: Limited battery life and processing capabilities of mobile devices and IoT devices pose challenges in executing complex machine learning algorithms. Federated learning algorithms need to be optimized to minimize computational overhead and energy consumption while maintaining model accuracy.

7.6 Key Algorithms for Federated Learning

Federated learning leverages several algorithms to effectively train models across decentralized data sources while ensuring data privacy and efficient communication.

Federated Averaging (FedAvg): This is a cornerstone algorithm in federated learning. In FedAvg, each participating client trains a local model using its own dataset and eventually sends model updates (instead of the raw data) to a central server. The central server aggregates these updates by averaging them to create an updated global model. Mathematically, this can be represented as: $w_{t+1} = \sum_{k=1}^{K} \frac{n_k}{n} w_{t+1}^{k}$

It is the total of the samples across all clients. FedAvg's performance depends on factors such as communication frequency, data heterogeneity, and network scalability. To optimize FedAvg, techniques like adjusting learning rates, managing stragglers (clients with slower processing speeds), and periodically rebalancing data distribution are employed [26].

- **Privacy-preserving Strategies:** Privacy-preserving strategies are crucial for maintaining data confidentiality in federated learning. Differential privacy is a widely used technique that involves adding random noise to the data or model updates to obscure individual data points, ensuring that the inclusion or exclusion of any single data point does not significantly affect the model's output [27]. This technique provides strong privacy guarantees while allowing meaningful model updates.
  Secure Multiparty Computation (SMPC): SMPC enables multiple parties to jointly compute a function over their inputs without revealing those inputs to each other. In federated learning, SMPC can be used to securely aggregate model updates from clients, ensuring that individual updates remain confidential [28]. These privacy-preserving techniques are essential for protecting against adversarial attacks and maintaining user trust (Table 7.2).

Personalization in federated learning aims to adapt the global model to better serve individual clients' needs [40]. Since clients may have diverse data distributions and requirements, a one-size-fits-all global model may not be optimal for all users [29]. Techniques for personalization include:

Table 7.2 Privacy-preserving techniques in federated learning.

Technique	Description
Differential Privacy	Adds noise to data or model updates to prevent the reconstruction of individual client data.
Homomorphic Encryption	Enables computation on encrypted data without decryption, preserving data confidentiality.
Secure Aggregation	Aggregates encrypted model updates, ensuring privacy during the global model update process.

Fine-Tuning: After the global model is trained, each client can fine-tune the model using its local data. This allows the model to adapt to the specific characteristics of the client's data, enhancing its performance on local tasks [39].
Meta-Learning: Meta-learning strategies enable the model to rapidly adapt to new tasks with minimal data. This is particularly useful in federated learning, where each client's data can be viewed as a unique task. By training the global model to be adaptable, meta-learning ensures that the model performs well across diverse client datasets [30].
Clustered Federated Learning: Clients with similar data distributions can be grouped into clusters, and separate models can be trained for each cluster. This approach strikes a balance between a fully personalized model and a single global model, improving performance for clients within each cluster [31].
Multi-Task Learning: This approach treats the federated learning process as a multi-task learning problem, where each client's data represents a different task. The model is trained to perform well across all tasks, leveraging shared data while adapting to individual client needs [32].

7.7 Model Aggregation and Optimization

7.7.1 Aggregation Techniques

Model aggregation is a critical step in federated learning, ensuring that the global model benefits from updates provided by all participating clients [33]. One common approach is weighted averaging, where each client's model update is proportional to the size of its dataset. Mathematically, this can be expressed as:

$$w_{t+1} = \sum_{k=1}^{K} \frac{n_k}{n} w_{t+1}^{k} \%u200B$$

Other aggregation methods may involve more complex approaches to account for data quality, model performance, or client trustworthiness [34].

7.7.2 Optimization Algorithms

Optimization in federated learning presents unique challenges due to the decentralized nature of the data and the variability in client resources and data distributions. Traditional optimization methods must be adapted to function effectively in this context [35].

Federated Stochastic Gradient Descent (FedSGD): FedSGD is a foundational algorithm used to optimize models in federated learning. In FedSGD, each client computes the gradient of the loss function with respect to its local data and sends these gradients to the central server. The server then averages these gradients to update the global model. While this method is straightforward, it can be communication-intensive, as gradients need to be exchanged frequently [36].

Federated optimization algorithms must address various challenges, including communication efficiency, handling non-IID data distributions, and accommodating heterogeneous client capabilities. Solutions to these challenges include:

Communication Efficiency: Techniques such as local updates (clients perform several local updates before communicating with the server), gradient compression (reducing the size of gradient updates), and periodic aggregation (reducing the frequency of communication) help mitigate communication overhead [37].

Handling Non-IID Data: Algorithms like FedProx introduce a proximal term into the optimization objective to better handle data heterogeneity by ensuring that local updates do not deviate significantly from the global model (Table 7.3).

Table 7.3 Federated averaging (FedAvg).

Aspect	**Details**
Concept	Federated averaging combines local model updates from multiple clients into a global model.
Mathematical Formulation	$w_{t+1} = \sum_{k=1}^{K} \frac{n_k}{n} w_{t+1}^{k} \%u200B$
Implementation	Involves periodic communication between clients and server, local model training, and global update steps.
Optimization	Techniques to improve efficiency, reduce communication costs, and enhance model accuracy.

Managing Heterogeneous Clients: Strategies such as adaptive learning rates and weighted aggregation can be employed to balance the contributions from clients with varying computational capabilities and data quality [38–40].

7.8 Conclusion

Federated learning represents a transformative approach in machine learning, addressing critical issues of data privacy, security, and scalability by decentralizing the training process.

Unlike conventional centralized models, federated learning allows collaborative model training across multiple clients without the need to share raw data, thereby preserving user privacy and complying with stringent data regulations. The architectural components, including clients, servers, and communication protocols, work in tandem to enable effective distributed learning while maintaining data integrity and privacy.

Key algorithms like Federated Averaging (FedAvg) and optimization techniques such as Federated Stochastic Gradient Descent (FedSGD) have been instrumental in advancing federated learning. These methods facilitate the aggregation of local updates into a robust global model, optimizing performance while minimizing communication overhead. Federated learning also addresses several inherent challenges, including data heterogeneity, communication efficiency, privacy and security, and system and computational constraints.

Techniques such as differential privacy, secure multiparty computation, and personalized models are crucial for mitigating these challenges, ensuring that the federated learning framework is resilient and adaptable to various real-world applications. Ongoing research focuses on enhancing algorithm efficiency, improving model accuracy across non-IID data distributions, and developing more sophisticated techniques to ensure client-level privacy and security.

The future of federated learning holds promise for broader adoption across various industries, enabling innovative applications that leverage decentralized data for smarter and more secure AI solutions.

References

1. Kairouz, P., McMahan, H.B., Avent, B., Bellet, A., Bennis, M., Bhagoji, A.N., Suresh, A.T., Advances and open problems in federated learning. arXiv preprint arXiv:1912.04977, 2019.

2. McMahan, H.B., Moore, E., Ramage, D., Hampson, S., y Arcas, B.A., Communication-efficient learning of deep networks from decentralized data, in: *Artificial Intelligence and Statistics*, pp. 1273–1282, PMLR, 2017.
3. Li, T., Sahu, A.K., Talwalkar, A., Smith, V., Federated learning: Challenges, methods, and future directions. *IEEE Signal Process. Mag.*, 37, 3, 50–60, 2020.
4. Bonawitz, K., Eichner, H., Grieskamp, W., Huba, D., Ingerman, A., Ivanov, V., Ramage, D., Towards federated learning at scale: System design. arXiv preprint arXiv:1902.01046, 2019.
5. Yang, Q., Liu, Y., Cheng, Y., Kang, Y., Chen, T., Yu, H., Federated learning. *Synth. Lect. Artif. Intell. Mach. Learn.*, 13, 3, 1–207, 2019.
6. Zhang, Z. and Zhou, J., Dynamic fusion-based federated learning for COVID-19 detection. arXiv preprint arXiv:2007.08197, 2020.
7. Aledhari, M., Razzak, R., Parizi, R.M., Dehghantanha, A., Federated learning: A survey on enabling technologies, protocols, and applications. *IEEE Access*, 8, 140699–140725, 2020.
8. Konečný, J., McMahan, H.B., Yu, F.X., Richtárik, P., Suresh, A.T., Bacon, D., Federated learning: Strategies for improving communication efficiency. arXiv preprint arXiv:1610.05492, 2016.
9. Sattler, F., Wiedemann, S., Müller, K.R., Samek, W., Robust and communication-efficient federated learning from non-iid data. *IEEE Trans. Neural Netw. Learn. Syst.*, 31, 9, 3400–3413, 2019.
10. Caldas, S., Wu, P., Li, T., Konecny, J., McMahan, H.B., Smith, V., Talwalkar, A., LEAF: A benchmark for federated settings. arXiv preprint arXiv:1812.01097, 2018.
11. Li, Q., Wen, Z., Wu, Z., Hu, S., Wang, N., He, B., A survey on federated learning systems: vision, hype and reality for data privacy and protection. arXiv preprint arXiv:1904.05072, 2019.
12. Wang, H., Yurochkin, M., Sun, Y., Papailiopoulos, D., Khazaeni, Y., Federated learning with matched averaging, in: *International Conference on Learning Representations*, 2020.
13. Sun, Y., Kairouz, P., Suresh, A.T., McMahan, H.B., Ramage, D., Can you really backdoor federated learning? arXiv preprint arXiv:1911.07963, 2019.
14. Mohri, M., Sivek, G., Suresh, A.T., Agnostic federated learning, in: *International Conference on Machine Learning*, pp. 4615–4625, PMLR, 2019.
15. Geyer, R.C., Klein, T., Nabi, M., Differentially private federated learning: A client level perspective. arXiv preprint arXiv:1712.07557, 2017.
16. Zhao, Y., Li, M., Lai, L., Smola, A., Federated learning with non-iid data. arXiv preprint arXiv:1806.00582, 2018.
17. Smith, V., Chiang, C.K., Sanjabi, M., Talwalkar, A., Federated multi-task learning, in: *Advances in Neural Information Processing Systems*, pp. 4424–4434, 2017.
18. Yu, H., Liu, R., Chen, T., Cong, G., Federated learning with attributed heterogeneity. arXiv preprint arXiv:2002.06440, 2020.

19. Wang, J., Zhao, Y., Li, M., Lei, J., An efficient communication method for federated learning. *IEEE Trans. Neural Netw. Learn. Syst.*, 31, 8, 2026–2039, Aug. 2019.
20. Xu, J., Wang, H., Li, Y., Federated learning in the sky: Aerial-ground air quality sensing framework with UAV swarms. *IEEE Internet Things J.*, 7, 9, 8792–8803, 2020.
21. McMahan, B., *et al.*, Federated Learning: Collaborative Machine Learning without Centralized Training Data. arXiv:1602.05629, 2017.
22. Bonawitz, K., *et al.*, Towards Federated Learning at Scale: System Design. *Proceedings of the 2nd SysML Conference*, 2019, arXiv:1902.01046.
23. Kairouz, P., *et al.*, Federated Learning: Challenges, Methods, and Future Directions. arXiv:1912.04977, 2019.
24. Li, T., *et al.*, Advances and Open Problems in Federated Learning. arXiv:1912.04977, 2020.
25. Wei, K., *et al.*, Differential Privacy for Federated Learning: A Comprehensive Survey. arXiv:2003.08119, 2020.
26. Mothukuri, V., *et al.*, A Survey on Federated Learning Systems: Vision, Hype and Reality for Data Privacy and Protection. arXiv:2103.05471, 2021.
27. Xu, J., *et al.*, Federated Learning: Privacy and Incentive. arXiv:1902.04885, 2019.
28. Zhou, Z., *et al.*, Edge Intelligence: The Confluence of Edge Computing and Artificial Intelligence. *IEEE Internet Things J.*, 7, 8, 7227–7239, 2019, DOI: 10.1109/JIOT.2019.2952134.
29. McMahan, H.B., *et al.*, Communication-Efficient Learning of Deep Networks from Decentralized Data. AISTATS. arXiv:1602.05629, 2017.
30. Google AI Blog, Federated Learning: The Future of Distributed Machine Learning. Google AI Blog, 2017. Retrieved from https://ai.googleblog.com.
31. Rieke, N., *et al.*, Federated Learning for Healthcare Informatics. *J. Am. Med. Inf. Assoc.*, 27, 2, 2020, DOI: 10.1093/jamia/ocz039.
32. Yang, Q., *et al.*, Privacy-Preserving Federated Learning for Wireless Communications. *IEEE Wireless Commun.*, 26, 5, 2019, DOI: 10.1109/MWC.001.1900175.
33. Lim, W.Y.B., *et al.*, Federated Learning in Mobile Edge Computing: A Comprehensive Survey. *IEEE Commun. Surv. Tutor.*, 22, 3, 2020, DOI: 10.1109/COMST.2020.2978306.
34. Li, T., Sahu, A.K., Talwalkar, A., Smith, V., Federated Learning: Challenges, Methods, and Future Directions. *IEEE Signal Process. Mag.*, 37, 3, 50–60, 2020, DOI: 10.1109/MSP.2020.2975749.
35. Liu, Y., *et al.*, Scalable and Privacy-Preserving Federated Learning for Industrial IoT. *IEEE Internet Things J.*, 7, 8, 2020, DOI: 10.1109/JIOT.2019.2952134.
36. Agarwal, N., *et al.*, Federated Learning with Differential Privacy: Algorithms and Performance Analysis. arXiv:1803.07389, 2018.

37. Grigorescu, S., Trasnea, B., Cocias, T., Macesanu, G., A Survey of Deep Learning Techniques for Autonomous Driving. *IEEE Trans. Intell. Transp. Syst.*, 22, 2, 7134–7149, 2020, DOI: 10.1109/TITS.2020.2998944.
38. Zhao, Z., Liu, P., Cheng, Y., Yu, H., Federated Learning: A Comprehensive Survey. *IEEE Internet Things J.*, 7, 5, 4642–4654, 2020, DOI: 10.1109/JIOT.2020.3001241.
39. Jiang, Y., *et al.*, Personalized Federated Learning: A Meta-Learning Approach. arXiv:1909.12488, 2019.
40. Wang, H., *et al.*, An Overview of Federated Learning for Wireless Communications. *IEEE Commun. Mag.*, 57, 6, 2019, DOI: 10.1109/MCOM.2019.1900108.

8

Reconstructing Healthcare Foundations: Building Blocks of Federated Systems in Medical Technology

Blessing Takawira* **and David Pooe**

University of Johannesburg, Johannesburg, South Africa

Abstract

This chapter thoroughly examines the fundamental components necessary to deploy federated healthcare systems effectively. It highlights the importance of decentralized data management and provides an overview of the essential technological prerequisites for federated systems, such as hardware, software, and network requirements. It also offers practical insights into their implementation. The text thoroughly examines critical subjects such as the incorporation of edge devices and the Internet of Medical Things (IoMT), the considerations regarding privacy and security, and the significance of blockchain technology. The chapter also emphasizes the capacity of federated learning to improve collaborative data analysis and safeguard patient privacy. The authors conduct a systematic literature analysis to examine how federated healthcare systems affect patient outcomes, promote precision medicine, and stimulate healthcare innovation. The discussion on future research areas and current trends offers valuable insights into the potential of federated systems to transform healthcare delivery and data management. It provides a roadmap for their practical application.

Keywords: Federated learning, healthcare systems, decentralized data management, IoMT, data privacy, blockchain technology, edge devices, precision medicine

**Corresponding author*: takawirablessing@gmail.com

S. Rakesh Kumar, N. Gayathri and Seifedine Kadry (eds.) Federated Intelligent System for Healthcare: A Practical Guide, (171–200) © 2025 Scrivener Publishing LLC

Introduction

Federated healthcare systems have emerged as a crucial medical technology model, revolutionizing healthcare delivery. This decentralized approach can increase accessibility, improve outcomes, and address healthcare supply disparities [1]. The COVID-19 pandemic has accelerated the development and use of telehealth, underscoring the importance of technology in maintaining consistent healthcare and extending services beyond face-to-face appointments [2]. The rise of open medical databases and digital health platforms has significantly transformed biomedical research and healthcare innovation. This shift has also highlighted the need for privacy-enhancing technology to ensure data openness and empower individuals to control their data-sharing preferences [3]. Furthermore, drones have demonstrated their potential to revolutionize emergency responses and healthcare provision in remote areas, offering cost-effective and flexible methods for transporting medical supplies and samples [4].

Joint imaging platforms have been created in federated clinical data analytics to assist with multicenter medical imaging trials and research. These platforms focus on the need to synchronize data, simplify analysis, and enable federated machine learning for large groups of participants [5]. Emerging strategies, such as utilizing blockchain and federated learning, have been suggested as solutions to tackle issues about data security, privacy, and trust within healthcare systems [6]. Ring-topology-based models are a type of decentralized, federated learning scheme that has been created to improve the usability of data and the efficiency of model training in healthcare applications [7]. Federated learning is crucial in healthcare systems as it utilizes data from different devices to propel technological progress and enhance patient care [8].

The integration of blockchain technology into medical systems has been on the rise. This integration aims to guarantee data integrity, prevent unauthorized alterations, and strengthen the security of healthcare data management [9]. The utilization of federated learning and blockchain technology in supplementary diagnoses, such as for COVID-19, has shown promise in addressing issues related to data sharing while ensuring the protection of privacy and security concerns [10]. Federated learning approaches have played a crucial role in training models across many healthcare units while maintaining data privacy. This has allowed disease discrimination and prediction using various knowledge sources [11]. In addition, the progress made in deep learning has substantially influenced the analysis of medical images, namely in the neurological, cardiovascular, digestive, and skeletal systems. This demonstrates the great potential of artificial intelligence in transforming healthcare [12].

Researchers have devised medical data-sharing schemes that utilize federated learning to provide precise access methods and facilitate proper screening of necessary medical data, all the while ensuring data security and privacy [13]. To guarantee reliable federated learning, designs based on blockchain technology have been suggested to improve the processes of auditing, traceability, and verification. This, in turn, encourages secure practices of sharing data in healthcare environments [14]. Technology transfer programs, particularly in public sector technology transfer, promote innovation, economic prosperity, and national security. These projects transfer knowledge from research to practical applications [15].

Privacy-preserving federated learning algorithms have been used in medical image classification to protect data privacy while maintaining model accuracy. This approach improves the robustness and security of models in healthcare applications [16]. The importance of technology in enhancing healthcare infrastructure, response mechanisms, and patient outcomes is highlighted by the use of intelligent algorithms to anticipate mortality and the need for preparedness in urban pandemics [17, 18]. The utilization of federated learning in interpreting thyroid ultrasound pictures has shown promise in safeguarding personal data while facilitating precise medical image analysis in authentic healthcare settings [19]. Incorporating socioeconomic determinants of health into electronic health records has gained significance in comprehending patient health and customizing interventions to enhance health outcomes across various healthcare systems [20].

Integrating blockchain management and federated learning in healthcare systems can improve data sharing and access control and facilitate medical research and treatment. This highlights the significance of implementing secure and efficient data management procedures [21]. The medical data model's portal and federated data capture initiatives emphasize the current research endeavors in federated data management systems, with the goal of optimizing data capture processes and improving data interoperability in healthcare contexts [22]. Models for information transmission in remote consultation systems have been created to mitigate medical errors, expedite replies, and enhance treatment adherence. These models aim to tackle the significant issues of managing chronic diseases [23]. Privacy-preserving frameworks, such as federated learning algorithms, have been suggested to train models without sharing data, guaranteeing patient information's confidentiality and safeguarding data integrity in healthcare applications [24].

Federated content distribution systems have been developed to create health data synchronization services independent of infrastructure. This allows organizations to implement services across various cloud environments while guaranteeing data synchronization and accessibility [25]. The German Medical Informatics Initiative highlights the significance of joint endeavors in developing medical informatics research and healthcare delivery. It emphasizes the necessity of interconnected data systems and interoperable healthcare solutions [26]. To achieve digital healthcare modernization and improve the quality of medical care delivery, it is essential to address the financial support difficulties in telemedicine and enhance ICT skills in healthcare settings [27, 28]. Including infertility treatment coverage in federally mandated insurance policies brings attention to the convergence of legislative structures, medical treatments, and patient care in addressing intricate healthcare requirements [29].

In addition to this introduction, this chapter examines the importance of federated healthcare systems in transforming healthcare delivery, boosting data management methods, and improving patient outcomes. This chapter aims to explore the function of federated systems in decentralizing healthcare delivery, diminishing inequalities, and enhancing the availability of healthcare services. It also aims to investigate the incorporation of technologies like telemedicine, blockchain, and federated learning into healthcare systems to tackle data security, privacy, and interoperability issues. Moreover, it evaluates the influence of federated clinical data analytics, deep learning, and medical image analysis on healthcare advancements and patient care quality. Furthermore, it investigates the capacity of federated learning models, oversees the integration of social determinants of health, and privacy-preserving strategies in improving healthcare data management and patient outcomes. Additionally, it analyses the consequences of technology transfer, financial support mechanisms, and policy concerns on developing federated healthcare systems and breakthroughs in medical technology.

Historical Context and Evolution of Healthcare Systems

Federated healthcare systems are a novel approach to delivering healthcare that involves decentralized data management and collaborative learning among multiple healthcare groups. Federated systems in healthcare include sharing data and knowledge while ensuring the preservation of data privacy and security [30]. This concept enables healthcare organizations to engage in collaborative data analysis and model training without the necessity of centralizing sensitive patient information, hence resolving concerns about data protection and confidentiality. Federated learning, an essential element of federated healthcare systems, allows training machine learning models on numerous decentralized devices or servers without sharing raw data, thus maintaining data privacy [31].

The emergence of federated healthcare systems has been propelled by the escalating quantity of healthcare data, the desire for seamless integration among healthcare providers, and tailored and streamlined healthcare services. Federated learning has become a potential option in the healthcare industry with the increasing use of big data. It allows for data utilization from various sources while still adhering to data ownership and privacy requirements [32]. Federated learning enhances data security and confidentiality in healthcare settings by enabling institutions to collaborate on data analysis without exposing sensitive information. This aligns with the increasing focus on patient privacy and data protection in the digital era [33].

Federated healthcare systems are crucial because they enable data exchange and cooperation among healthcare practitioners, researchers, and institutions while ensuring patient privacy and confidentiality. Federated learning has played a vital role in facilitating collaborative analysis of genomic data in oncology and cancer research. This has allowed many healthcare organizations to work together, resulting in progress in precision medicine and personalized treatment methods [34]. Federated healthcare systems enable stakeholders to leverage the combined knowledge of remote datasets while ensuring individual privacy through a safe and privacy-focused data-sharing methodology [33].

The notion of federated healthcare systems aligns with the overarching objectives of boosting healthcare quality, improving patient outcomes, and promoting medical research using collaborative data analysis and knowledge exchange. Integrating federated learning frameworks into healthcare informatics allows organizations to enhance data analysis processes, strengthen predictive modeling skills, and foster innovation in healthcare delivery [35]. When applied in intelligent healthcare systems, Federated learning can transform patient care by facilitating real-time data analysis, personalized treatment suggestions, and proactive health monitoring [36].

The development of federated healthcare systems has also been impacted by the requirement for data interoperability, smooth information transmission, and effective resource utilization across healthcare networks. Australia has shown the benefits of collaborative data sharing in enhancing precision medicine and diagnosing uncommon diseases by using federated models to integrate genomics into healthcare [37]. Federated healthcare systems provide a means to address the problem of isolated data storage, encourage collaboration between different institutions, and facilitate the use of evidence-based decision-making in healthcare policy and practice [38].

Thus, federated healthcare systems are a notable progression in healthcare delivery, prioritizing cooperative data analysis, distributed learning, and privacy-preserving methods to stimulate innovation and enhance patient care. Healthcare organizations can utilize federated learning frameworks to utilize the combined intelligence of distributed datasets, improve predictive modeling capabilities, and progress precision medicine programs. The development and significance of federated healthcare systems highlight the revolutionary capacity of decentralized data management in transforming healthcare delivery and defining the future of medical technology.

Fundamental Concepts of Federated Healthcare Systems

Integrating and operating federated healthcare systems in healthcare settings provides several issues that must be resolved for successful implementation. A significant obstacle lies in the intricate nature of data exchange and interoperability across many healthcare bodies, all the while ensuring data privacy and security [1]. The distributed nature of federated systems requires robust procedures to enable smooth communication while protecting sensitive patient data, which can pose a substantial challenge during deployment. Moreover, the absence of established protocols and frameworks for federated learning in healthcare might result in inconsistencies in data management and analysis, which presents obstacles to attaining dependable and precise findings [39].

A further crucial concern with the establishment of federated healthcare systems is the requirement for capacity development and training initiatives to improve the expertise of healthcare practitioners and administrators at both the federal and regional levels [40]. It is crucial to ensure that stakeholders possess the requisite expertise to efficiently navigate the intricacies of federated systems and make optimal use of new technology. This is vital for the successful implementation and long-term viability of such systems. Moreover, the incorporation of federated networks for decentralized analysis of health data necessitates a thorough comprehension of computer science and significant data principles to enhance the efficiency of data processing and analysis workflows [41].

The diagram depicted in Figure 8.1 visually represents the fundamental problems and disputes related to the adoption of federated systems in medical technology. The central focus of this map is the main topic, Federated Healthcare Systems, which is linked to several primary nodes that represent the main categories of concern: Ethical Considerations, Interoperability, Data Governance, and Privacy and Security. Each principal node expands into associated sub-topics, indicating a hierarchical and interwoven correlation among the different issues encountered in the field.

Ethical considerations are associated with bias and fairness, emphasizing the rigorous examination of algorithms and processes for possible systemic flaws or discriminatory impacts. Interoperability encompasses the integration and standardization of data, highlighting the importance of smooth information transmission and consistent standards within the interconnected healthcare system. Data Governance involves the management of data access, distribution, and the rights of individuals and institutions over their data. It includes the aspects of Data Sharing and Ownership. Privacy and security are essential components of federated healthcare systems. These aspects can be further categorized into data breaches and protection concerns. Establishing solid methods to protect sensitive health information from unauthorized access and exploitation is crucial.

Figure 8.1 below presents a comprehensive summary of the intricate and diverse discussions surrounding the creation and functioning of federated

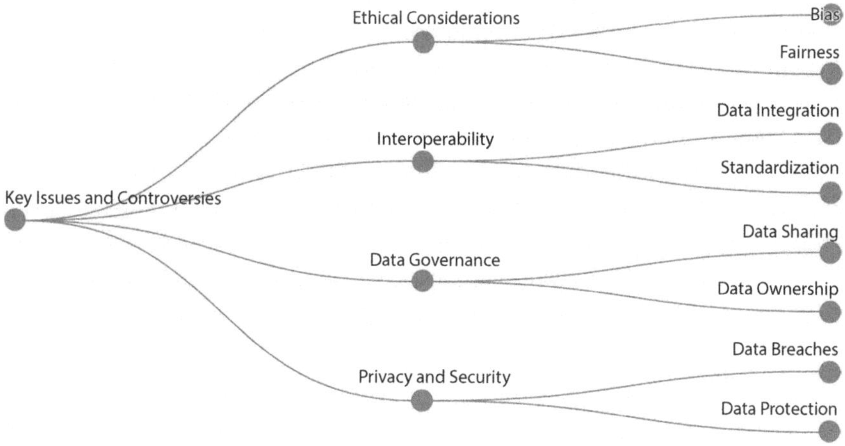

Figure 8.1 Key issues and controversies.

systems in healthcare. It offers a structured perspective that highlights the interconnectedness of these crucial matters.

Another controversial matter that requires attention is the discussion on the fair allocation of resources and finance in federated healthcare systems. Discrepancies in healthcare funding across state and federal levels can result in inequalities in the availability of necessary healthcare treatments across various healthcare facilities, affecting patient results and healthcare quality [37]. The problem is effectively distributing resources to enable equitable access to critical financing and support for all healthcare institutions, irrespective of their geographical location or affiliation.

One suggested approach to tackle these problems is to create federated models integrating genomics into healthcare. This has been exemplified by projects such as Australian Genomics, which seek to improve the identification of uncommon diseases and promote using genomic medicine based on solid evidence [42]. Federated models can enhance innovation and patient care outcomes by encouraging collaboration and knowledge exchange among healthcare professionals. Incorporating privacy-first strategies using federated learning frameworks can bolster data security and confidentiality in healthcare environments, addressing concerns regarding data privacy and ownership [43].

The CAreFL framework and other contribution-aware federated learning frameworks seek to improve data analysis processes and expand predictive modeling skills in healthcare applications, enhancing innovative healthcare systems [44]. Federated learning approaches can enhance the quality and efficacy of healthcare delivery by prioritizing personalized healthcare solutions and utilizing adaptive batch normalization techniques. This allows for tailoring treatment recommendations to patient needs [45]. In addition, the emergence of open-source front-end frameworks such as Fed-BioMed can simplify the implementation of federated learning solutions in the healthcare sector. This facilitates transparency and accessibility in data analysis and model training [35].

Unlike the existing methods, the future of federated healthcare systems may incorporate advanced technologies that analyze patient data collected from the Internet of Things (IoT) to improve the accuracy of diagnoses and treatment results [46]. Healthcare systems can enhance patient care and promote healthcare efforts by utilizing modern technology, such as fused weighted federated deep extreme machine learning to construct intelligent disease prediction models [47]. The advancement of federated systems in healthcare is positioned to transform the provision of care, enhance the allocation of resources, and stimulate innovation in medical technology, leading to a more effective and patient-focused healthcare ecosystem.

Technological Foundations

Establishing a solid technological foundation for federated healthcare systems requires a complete approach that includes hardware, software, and network components. Federated healthcare systems often necessitate a network of servers or edge devices dispersed throughout healthcare facilities to enable data processing, storage, and analysis. The servers must possess ample computing power, memory capacity, and storage capabilities to manage the varied healthcare datasets associated with federated learning and data sharing [31]. In federated healthcare applications, the performance of machine learning algorithms can be improved by using specialized hardware accelerators such as GPUs or TPUs [46].

Federated healthcare systems heavily depend on sophisticated software frameworks and tools to facilitate safe data sharing, model training, and collaborative analysis among remote healthcare institutions. Frameworks such as TensorFlow Federated and PySyft offer the essential infrastructure for implementing federated learning algorithms and guaranteeing data privacy and confidentiality during model training [31]. Furthermore, software solutions such as data encryption, secure communication protocols, and access control mechanisms are essential to safeguard sensitive patient information within federated healthcare systems [46].

Network requirements are crucial for the smooth functioning of federated healthcare systems since they enable communication and data exchange between distant healthcare entities. An efficient network architecture with ample bandwidth, minimal latency, and secure connections is crucial for facilitating instantaneous data transmission, updating models, and enabling collaborative learning in federated environments [48]. Virtual private networks (VPNs), secure sockets layer (SSL) protocols, and firewalls are frequently used to guarantee the security and privacy of data when it is being exchanged within federated healthcare networks [49].

To establish federated healthcare systems, it is essential to include data interoperability standards like Health Level Seven (HL7) and Digital Imaging and Communications in Medicine (DICOM). These standards enable the smooth integration and exchange of healthcare information among various systems and devices [50]. Federated healthcare systems can improve data exchange, interoperability, and collaboration among healthcare stakeholders by following standardized data formats and protocols [51]. In addition, federated learning architectures such as FLRA (Federated Learning Reference Architecture) can offer a standardized framework for developing federated learning solutions, guaranteeing uniformity and effectiveness in the training and deployment of models [52].

To tackle the issues of scalability and resource monitoring in federated healthcare systems, novel solutions like FEDARGOS-V1 (Federated Architecture for Monitoring in Cloud Computing Infrastructures) have been suggested. These solutions aim to facilitate quicker and more scalable resource monitoring in federated cloud environments [53]. These monitoring architectures can be used in private or public cloud infrastructures to maximize resource utilization, improve performance, and guarantee the dependability of federated healthcare systems [54]. Incorporating edge computing methods and federated deep extreme learning can improve data privacy, expedite data transmission, and enable intelligent disease prediction in healthcare applications [42].

Thus, the technological framework for federated healthcare systems consists of a complex network of advanced hardware, software, and network components designed to provide safe data sharing, collaborative learning, and interoperability among various geographically dispersed healthcare institutions. Federated healthcare systems have the potential to transform healthcare delivery, promote medical advancements, and enhance patient outcomes in a decentralized and privacy-focused way by utilizing modern technologies, standardized protocols, and creative solutions.

Building Blocks of Federated Healthcare Systems

Federated healthcare systems rely on certain fundamental elements that together facilitate distributed data management, secure data exchange, and collaborative knowledge acquisition across multiple healthcare organizations. These components consist of various data sources, advanced algorithms, and strong communication protocols, all of which have important roles in ensuring the efficient operation of the systems.

Data Sources

The fundamental basis of a federated healthcare system is its data sources, which are usually varied and spread out across different healthcare providers, research organizations, and medical devices. The data sources encompass electronic health records (EHRs), medical imaging databases, genomic data repositories, and real-time health monitoring data from wearable devices and IoMT (Internet of Medical Things) sensors. To ensure smooth integration and exchange of data from diverse sources, standardized data formats and interoperability frameworks like Health Level Seven (HL7) and Digital Imaging and Communications in Medicine (DICOM) are necessary [50, 51]. Using these standardized protocols, federated healthcare systems can enable the gathering and examination of extensive and diverse information while upholding the integrity and consistency of the data.

Algorithms

Federated healthcare systems rely on sophisticated machine learning and artificial intelligence algorithms to provide collaborative data analysis while ensuring patient privacy remains intact. Federated learning techniques, such as Federated Averaging (FedAvg), are designed to train models using decentralized datasets stored locally at each participating entity. These methods enable the global model to be updated by combining locally trained models, ensuring that raw data remains at its source and maintaining data privacy and security [55]. Furthermore, the integration of explainable AI (XAI) algorithms into federated systems is becoming more common. This integration aims to improve the transparency and interpretability of model predictions, thereby enhancing clinical decision-making and fostering patient trust [56]. These advanced algorithms are crucial for creating prediction models that can utilize the diverse and varied nature of healthcare data.

Communication Protocols

The effectiveness of federated healthcare systems is highly dependent on the deployment of secure and efficient communication protocols. These protocols enable the transfer of model updates and other pertinent information between the central server and the participating nodes. Secure communication protocols, such as Secure Sockets Layer (SSL) and Transport Layer Security (TLS), are used to encrypt data while it is being transmitted. This helps to safeguard the data from cyber threats and unauthorized access [49]. In addition, the security and confidentiality of the shared data are further improved by including privacy-preserving technologies such as homomorphic encryption and differential privacy [57]. These protocols are essential for preserving the integrity and confidentiality of data flows in a federated context.

Figure 8.2 illustrates a hierarchical framework that identifies the fundamental components of federated healthcare systems. 'Health Data Sources' are positioned as the key input for the system at the highest layer.

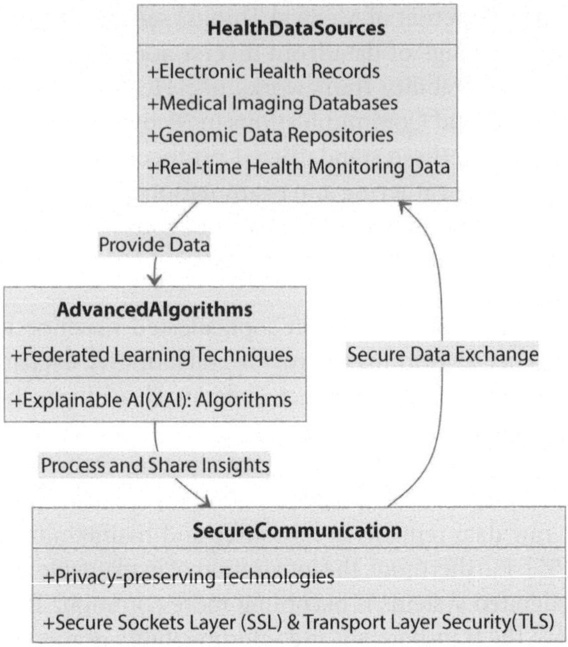

Figure 8.2 Building blocks of federated healthcare systems. Source: Takawira and Pooe (2024).

This category includes a wide range of important data types that are essential to the healthcare process, such as Electronic Health Records, Medical Imaging Databases, Genomic Data Repositories, and Real-time Health Monitoring Data. These sources are shown as the fundamental basis of the federated system, supplying the unprocessed material from which value is obtained through further analysis procedures.

The second level, referred to as 'Advanced Algorithms,' represents the analytical engines that handle the data provided by the previously described sources. Two significant elements within this tier are Federated Learning Techniques and Explainable AI (XAI) Algorithms. Federated Learning Techniques enable the training of machine learning models on several decentralized devices or servers that store local data samples, without the need to exchange the data. Preserving the privacy of sensitive health data is of utmost importance. Explainable AI pertains to algorithms that are intentionally created to possess transparency and interpretability. This enables humans to comprehend the decision-making procedures of AI systems, which is crucial for establishing trust and accountability in medical environments.

The process of Secure Data Exchange occurs between the 'sophisticated Algorithms' and 'Secure Communication' levels, emphasizing the significance of data security while sharing insights obtained from sophisticated analytical tools. This statement highlights the need to safeguard the accuracy and secrecy of data while transferring it from analysis to transmission.

The third and last level, known as 'Secure Communication,' focuses on the crucial element of data security within the federated system. This tier encompasses Privacy-preserving Technologies, which refer to methodologies and instruments specifically developed to safeguard individual privacy during the process of data analysis. These approaches enable the utilization of data without compromising the confidentiality of individual identities. The Secure Sockets Layer (SSL) and Transport Layer Security (TLS) protocols are designated as the standard technology for creating a secure connection between a web server and a browser. This connection encrypts all data transmitted between the two, guaranteeing its confidentiality and integrity.

This structured graphic illustrates the intricate relationship between data, analytics, and security that is the foundation of federated healthcare systems. The statement emphasizes the importance of reliable data sources, advanced analytical techniques, and strong security measures as the three essential foundations on which such systems are constructed and upheld.

The core components of federated healthcare systems, such as diverse data sources, sophisticated algorithms, and robust communication protocols, synergistically enable decentralized, secure, and collaborative data administration and analysis. Federated healthcare systems can employ defined data formats, sophisticated machine learning techniques, and secure communication methods to access and utilize distant datasets. This facilitates the incorporation of collective wisdom, resulting in innovation and enhanced patient outcomes. In addition, data privacy and security are efficiently upheld. The building above blocks function as the essential elements of federated healthcare systems, ensuring their efficacy and long-term sustainability in the ever-evolving realm of healthcare technology [31, 36].

Edge Devices and IoMT Integration

Integrating edge devices with the IoMT is crucial for the operation and efficiency of federated healthcare systems. The proximity of edge devices to data sources allows for immediate processing, analysis, and decision-making at the edge of the network, resulting in less delay and enhanced system responsiveness [58]. Edge devices play a critical role in federated healthcare systems by gathering and analyzing medical data from different sources such as wearable devices, sensors, and medical equipment. This data is then sent to centralized servers for further analysis [59].

The IoMT refers to a system of interconnected medical devices, sensors, and applications that collect and transmit health-related data with the goal of monitoring, diagnosing, and treating patients [60]. IoMT devices have a crucial role in monitoring patients from a distance, delivering personalized treatment, and collecting data from various healthcare settings in federated healthcare systems [61]. IoMT technology enables healthcare professionals to get up-to-date patient information, track health indicators, and make well-informed choices to improve patient results and optimize healthcare delivery procedures [62].

Incorporating edge devices and the IoMT in federated healthcare systems enables smooth gathering, analysis, and exchange of medical data while guaranteeing data security and confidentiality. Edge devices serve as gateways to collect data from IoMT devices, perform initial data processing activities, and transport the aggregated data to centralized servers for further analysis [63]. The distributed design improves data processing efficiency, decreases network congestion, and allows for real-time monitoring and decision-making in healthcare settings [64]. Incorporating blockchain technology into IoMT systems can enhance data security by offering immutable data storage and safe transaction processes [65].

Moreover, the combination of edge computing and the IoMT in federated healthcare systems enables the creation of advanced healthcare applications that utilize machine learning algorithms for predictive analysis, anomaly identification, and personalized treatment suggestions [66]. Healthcare providers can leverage machine learning models deployed at the network edge to extract valuable insights from medical data in real-time, optimize resource allocation, and improve clinical decision-making processes [67].

The function of edge devices and IoMT in federated healthcare systems goes beyond processing and analyzing data. It includes implementing proactive security measures, detecting anomalies, and employing adaptive response mechanisms to reduce cybersecurity risks [68]. Using intrusion detection systems, anomaly-based monitoring, and security mechanisms enabled by blockchain technology, edge devices and IoMT systems can protect healthcare data, thwart unauthorized access, and guarantee the integrity and confidentiality of patient information [69].

Integrating edge devices and the IoMT in federated healthcare systems is crucial for facilitating real-time data processing, ensuring safe data transfer, and enabling intelligent decision-making in healthcare settings. By utilizing edge computing capabilities and IoMT technology, healthcare providers can improve patient care, streamline healthcare delivery processes, and safeguard data security and privacy in a decentralized and networked healthcare ecosystem.

Privacy and Security Considerations

The privacy and security challenges in federated healthcare systems are of utmost importance due to the sensitive nature of medical data and the decentralized character of the system. Various approaches can be utilized to address these problems and guarantee the secrecy, accuracy, and accessibility of healthcare information. This chapter has implemented the following measures to reduce the impact, as depicted in Figure 8.3 below. The picture presents a thorough strategy for establishing a federated healthcare system that places utmost importance on data security and privacy right from the beginning. The process commences by deploying cutting-edge privacy technology and proceeds by reinforcing encryption and access control. The utilization of blockchain technology is emphasized due to its ability to uphold data integrity and transaction records, indicating a dependence on this technology for secure data management.

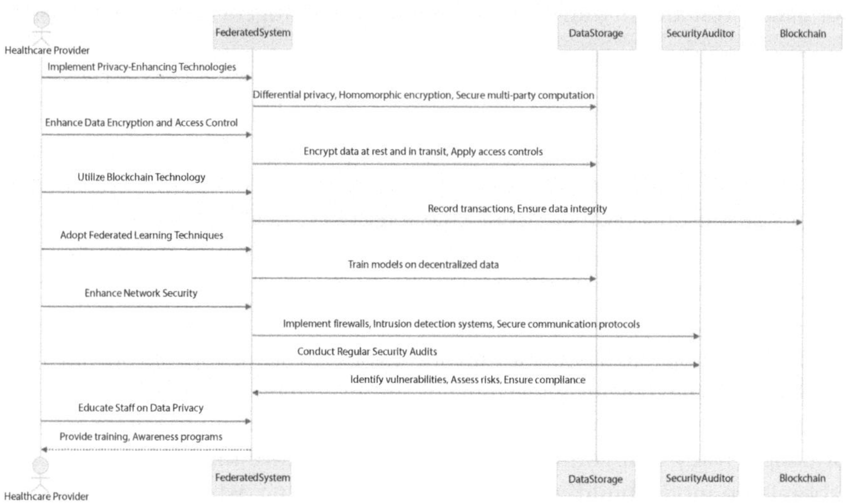

Figure 8.3 Privacy and security challenges and mitigation strategies. Source: Takawira and Pooe (2024).

Adopting federated learning approaches shows an evident dedication to utilizing decentralized data for training models, which is crucial for a federated system. Network security is prioritized by implementing a range of preventative measures. The ongoing processes of staff education on data protection and regular security audits reflect a culture of constant learning and vigilance. This is reinforced by training and awareness programs that circle back to the Healthcare Provider, indicating that these initiatives are both an initial step and an ongoing component of the system's functioning.

Implement Privacy-Enhancing Technologies

Privacy-enhancing technologies, such as differential privacy, homomorphic encryption, and secure multi-party computation, can be included in federated healthcare systems to safeguard sensitive patient data while sharing data and training models [70]. By implementing Privacy Enhancing Technologies (PETs), healthcare organizations can improve the protection of data privacy while yet preserving the usefulness of shared data for analysis and decision-making purposes.

Enhance Data Encryption and Access Control

Employ resilient data encryption protocols enforce stringent access control measures to protect healthcare data from unauthorized intrusion, and guarantee that only unauthorized staff can access and manipulate confidential information [46]. Healthcare organizations can avoid data breaches and unauthorized disclosures of patient information by employing encryption for data at rest and in transit and implementing stringent access restrictions.

Utilize Blockchain Technology

Implement blockchain technology to provide a reliable and unchangeable record-keeping system for transactions and guarantee the accuracy of data in federated healthcare systems [71]. By utilizing blockchain technology's decentralized and tamper-proof characteristics, healthcare organizations may improve data security, traceability, and transparency in data sharing and access control.

Adopt Federated Learning Techniques

Utilize federated learning methods to train models using distributed data without the need to share the raw data, thereby ensuring the preservation of data privacy and confidentiality [72]. Healthcare institutions can collaborate on model building using federated learning, which helps preserve sensitive patient information and reduces privacy risks associated with centralized data sharing.

Enhance Network Security

To enhance network security in federated healthcare systems, it is recommended to use firewalls, intrusion detection systems, and secure communication protocols. These measures will safeguard data transmission and mitigate the risk of cyber threats [73]. Healthcare organizations can reduce the likelihood of data breaches, unauthorized access, and cyberattacks by implementing measures to protect their network infrastructure.

Conduct Regular Security Audits

Conduct routine security audits and assessments to detect weaknesses, evaluate potential dangers, and guarantee adherence to data protection rules in federated healthcare systems [74]. Healthcare organizations can improve their data security by undertaking proactive security assessments. These assessments help identify and fix security holes, apply relevant policies, and increase the overall data security posture.

Educate Staff on Data Privacy

Deliver extensive training and awareness initiatives to healthcare personnel regarding data privacy best practices, security measures, and compliance standards. This is to ensure that all staff members have a clear understanding of their duties and obligations in protecting patient data [75]. Healthcare businesses can reduce the impact of human errors and insider threats that could jeopardize data security by promoting a culture of knowledge regarding data privacy and security.

Hence, healthcare organizations can proficiently address privacy and security issues in federated healthcare systems by deploying a blend of privacy-enhancing technologies, encryption protocols, blockchain integration, federated learning techniques, network security measures, periodic audits, and staff training. These solutions can safeguard patient data, preserve data confidentiality, and guarantee the integrity of healthcare information in a decentralized and networked healthcare setting.

Systematic Literature Review Process

This chapter presents a carefully organized systematic literature review (SLR) process to extract and synthesize knowledge on federated healthcare systems and their components from the scholarly work of the past two decades. This review sets itself apart from past literature studies for example, Jones, Keil [76] and Page, Sterne [77] by employing numerous unique methodologies. Firstly, it encompasses a wide array of fields, such as Medicine, Computer Science, Engineering, and Health Informatics. This study primarily focuses on literature relating to healthcare and technology management. However, it also includes pertinent works from allied domains to ensure a comprehensive understanding of federated systems. This interdisciplinary approach recognizes that the progress and execution of federated healthcare systems are impacted by breakthroughs and practices in many fields.

The sample chosen for this review intends to be inclusive and reliable rather than comprehensive to ensure the validity of the findings [78, 79]. The maintenance of this equilibrium is essential to get significant conclusions while avoiding the drawbacks of excessive concentration. Furthermore, this review examines many fundamental conceptualizations and frameworks present in the literature on federated healthcare systems. The chapter conducts a thorough analysis of these theoretical foundations, identifying and comparing significant concepts, similarities, and differences among them. This thorough examination emphasizes the development of ideas in the subject and emphasizes the areas where a clear understanding of concepts is still required.

Moreover, this review extends beyond the traditional examination of the advantages and difficulties associated with federated healthcare systems. Additionally, it examines research that addresses the role of federated systems in modulating healthcare outcomes. This added emphasis enhances the scholarly discourse by analyzing the intricate functions and secondary impacts of federated systems in different healthcare settings. The chapter tries to broaden the comprehension of federated healthcare systems beyond their immediate uses and implications, offering a more intricate and comprehensive perspective on their potential influence on healthcare delivery and innovation.

Solutions and Recommendations

Figure 8.4 below depicts a methodical and gradual strategy for developing federated healthcare systems. The initial focus is on prioritizing privacy and technology, followed by engaging stakeholders and ensuring data interoperability during the intermediate stage. Ultimately, the goal is to implement the federated architecture. Quality assurance is a primary concern throughout the advanced phase, signifying a shift from the initial setup to the process of improvement.

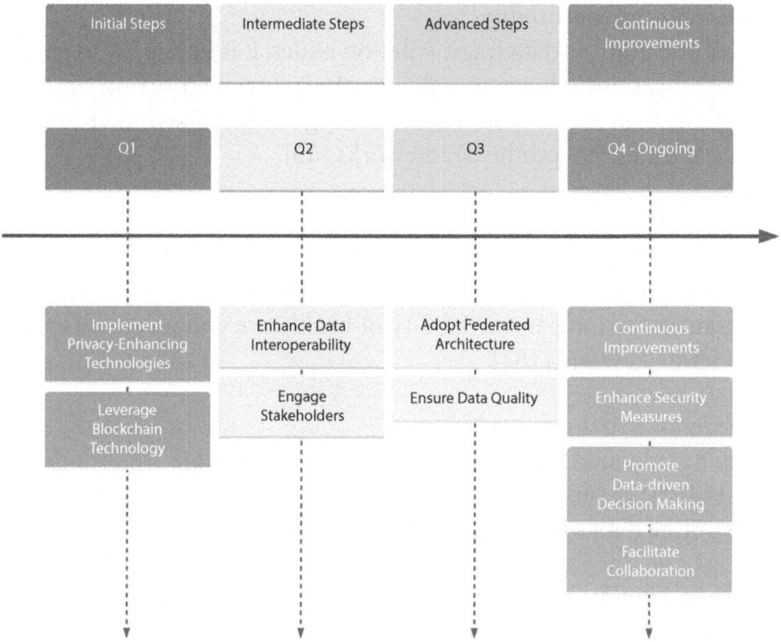

Figure 8.4 Implementation timeline for federated healthcare systems. Source: Takawira and Pooe (2024).

The last stage, Continuous Improvements, proposes an iterative approach to sustaining and improving the system. This includes continuous initiatives aimed at enhancing security, advocating for data-driven decision-making, and cultivating collaboration, all of which are vital for the system's long-term performance and adaptability.

Implement Privacy-Enhancing Technologies

Implement privacy-enhancing technologies, such as differential privacy, homomorphic encryption, and secure multi-party computation, to safeguard sensitive healthcare data while conducting collaborative model training. This ensures data privacy without any compromises, as suggested by [80].

Leverage Blockchain Technology

Examine the application of blockchain technology in creating reliable and unchangeable records for transactions and maintaining the accuracy of data in healthcare systems that are decentralized, hence resolving issues related to data security and integrity [81].

Enhance Data Interoperability

To resolve and address data fragmentation issues, it is necessary to enhance research and service efficiency, enhance clinical trial reporting, and guarantee patient data security by implementing standardized data exchange protocols and interoperability frameworks [45].

Engage Stakeholders

Facilitate the involvement and cooperation of stakeholders to establish pertinent research inquiries, enhance the efficiency of implementation, and guarantee the long-term viability of healthcare enhancement endeavors in federated systems [82].

Adopt Federated Architecture

Develop a federated architecture for Fast Healthcare Interoperability Resources (FHIR) servers to distribute data storage, improve data security, and streamline data interchange in healthcare systems.

Ensure Data Quality

Highlight the significance of data quality in healthcare systems through the implementation of data validation methods, data cleansing techniques, and data governance frameworks to enhance the precision and dependability of healthcare data.

Continuous Improvement

Adopt a culture of ongoing improvement by utilizing implementation science approaches, involving stakeholders, and closely monitoring progress to maximize the effectiveness of implementing federated healthcare systems.

Enhance Security Measures

To enhance network security in federated healthcare environments, robust mechanisms such as firewalls, intrusion detection systems, and secure communication protocols must be incorporated. These measures are essential for safeguarding data transmission, preventing cyber threats, and ensuring the confidentiality of sensitive information.

Promote Data-driven Decision Making

Employ data-driven solutions to improve patient outcomes, streamline healthcare procedures, and guide strategic decision-making in healthcare organizations, with a focus on evidence-based practices.

Facilitate Collaboration
Facilitate cooperation among healthcare providers, researchers, and policymakers to synchronize implementation tactics with improvement models, increase healthcare delivery, and promote favorable healthcare outcomes.

By using these solutions and methods, healthcare businesses can overcome the hurdles associated with implementing federated healthcare systems, enhance data security and privacy, improve interoperability, and optimize healthcare delivery to achieve better patient outcomes.

Future Research Directions

The future of federated healthcare systems holds great potential for revolutionizing healthcare delivery, improving patient outcomes, and fostering innovation in the healthcare sector. The landscape of healthcare technology and data management is set to be transformed by emerging trends and research directions in federated healthcare systems. The incorporation of multi-omics data into federated healthcare systems has great potential for developing precision medicine, personalized treatment strategies, and disease management. Healthcare professionals can enhance their understanding of individual health profiles and customize interventions to enhance patient outcomes by utilizing multi-omics data [83]. Implementing Explainable AI (XAI) and personalized medicine in federated healthcare systems can improve clinical decision-making, treatment planning, and patient care. Healthcare companies can enhance treatment methods, improve diagnosis accuracy, and increase patient involvement by integrating XAI models and personalized medicine approaches [84].

Collaborative open science projects within federated healthcare systems can promote the exchange of knowledge, facilitate research cooperation, and enhance data transparency among healthcare organizations. Healthcare organizations can expedite medical research, foster innovation, and enhance healthcare results by advocating for open science principles, as demonstrated by [85]. Implementing federated learning-based AI methods in smart healthcare environments has the potential to completely transform the way data is shared, models are trained, and predictive analytics are conducted. Healthcare businesses can utilize federated learning strategies to maintain data privacy, improve data security, and optimize collaborative model training across dispersed datasets [86]. The incorporation of IoT technologies in healthcare monitoring systems allows for the immediate gathering of health data, remote monitoring of patients, and tailored healthcare interventions. Healthcare providers can increase patient care, improve treatment outcomes, and optimize healthcare delivery procedures by utilizing IoT devices and sensors [87].

Federated X learning, which combines federated learning with other learning paradigms, has the potential to revolutionize healthcare applications by enabling model fusion, multitask learning, meta-learning, transfer learning, and reinforcement learning. Healthcare organizations can improve predictive modeling, decision support, and clinical insights by incorporating federated X-learning methods [88]. Thus, the future of federated healthcare systems is marked by the integration of cutting-edge technologies, data-centric strategies, and cooperative endeavors to revolutionize healthcare provision, enhance patient care, and foster medical advancement. Healthcare companies can capitalize on growing trends and research directions in federated healthcare systems to seize new opportunities, tackle intricate healthcare difficulties, and establish a more streamlined, patient-focused, and data-powered healthcare ecosystem.

Conclusion

This chapter has examined federated healthcare systems' complex and diverse characteristics, highlighting their ability to transform healthcare delivery by decentralizing data management, improving privacy, and fostering collaborative learning. The fundamental elements of federated healthcare systems, including the technological infrastructure, incorporation of edge devices and IoMT, and strong privacy and security protocols, were thoroughly examined. In addition, we analyzed the fundamental components necessary for the successful execution of these systems, which encompass hardware, software, and network prerequisites. Furthermore, we explored the significance of cutting-edge technologies such as blockchain and federated learning.

Integrating multi-omics data in federated healthcare systems offers a great opportunity to advance precision medicine and personalized treatment methods. This integration allows for a more comprehensive understanding of individual health profiles and facilitates customized interventions. Explainable AI and personalized medicine boost clinical decision-making and patient care by optimizing treatment options and enhancing diagnostic accuracy. The potential of collaborative open scientific programs to promote knowledge sharing, expedite medical research, and stimulate innovation through joint endeavors was emphasized.

Using federated learning-based artificial intelligence methods in innovative healthcare environments has demonstrated the potential to transform data sharing, model training, and predictive analytics. This strategy effectively safeguards data privacy and strengthens data security. Integrating IoT technologies with healthcare monitoring systems enables the immediate collection of health data, remote monitoring of patients, and customized healthcare interventions, leading to substantial enhancements in patient care and treatment results.

In addition, the chapter explored future research paths and upcoming developments in federated healthcare systems, including federated X learning. This approach combines many learning paradigms to enable model fusion, multitask learning, and meta-learning, opening up new opportunities. These developments are expected to improve predictive modeling, decision support, and clinical insights, leading to a more efficient, patient-centered, and data-driven healthcare system.

To summarize, federated healthcare systems are a revolutionary method of modern healthcare that utilizes cutting-edge technologies and decentralized data management to increase patient outcomes, foster innovation, and optimize the overall efficiency of healthcare delivery. Healthcare organizations can tackle intricate challenges, optimize resource distribution, and establish a more robust and adaptable healthcare system by adopting these emerging trends and research directions. This will prioritize patient privacy and data security. The ongoing advancement and application of federated healthcare systems have the potential to significantly influence the future of medical technology, promoting a more cooperative and open healthcare environment.

References

1. Thapa, R., *et al.*, Implementing Federalism in the Health System of Nepal: Opportunities and Challenges. *Int. J. Health Policy Manage.*, 8, 4, 195–198, 2018.
2. Shah, N.D., *et al.*, The Evolution and Utilization of Telehealth in Ambulatory Nutrition Practice. *Nutr. Clin. Pract.*, 36, 4, 739–749, 2021.
3. Yang, A., *Assessing the Evolution and Influence of Medical Open Databases on Biomedical Research and Healthcare Innovation: A 25-Year Perspective With a Focus on Privacy and Privacy-Enhancing Technologies (Preprint)*, JMIR, Canada, 2024.

4. Frith, K.H. and Amiri, A., Drones Could Offer Solutions for Emergency Responses and Health Care in Remote Areas. *Nurs. Educ. Perspect.*, 43, 3, 203–204, 2022.
5. Scherer, J., *et al.*, Joint Imaging Platform for Federated Clinical Data Analytics. *Jco Clin. Cancer Inf.*, 4, 1027–1038, 2020.
6. Wang, B., *et al.*, A Novel Disease Prediction Model Based on Blockchain and Federated Learning. *J. Phys. Conf. Ser.*, 2504, 1, 012049, 2023.
7. Wang, Z., *et al.*, Efficient Ring-Topology Decentralized Federated Learning With Deep Generative Models for Medical Data in eHealthcare Systems. *Electronics*, 11, 10, 1548, 2022.
8. Rana, N. and Marwaha, H., Role of Federated Learning in Healthcare Systems: A Survey. *Math. Found. Comput.*, 2024, 7, 4, 459–484, 2023.
9. Qu, J., Research on Medical System Based on Blockchain Technology. *Medicine*, 100, 16, e25625, 2021.
10. Wang, Z., *et al.*, A COVID-19 Auxiliary Diagnosis Based on Federated Learning and Blockchain. *Comput. Math. Methods Med.*, 2022, 1–12, 2022.
11. Ao, B. and Fan, B., An Automatic Annotation Method Based on Federated Learning, Proceedings Volume 12626, International Conference on Signal Processing, Computer Networks, and Communications (SPCNC 2022); 126260I, 2023. https://doi.org/10.1117/12.2674584.
12. Liu, X., *et al.*, Advances in Deep Learning-Based Medical Image Analysis. *Health Data Sci.*, 2021, 1–14, 2021.
13. Liu, W., *et al.*, A fine-grained medical data sharing scheme based on federated learning. *Concur. Comput. Pract. Exper.*, 35, 20, e6847, 2023.
14. Gao, H., Towards Trustworthy Federated Learning: A Blockchain-Based Architecture for Auditing, Traceability, and Verification, Proceedings Volume 12918, Fourth International Conference on Computer Science and Communication Technology (ICCSCT 2023); 1291823, 2023. https://doi.org/10.1117/12.3009373.
15. Link, A.N., Why Public Sector Technology Transfer?, in: *Public Sector Technology Transfer*, pp. 1–16, Edward Elgar Publishing, 2024.
16. Yang, P., *et al.*, Study of Medical Image Classification With Privacy-Preserving Federated Learning: Chest X-ray Images Classification as an Example, Research Square, 1–21, 2023. https://doi.org/10.21203/rs.3.rs-3124682/v1.
17. Alaria, S.K., Design Simulation and Assessment of Prediction of Mortality in Intensive Care Unit Using Intelligent Algorithms. *Math. Stat. Eng. Appl.*, 71, 2, 355–367, 2022.
18. Madad, S., *et al.*, Ready or Not, Patients Will Present: Improving Urban Pandemic Preparedness. *Disaster Med. Public Health Prep.*, 15, 3, 267–270, 2020.
19. Lee, H., *et al.*, Federated Learning for Thyroid Ultrasound Image Analysis to Protect Personal Information: Validation Study in a Real Health Care Environment. *JMIR Med. Inf.*, 9, 5, e25869, 2021.

20. Freij, M., *et al.*, Incorporating Social Determinants of Health in Electronic Health Records: Qualitative Study of Current Practices Among Top Vendors. *JMIR Med. Inf.*, 7, 2, e13849, 2019.
21. Turgay, S., Blockchain Management and Federated Learning Adaptation on Healthcare Management System. *Int. J. Intell. Syst. Appl.*, 14, 5, 1–13, 2022.
22. Ganzinger, M., Blumenstock, M., Niklas, C. and Dugas, M., Portal of Medical Data Models: Application in Federated Data Capture. In MIE, pp. 137–138, 2023, May.
23. Ilin, I.V., Iliashenko, V., Iliashenko, O., Information Exchange Model for Remote Consulting Systems in the Russian Federation. *E3s Web Conf.*, 110, 02047, 2019.
24. Cheng, W., *et al.*, A Privacy-Protection Model for Patients. *Secur. Commun. Netw.*, 2020, 1–12, 2020.
25. Carrizales-Espinoza, D., Sánchez-Gallegos, D.D., Gonzalez-Compean, J.L. and Carretero, J., A federated content distribution system to build health data synchronization services, in: *2021 29th Euromicro International Conference on Parallel, Distributed and Network-Based Processing (PDP)*, pp. 1–18, IEEE, 2021, March.
26. Semler, S.C., Wissing, F., Heyder, R., German Medical Informatics Initiative. *Methods Inf. Med.*, 57, S 01, e50–e56, 2018.
27. Razgildieva, M.B. and Malysheva, A.A., Financial Support Problems That Telemedicine Faces In Russia, *European Proceedings of Social and Behavioural Sciences*, 2022.
28. Soyemi, O.D., Information and Communication Technology (ICT) Skill and Quality Medical Care in Federal Medical Centre, Owo, Ondo State, Nigeria. *Int. J. Multi. Res. Anal.*, 05, 02, 338–342, 2022.
29. Tutt, T., Healthcare Policy: Federally Mandated Insurance Coverage for Infertility Treatment. *C. Soc. Work Rev.*, 19, 1, 2–19, 2021.
30. Xu, J., *et al.*, Federated Learning for Healthcare Informatics. *J. Healthc. Inf. Res.*, 5, 1, 1–19, 2020.
31. Budrionis, A., *et al.*, Benchmarking PySyft Federated Learning Framework on MIMIC-III Dataset. *IEEE Access*, 9, 116869–116878, 2021.
32. Righolt, A.J., *et al.*, An International Working Definition for Quality of Oral Healthcare. *JDR Clin. Transl. Res.*, 5, 2, 102–106, 2019.
33. Sadilek, A., Liu, L., Nguyen, D., Kamruzzaman, M., Serghiou, S., Rader, B., Ingerman, A., Mellem, S., Kairouz, P., Nsoesie, E.O. and MacFarlane, J., Privacy-first health research with federated learning. *NPJ Digit. Med.*, 4, 1, 132, 2021.
34. Chowdhury, A., Kassem, H., Padoy, N., Umeton, R. and Karargyris, A., A review of medical federated learning: Applications in oncology and cancer research, in: *International MICCAI Brainlesion Workshop*, pp. 3–24, , Cham: Springer International Publishing, 2021, September.
35. Mishra, A., *et al.*, A Federated Learning Approach for Smart Healthcare Systems. *Csi Trans. Ict*, 11, 1, 39–44, 2023.

36. Liu, Z., *et al.*, CAreFL: Enhancing Smart Healthcare With Contribution-Aware Federated Learning. *Ai Mag.*, 44, 1, 4–15, 2023.
37. Stark, Z., *et al.*, Australian Genomics: A Federated Model for Integrating Genomics Into Healthcare. *Am. J. Hum. Genet.*, 105, 1, 7–14, 2019.
38. Nokkala, T. and Dahlberg, T., Empowering citizens through data interoperability - data federation applied to consumer-centric healthcare. *Finnish J. Ehealth Ewelfare*, 11, 4, 246–257, 2019.
39. Azab, E.F.E. and Mostafa, H.S., Geraniol Ameliorates the Progression of High Fat-diet/Streptozotocin-induced Type 2 Diabetes Mellitus in Rats via Regulation of Caspase-3, Bcl-2, and Bax Expression. *J. Food Biochem.*, 46, 7, e14142, 2022.
40. Said, A.S. and Kicha, D.I., Implementing health system and the new federalism in Somalia: challenges and opportunities. *Front. Public Health*, 12, 1205327, 2024.
41. Hallock, H., Marshall, S.E., 't Hoen, P.A., Nygård, J.F., Hoorne, B., Fox, C. and Alagaratnam, S., Federated networks for distributed analysis of health data. *Front. Public Health*, 9, 712569, 2021.
42. Bhurtel, K.K., Health Equity Through Structural Adjustment by Nepal for Public Health. *Orchid Acad. Siraha*, 2, 1, 80–86, 2023.
43. Duncan, D.F., *et al.*, Health Care Administration and Drug Policy. *Int. J. Health Plann. Manage.*, 38, 3, 735–746, 2023.
44. Brown, N., Reimbursement of Interventional Oncology in Australia: How It Works and How It Does Not. *J. Med. Imaging Radiat. Oncol.*, 67, 8, 915–925, 2023.
45. Baldridge, A.S., Aluka-Omitiran, K., Orji, I.A., Shedul, G.L., Ojo, T.M., Eze, H., Shedul, G., Ugwuneji, E.N., Egenti, N.B., Okoli, R.C. and Ale, B.M., Hypertension Treatment in Nigeria (HTN) Program: rationale and design for a type 2 hybrid, effectiveness, and implementation interrupted time series trial. *Implement. Sci. Commun.*, 3, 1, 84, 2022.
46. Abbas, S., *et al.*, Fused Weighted Federated Deep Extreme Machine Learning Based on Intelligent Lung Cancer Disease Prediction Model for Healthcare 5.0. *Int. J. Intell. Syst.*, 2023, 1–14, 2023.
47. Amri, B. and Menazla, N., Obamacare During the Pandemic: A Historical, Economic and Sociopolitical Evaluation of the Initial Response of the US Government. *Tech. Soc. Sci. J.*, 33, 638–647, 2022.
48. Nzanzu, V.P., *et al.*, FEDARGOS-V1: A Monitoring Architecture for Federated Cloud Computing Infrastructures. *IEEE Access*, 10, 133557–133573, 2022.
49. Ansari, M.T.J., Al-Zahrani, F.A., Pandey, D. and Agrawal, A., A fuzzy TOPSIS based analysis toward selection of effective security requirements engineering approach for trustworthy healthcare software development. *BMC Med. Inform. Decis. Mak.*, 20, 1–13, 2020.
50. Patel, V.A., *et al.*, Adoption of Federated Learning for Healthcare Informatics: Emerging Applications and Future Directions. *IEEE Access*, 10, 90792–90826, 2022.

51. Javed, I., *et al.*, Next Generation Infectious Diseases Monitoring Gages via Incremental Federated Learning: Current Trends and Future Possibilities. *Comput. Intell. Neurosci.*, 2023, 1–12, 2023.
52. Tariq, U., *et al.*, An Effective Self-Configurable Ransomware Prevention Technique for IoMT. *Sensors*, 22, 21, 8516, 2022.
53. McMurry, A.J., Gottlieb, D.I., Miller, T.A., Jones, J.R., Atreja, A., Crago, J., Desai, P.M., Dixon, B.E., Garber, M., Ignatov, V., Kirchner, L.A., Payne, P.R.O., Saldanha, A.J., Shankar, P.R.V., Solad, Y.V., Sprouse, E.A., Terry, M., Wilcox, A. B. and Mandl, K.D. Cumulus: A federated EHR-based learning system powered by FHIR and AI. medRxiv, 2024, 2024.2002.2002.24301940 https://doi.org/10.1101/2024.02.02.24301940.
54. Castellanos, J., Raposo, G., Antúnez, L., Data Federation in Healthcare for Artificial Intelligence Solutions, in: *Advances in Informatics, Management and Technology in Healthcare*, pp. 167–170, IOS Press, 2022.
55. McMahan, H.B., A survey of algorithms and analysis for adaptive online learning. *J. Mach. Learn. Res.*, 18, 90, 1–50, 2017.
56. Nasarian, E., Alizadehsani, R., Acharya, U. R. and Tsui, K.-L., Designing interpretable ML system to enhance trust in healthcare: A systematic review to proposed responsible clinician-AI-collaboration framework. *Inf. Fusion*, 108, 102412, 2024, https://doi.org/https://doi.org/10.1016/j.inffus.2024.102412.
57. Abadi, M. and Andersen, D.G., Learning to protect communications with adversarial neural cryptography. arXiv preprint arXiv:1610.06918, 2016.
58. Seid, A.M., *et al.*, Multiagent Federated Reinforcement Learning for Resource Allocation in UAV-Enabled Internet of Medical Things Networks. *IEEE Internet Things J.*, 10, 22, 19695–19711, 2023.
59. Lakhan, A., *et al.*, Federated-Learning Based Privacy Preservation and Fraud-Enabled Blockchain IoMT System for Healthcare. *IEEE J. Biomed. Health. Inf.*, 27, 2, 664–672, 2023.
60. Hasan, M.K., *et al.*, A Review on Security Threats, Vulnerabilities, and Counter Measures of 5G Enabled Internet-of-Medical-Things. *IET Commun.*, 16, 5, 421–432, 2021.
61. Bhan, R., *et al.*, Blockchain-Enabled Secure and Efficient Data Sharing Scheme for Trust Management in Healthcare Smartphone Network. *J. Supercomput.*, 79, 14, 16233–16274, 2023.
62. Tariq, U., Proactive Ransomware Prevention in Pervasive IoMT via Hybrid Machine Learning. *Indones. J. Electr. Eng. Comput. Sci.*, 34, 2, 970, 2024.
63. Papaioannou, M., Karageorgou, M., Mantas, G., Sucasas, V., Essop, I., Rodriguez, J. and Lymberopoulos, D., A survey on security threats and countermeasures in internet of medical things (IoMT). *Trans. Emerg. Telecommun. Techno*l., 33, 6, e4049, 2022.
64. Pelekoudas-Oikonomou, F., *et al.*, Blockchain-Based Security Mechanisms for IoMT Edge Networks in IoMT-Based Healthcare Monitoring Systems. *Sensors*, 22, 7, 2449, 2022.

65. Priyadarshi, R., Gheisari, M., Security and Privacy in Machine Learning for IoHT and IoMT: A Review. Preprints 2024, 2024030329. https://doi.org/10.20944/preprints202403.0329.v1.
66. Yang, C.-H., *et al.*, National IoMT Platform Strategy Portfolio Decision Model Under the COVID-19 Environment: Based on the Financial and Non-Financial Value View. *Ann. Oper. Res.*, 328, 1, 1151–1179, 2022.
67. Ahmed, Z., *et al.*, Artificial intelligence with multi-functional machine learning platform development for better healthcare and precision medicine. *Database*, 2020, baaa010, 2020.
68. Ali, N.J., 5g-Backed Resilience and Quality Enhancement in Internet of Medical Things Infrastructure for Resilient Infrastructure. *Telkomnika (Telecommun. Comput. Electron. Control)*, 22, 2, 372, 2024.
69. Dai, H.-N., Imran, M., Haider, N., Blockchain-Enabled Internet of Medical Things to Combat COVID-19. *IEEE Internet Things Mag.*, 3, 3, 52–57, 2020.
70. Asif, H., U.S.-U.K. PETs Prize Challenge: Anomaly Detection via Privacy-Enhanced Federated Learning. *IEEE Trans. Privacy*, 1, 3–18, 2024.
71. Ismail, L., Materwala, H., Hennebelle, A., A Scoping Review of Integrated Blockchain-Cloud (BcC) Architecture for Healthcare: Applications, Challenges and Solutions. *Sensors*, 21, 11, 3753, 2021.
72. Woubie, A., Maintaining Privacy in Face Recognition Using Federated Learning Method. *IEEE Access*, 12, 39603–39613, 2024.
73. Sun, Y., Lo, F.P., Lo, B., Security and Privacy for the Internet of Medical Things Enabled Healthcare Systems: A Survey. *IEEE Access*, 7, 183339–183355, 2019.
74. Hu, C., Lei, T., Wang, S., Yao, Z., Wang, P. and Zhang, T., August. Privacy preservation for federated learning based on Gaussian noise scrambling, in: *Sixth International Conference on Advanced Electronic Materials, Computers, and Software Engineering (AEMCSE 2023)*, vol. 12787, pp. 337–342, SPIE, 2023.
75. Seh, A.H., *et al.*, Machine Learning Based Framework for Maintaining Privacy of Healthcare Data. *Intell. Autom. Soft Comput.*, 29, 3, 697–712, 2021.
76. Jones, C.W., *et al.*, Comparison of registered and published outcomes in randomized controlled trials: a systematic review. *BMC Med.*, 13, 1–12, 2015.
77. Page, M.J., *et al.*, Investigating and dealing with publication bias and other reporting biases in meta-analyses of health research: A review. *Res. Synth. Methods*, 12, 2, 248–259, 2021.
78. Munn, Z., *et al.*, *Systematic review or scoping review? Guidance for authors when choosing between a systematic or scoping review approach. BMC Med. Res. Methodol.*, 18, 1–7, 2018.
79. Donthu, N., *et al.*, How to conduct a bibliometric analysis: An overview and guidelines. *J. Bus. Res.*, 133, 285–296, 2021.
80. Loftus, T.J., *et al.*, Federated Learning for Preserving Data Privacy in Collaborative Healthcare Research. *Digit. Health*, 8, 205520762211344, 2022.

81. Ahmed, J., Schneider, C.H., Alam, A. and Raynes-Greenow, C., An analysis of the impact of newborn survival policies in Pakistan using a policy triangle framework. *Health Res. Policy and Syst.*, 19, 1, 86, 2021.
82. Naamati-Schneider, L., The Effect of Digitalization on Service Orientation and Service Perception Among Israeli Healthcare Professionals: A Qualitative Study. *Digit. Health*, 9, 9, 2023.
83. Olorunsogo, T., Ethical Considerations in AI-enhanced Medical Decision Support Systems: A Review. *World J. Adv. Eng. Technol. Sci.*, 11, 1, 329–336, 2024.
84. Okolo, C.A., *et al.*, Reviewing the impact of health information technology on healthcare management efficiency. *Int. Med. Sci. Res. J.*, 4, 4, 420–440, 2024.
85. Adeghe, E.P., Okolo, C.A., Ojeyinka, O.T., Integrating IoT in pediatric dental health: A data-driven approach to early prevention and education. *Int. J. Front. Life Sci. Res.*, 6, 01, 022–035, 2024.
86. Rahman, A., *et al.*, Federated Learning-Based AI Approaches in Smart Healthcare: Concepts, Taxonomies, Challenges and Open Issues. *Cluster Comput.*, 26, 4, 2271–2311, 2022.
87. Abdulmalek, S., *et al.*, IoT-Based Healthcare-Monitoring System Towards Improving Quality of Life: A Review. *Healthcare*, 10, 10, 1993, 2022.
88. Ji, S., Tan, Y., Saravirta, T., Yang, Z., Liu, Y., Vasankari, L., Pan, S., Long, G. and Walid, A., Emerging trends in federated learning: From model fusion to federated x learning. *Int. J. Mach. Learn. Cybern.*, 1–22, 2024.

Key Terms and Definitions

Data Privacy: The protection of sensitive healthcare data from unauthorized access or disclosure, ensuring patient confidentiality and compliance with data protection regulations.
Federated Learning: A decentralized machine learning approach where models are trained across multiple devices or servers holding local data without exchanging raw data to preserve privacy and security.
Healthcare Interoperability: The ability of different healthcare systems and applications to exchange and interpret data seamlessly, facilitating coordinated patient care and data sharing.
IoMT: A network of interconnected medical devices, sensors, and applications that collect and transmit health-related data for monitoring, diagnosis, and treatment purposes.

Patient-Centric Care: A healthcare approach that prioritizes the individual patient's needs, preferences, and outcomes, focusing on personalized and tailored treatment plans.
Secure Data Sharing: The practice of securely exchanging healthcare data among authorized parties, ensuring data integrity, confidentiality, and compliance with privacy regulations.
Stakeholder Engagement: Involving all relevant stakeholders, including healthcare providers, patients, policymakers, and technology vendors, in the decision-making process to ensure alignment and collaboration in healthcare initiatives.

9

Federated Learning in Brain Tumor Segmentation in Medical Imaging

Jyoti Kataria[1*] **and Supriya P. Panda**[2]

[1]*K. R. Mangalam University, Gurugram, India*
[2]*Manav Rachna International Institute of Research and Studies, Faridabad, India*

Abstract
Federated Learning (FL) is revolutionizing the field of medical imaging by enabling joint model training among multiple institutions while protecting the privacy of data. The application of FL to brain tumor segmentation is discussed in this chapter. It goes over the benefits, challenges, processes, necessary technology, and possible advancements of this strategy in the future. In medical imaging, brain tumor segmentation is an essential process that seeks to define the borders of tumors in brain images accurately. Brain tumor diagnosis, treatment planning, and tracking the growth or shrinkage of tumors all depend on segmentation. Radiologists have historically completed this task by hand, which is accurate but labor-intensive and subject to error. Artificial intelligence (AI) and machine learning (ML)-based automated segmentation algorithms have significantly increased the accuracy and efficiency of this process. This chapter looks at the importance of accurate segmentation, comparing traditional and AI-driven methods, and discussing the advantages and disadvantages of each. This chapter delves into the automation of segmentation in the diagnosis and treatment planning of brain tumors known as gliomas, which are known for their extreme aggression. The focus is primarily on the utilization of Neural Networks (NN) and Deep Learning (DL) in this process. This study provides a comprehensive analysis of many recognized methodologies, accompanied by real-life instances that showcase the numerous advantages and uses of artificial intelligence in the categorization of brain tumors. The text discusses the difficulties and potential future paths of FL in the field of medical imaging. These problems encompass the necessity to establish uniform data formats, tackle data biases, and enhance the scalability and efficacy of FL systems. When effectively handled, FL has the capacity to entirely revolutionize the categorization

**Corresponding author*: jyoti.kataria87@gmail.com

S. Rakesh Kumar, N. Gayathri and Seifedine Kadry (eds.) Federated Intelligent System for Healthcare: A Practical Guide, (201–232) © 2025 Scrivener Publishing LLC

of brain tumors, leading to better treatment results, heightened diagnostic precision, and ultimately improved patient care.

Keywords: Automated segmentation, brain tumor segmentation, convolutional neural networks, federated learning, medical imaging, region-based methods, thresholding methods, U-Net

9.1 Introduction to Federated AI in Medical Imaging

Federated learning (FL) is an innovative method for Artificial Intelligence (AI) and Machine Learning (ML) that ensures privacy. It is beneficial in areas such as medical imaging, where maintaining the confidentiality of data is of utmost importance. Medical imaging produces substantial quantities of patient data that are exchanged throughout many healthcare organizations. Conventional approaches to training AI models include consolidating all the data into a single location, hence giving rise to substantial administrative and privacy vulnerabilities. FL enables collaborative model training without the need for centralized data storage, therefore addressing these difficulties [1]. Every participating medical facility locally keeps its dataset within the FL architecture. Instead of sharing raw data, institutions choose to train their models on datasets of their own and then share only the model parameters or updates (gradients) with a central server. This approach complies with strict privacy regulations like Health Insurance Portability and Accountability Act (HIPAA) and General Data Protection Regulation (GDPR) by ensuring that private patient data stays on the institution's property. These modifications are combined by the central server to create an all-encompassing model that uses the diverse data from every institution. There are several advantages to the decentralized approach. Firstly, because no raw data is sent, it significantly reduces the risk of data breaches. Additionally, FL facilitates the ongoing enhancement of AI models. It makes use of diverse data sources and integrated expertise from several institutions [2]. Institutions have the ability to consistently train and update their models as they get new data at the local level. Subsequently, they can regularly submit these modifications to the central server. This iterative procedure enables the global model to progress and enhance gradually, staying up-to-date with new medical information and evolving data patterns.

Medical imaging could undergo major transformations as a result of federated learning. A high-accuracy model is crucial for brain tumor

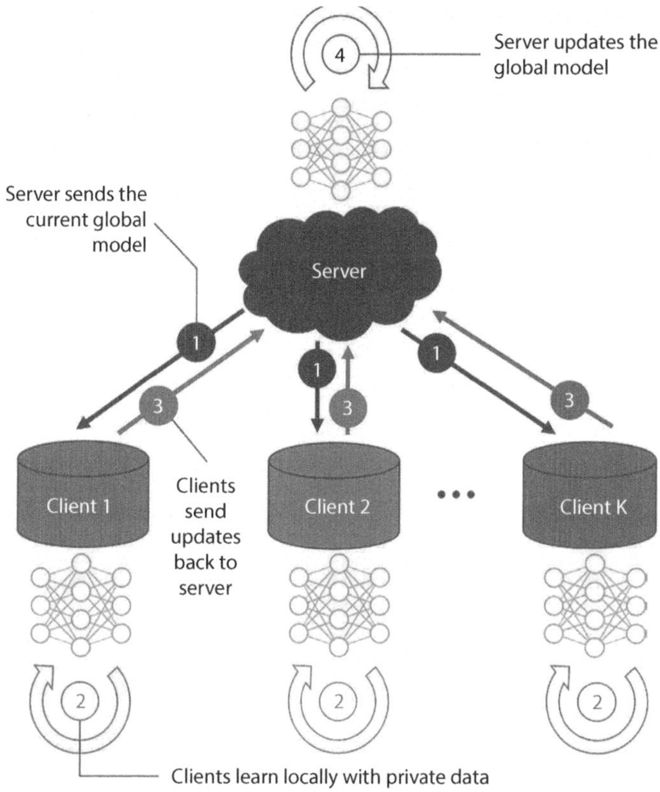

Figure 9.1 A schematic for FL and its training procedure, Source: [4].

segmentation since it helps with diagnosis, treatment planning, and monitoring, among other things. By leveraging FL, organizations may develop and refine models with more accuracy and reliability, which will ultimately lead to better patient outcomes. Additionally, federated learning's cooperative component fosters a collaborative environment among healthcare professionals by allowing the sharing of knowledge and expertise while maintaining data confidentiality. FL is a significant advancement in AI and ML that offers a workable solution to the problems with data security and privacy in medical imaging [3]. A schematic for FL and its training procedure is portrayed in Figure 9.1.

9.1.1 Federated Learning Key Concepts

Federated Learning is a machine learning technique that ensures data privacy while enabling cooperative model training with data from several

Table 9.1 Federated learning vs. conventional centralized methods.

Aspect	Federated learning	Conventional centralized methods
Data Storage	Data stays in each source's local storage	Data is gathered into one central storage for training
Data Privacy	High (sensitive information stays in its original place)	Low (data is transferred and aggregated centrally)
Model Training	Models are trained collectively using decentralized data	Models are trained on centralized, aggregated data
Model Updates	Changes to the model (not raw data) are exchanged and combined	Not applicable (data is centrally located)
Security Risks	Low, as data is not transferred, reducing potential breaches	High (owing to data transfer and central aggregation)
Compliance	Aligns with GDPR and HIPAA standards	Often challenging to comply with strict data protection
Collaboration	Collaborative training enabled without data sharing	Requires data sharing for collaborative efforts
Process Steps	1. Data segmentation 2. Local model training 3. Model updates 4. Global model aggregation	1. Data collection 2. Centralized storage 3. Model training

decentralized sources as shown in Table 9.1. In contrast to traditional centralized techniques, which combine data from multiple sources into a single training repository, FL assures that data stays in its local storage. By only transmitting model updates rather than raw data, this decentralized structure improves data privacy by preserving sensitive information in its original location. This approach complies with strict data protection laws like GDPR and HIPAA because it handles the significant privacy and security risks presented by centralized data transfers. The workflow of FL [4] can be divided into key steps including:

i) Data segmentation
ii) Local model training

iii) Model updates, and
iv) Global model aggregation.

Data Partitioning and Local Model Training: Every institution maintains its own dataset and uses it to train a machine learning model specific to their organization. This guarantees data confidentiality since only the model gains knowledge from the local data, without any raw data being exchanged.
Model Updates: Regularly, every institution transmits updates (such as gradients or model parameters) from its locally trained model to a central server. These updates incorporate the knowledge gained from the institution's specific data, but they do not include any unprocessed data.
Global Model Aggregation and Distribution: The central server utilizes algorithms such as federated averaging to consolidate the updates from all participating universities, resulting in an enhanced global model. To create an iterative cycle of collaborative learning, the combined global model is distributed back to each school for further instruction.

9.1.2 Overview of AI Techniques and Key Architectures Used in Segmentation

Artificial intelligence (AI) has led to the development of modern techniques that enhance the accuracy and efficiency of brain tumor segmentation in medical imaging. Machine learning, a core component of AI, is the utilization of data to train algorithms for predictions. It encompasses concepts such as unsupervised learning, supervised learning, and reinforcement learning. In this field, deep learning, a subclass of ML that takes cues from the human

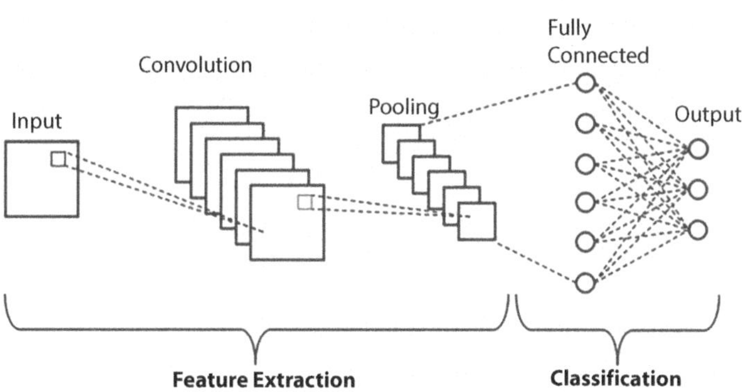

Figure 9.2 Basic CNN architecture, Source [Internet].

brain is especially adept at deciphering complicated input, such as voice and images. Neural networks, specifically recurrent neural networks (RNNs) and convolutional neural networks (CNN) serve as its foundation. CNNs are one of the primary AI architectures used in segmentation; as Figure 9.2 illustrates, CNNs are especially well-suited for image analysis. They have convolutional, pooling, and fully connected layers to extract hierarchical information from images for exact segmentation. A specialized CNN architecture called U-Net is frequently employed for segmentation [5].

9.1.3 Importance of Accurate Segmentation in Diagnosis and Treatment

For several reasons, precise brain tumor segmentation is essential. This procedure is crucial for both the care of individual patients and the larger medical community since it opens the door to novel therapies and better results. In the context of managing brain tumors, accurate segmentation is essential for the reasons that follow.

i) **Diagnosis and Staging:** The appropriate diagnosis and staging of a tumor depend on the physicians' ability to precisely define the size, location, and extent of the tumor.
ii) **Therapy Planning:** Precise segmentation facilitates focused treatment of the tumor while preserving healthy tissue, which helps in the treatment regimens involving surgery, radiation therapy, and chemotherapy.
iii) **Monitoring Treatment Response:** Clinicians can assess the tumor's response to treatment and modify therapy techniques based on segmented images obtained at different time intervals.
iv) **Research and Development:** Reliable segmentation is essential for gathering high-quality data for clinical trials and machine learning models, directly affecting medical research and the development of new medications.

9.2 Traditional Segmentation Methods

It is essential to comprehend the development and constraints of conventional brain tumor segmentation methods to appreciate the advances in contemporary approaches. Current procedures are rooted in traditional methods, which have been developed over time to provide fundamental knowledge and approaches. Even if these techniques work in some situations, they frequently run into problems that highlight the need for ongoing innovation and development. An outline of these conventional methods is given in the section that follows, emphasizing both their advantages and disadvantages.

9.2.1 Overview of Traditional Techniques

The text presents several conventional methods, emphasizing their advantages and drawbacks. Figure 9.3 illustrates conventional techniques for Brain Tumor Segmentation.

i) **Manual Segmentation:** Manual segmentation accurately delineates brain tumors using specialized imaging software by trained specialists, typically radiologists or medical practitioners. This process is highly dependent on the skill and expertise of the individual performing the segmentation. Manual segmentation is considered the gold standard method

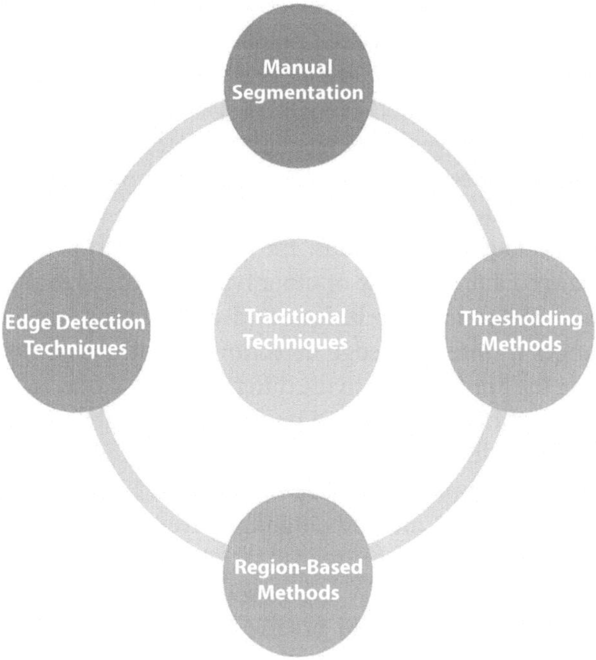

Figure 9.3 Traditional methods of brain tumor segmentation, Source: self.

as it may incorporate clinical skills with outstanding precision. However, due of the difficulty, duration, and inter-observer variability of this process, different experts may produce different segmentation findings for the same image [6].

ii) **Thresholding Methods:** One simple technique that is frequently used in picture segmentation is thresholding. To distinguish objects of interest from the background, the procedure involves setting a specific intensity level, also called the threshold. Pixels with values below the threshold are classified as the backdrop, and those with intensity levels over the threshold are classified as the object, such as a tumor. When a discernible difference exists between the object's brightness or strength and the background, this method works well. However, when thresholding is applied to images that contain noise, tumor patches with varying intensities, or insufficient contrast between the tumor and the surrounding tissue, problems may arise [6].

iii) **Region-Based Methods:** Using preset criteria, like texture or intensity similarity, a picture can be divided into discrete portions using region-based segmentation techniques. Region growth is a frequently used technique that starts with segmentation by choosing seed points, or individual pixels, then expands the region by adding neighboring pixels with comparable features. Another method is area splitting and merging, which involves breaking an image into smaller pieces and combining them according to specific homogeneity requirements. While region-based methods perform well on photos with homogeneous regions, they may not perform well on images containing noise or other types of structures [7].

v) **Edge Detection Techniques:** By detecting significant changes in intensity, edge detection algorithms are used to locate the borders that divide different areas within an image. These tactics are predicated on the idea that abrupt changes in intensity levels are connected to boundaries. Several edge detection techniques include the Prewitt, Canny, and Sobel operators. These methods highlight areas with large gradients (sharp changes in intensity), which are likely markers of object boundaries, by applying convolution filters. While edge detection can yield precise boundary information, it may struggle with images with noisy or faint edges, leading to segmentations that are incomplete or jumbled [8].

9.2.2 Advantages of Traditional Methods

For many years, conventional techniques for segmenting brain tumors have served as the mainstay of medical imaging. They have been widely used and accepted because they provide several advantages. The main benefits of these techniques are outlined in this section:

i) **Established Techniques:** Clinicians and researchers have a good understanding of traditional approaches, which have experienced substantial advancements throughout the years.
ii) **Cost-Effective:** These techniques are frequently more accessible and less expensive because they require fewer specialized gear and processing resources.
iii) **Interpretability:** Medical personnel may readily comprehend and modify the outcomes generated by conventional procedures, which aids in clinical decision-making.
iv) **Widespread Availability:** Medical imaging software packages frequently incorporate traditional segmentation techniques, guaranteeing widespread accessibility and application in clinical settings.

9.2.3 Limitations of Traditional Methods

Traditional techniques have been fundamental to the segmentation of brain tumors, but they have several drawbacks that may reduce their efficacy. The following section delineates the principal obstacles linked to these techniques:

i) **Labor-Intensive:** Manual segmentation is labor-intensive and time-consuming, requiring experts, which can cause delays and higher labor expenses.
ii) **Subjectivity:** Human judgment introduces variability, which can affect the precision and reliability of segmentation results.
iii) **Limited Automation:** The automation potential of conventional techniques like thresholding and edge detection is typically limited by the need for human tweaks.
iv) **Complex Cases:** Traditional approaches may not be able to accurately define tumors with complicated forms or invasive development patterns, which can affect their accuracy.

v) **Scalability:** The scalability of standard approaches is limited when handling large and complicated imaging datasets due to the major obstacles involved in adapting them.

vi) **Limited Quantitative Analysis:** Conventional techniques frequently yield qualitative or semi-quantitative evaluations that lack the accuracy required for in-depth study and judgment.

Comprehending the benefits and drawbacks of conventional techniques is imperative in assessing their function in brain tumor segmentation and investigating possible enhancements and substitutes.

9.3 AI-Based Segmentation Methods

The development of AI has resulted in novel approaches to brain tumor segmentation that promise notable gains in efficiency and accuracy. This section covers in detail the different AI-based methods that have transformed this field.

9.3.1 Convolutional Neural Networks (CNNs)

Convolutional Neural Networks (CNNs) are a subclass of DL models that are particularly good at segmentation and other image analysis tasks. Their model is inspired by the animal visual cortex, which has a hierarchical structure and neurons that respond to areas in the visual field that overlap.

As seen in Figure 9.4, CNNs are made up of multiple layers, often consisting of convolutional, pooling, and fully connected layers.

i) **Convolutional Layers:** The convolutional layers in this model perform convolution operations on the input data by

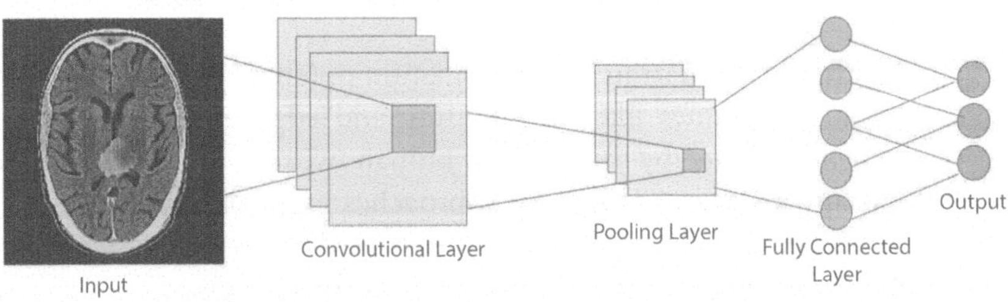

Figure 9.4 Semantic diagram of basic convolutional neural networks, source: self.

sliding a tiny filter, also called a kernel, across the input picture to extract features.

ii) **Pooling Layers:** Pooling layers decrease the spatial dimensions of the input, significantly reducing the feature maps' size created from convolutional layers.

iii) **Fully Connected Layers:** The interconnections between neurons in each layer facilitate the transmission of information from every neuron in one layer to every neuron in the subsequent layer, so enabling the ultimate determination of categorization or segmentation.

CNNs are utilized in segmentation to acquire hierarchical representations of pictures, allowing for precise classification or segmentation of regions of interest, such as brain tumors, based on acquired characteristics [6].

9.3.1.1 The Benefits of CNN-Based Segmentation

CNN-based segmentation offers several advantages over traditional methods:

i) **Automation:** Freeing Up Valuable Time for Medical Professionals: Convolutional Neural Networks (CNNs) streamline the segmentation process. The CNN, which has been trained, receives the MRI scan as input and automatically produces the segmentation map. This enables medical practitioners to allocate their time more efficiently, prioritizing crucial responsibilities such as treatment planning and direct engagement with patients.

ii) **Accuracy:** Towards More Reliable Diagnoses: CNNs are trained using extensive datasets that consist of thousands of MRI scans that have been labeled and segmented to identify tumors. Through this extensive exposure, they acquire knowledge of intricate patterns and distinctive characteristics that differentiate cancers from normal brain tissue.

iii) **Reduced Inter-observer Variability:** Reducing inter-observer variability, a prevalent problem in traditional segmentation methods is one of the major benefits of CNN-based segmentation approaches. Due to human biases, experience level, and subjective interpretation, various radiologists or technicians in the medical imaging field may segment the same image differently. Inconsistencies in diagnosis, treatment planning, and outcome assessment may result from this variability.

iv) **Consistent Results for Reliable Analysis:** Convolutional Neural Networks (CNNs) produce unbiased and uniform results regardless of the operator identity. The CNN architecture's learned patterns guide the segmentation process, lessening the influence of human judgments. Precise classification results provide enhanced communication and cooperation among medical professionals. As a result, individuals with brain tumors can receive analysis and treatment more accurately and effectively.

As a result, Convolutional Neural Networks (CNNs) are able to achieve a high degree of segmentation precision, possibly even exceeding human performance in some cases. Better tumor characterization and identification result from enhanced segmentation. This may significantly impact diagnosis, allowing for earlier identification and better-informed treatment choices.

9.3.2 U-Net and its Variants

A specific CNN called U-Net architecture was developed for accurate biological picture segmentation, especially for applications like brain tumor segmentation. The unique feature of Ronneberger *et al.*'s U-Net is its symmetric encoder-decoder architecture and is portrayed in Figure 9.5.

i) **Encoder Path:** Convolution and pooling techniques are used by the encoder to extract the context from the input image. This procedure increases the number of feature channels while decreasing the image's spatial dimensions.

ii) **Decoder Path:** Transposed convolutions, sometimes referred to as deconvolutions or upsampling layers, and are used in the decoder step to upsample the encoded features back to the original input resolution. By using skip connections between corresponding layers in the circuits of the encoder and decoder, spatial information is preserved and accurate segmentation is facilitated [9].

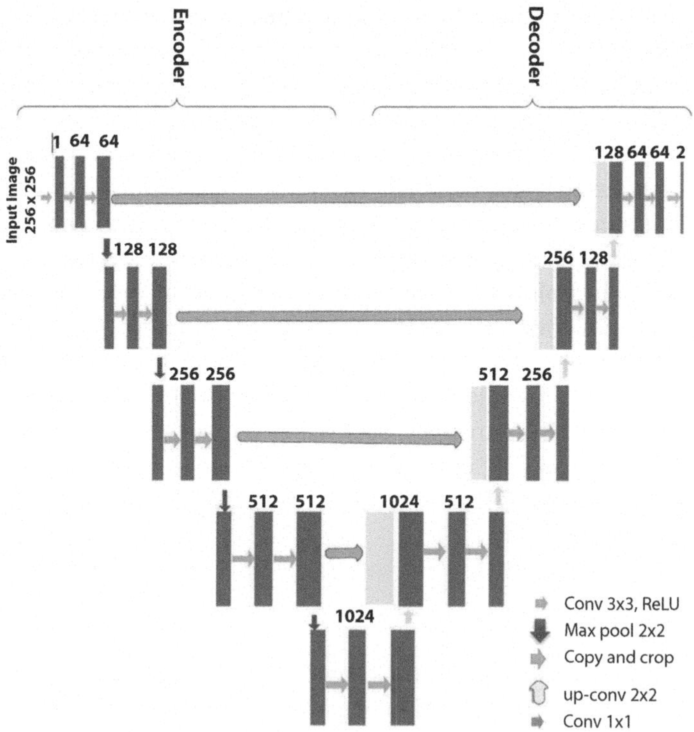

Figure 9.5 U-Net architecture, Source: self.

9.3.2.1 U-Net's Advantages for Brain Tumor Segmentation

U-Net's architecture boasts several key advantages that make it particularly effective for brain tumor segmentation. Some are listed below:

i) **Effective Feature Extraction at Multiple Scales:** The contracting route, comprising convolutional and pooling layers, functions akin to a detective meticulously examining the crime scene. It captures characteristics at various magnitudes. Convolutional layers detect and analyze edges, textures, and variations in intensity thereby contributing to a fundamental comprehension of brain anatomy. Pooling layers subsequently compress this information, capturing more extensive contextual details regarding the brain structure.

ii) **Precise Localization with Feature Concatenation:** By integrating this accurate location data, U-Net can preserve spatial resolution during the upsampling procedure. The network is capable of producing a segmentation map that precisely outlines the boundaries of tumors, including those that are complex or small [10].

iii) **Reduced Memory Footprint for Practical Applications:** The contracting path employs pooling layers to decrease the spatial resolution of feature maps. Although it may appear as a reduction in data, this actually aids in the management of memory utilization during the training process. U-Net becomes a feasible choice for applications with limited computational resources by decreasing memory requirements. This is especially crucial in healthcare environments where there may be restricted availability of advanced computing resources.

9.3.3 ResNet50

ResNet-50 makes use of a notion known as residual blocks. The network can learn from the direct addition of previous layer outputs to the current layer's output; thanks to the skip connections in these blocks that bypass certain layers. Better gradients can flow back during training; thanks to this direct path's ability to address the vanishing gradient problem, as seen in Figure 9.6.

The architecture consists of convolutional layers stacked within these residual blocks. These layers extract features from the input image at various levels of complexity. The network progressively increases the number of channels in the convolutional layers to capture intricate details. Finally, average pooling and fully connected layers analyze the features and predict image class probabilities.

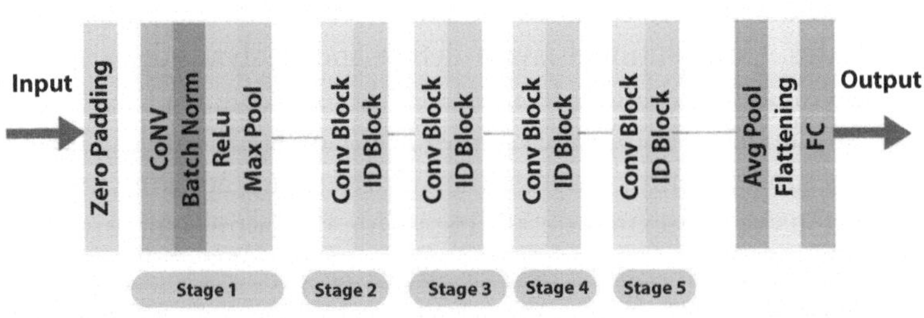

Figure 9.6 The architecture of ResNet-50, source: self.

ResNet-50's design allows for deeper networks compared to traditional CNNs, enhancing its feature learning ability. This depth makes it a popular choice for computer vision tasks like image classification and object detection [11].

9.3.3.1 ResNet's Advantages for Brain Tumor Segmentation

i) **Improved Gradient Flow and Deeper Learning:** The main novelty of ResNet is the use of residual connections, which allow data to skip the usual flow channel inside a block. This facilitates the direct propagation of the gradient from the preceding layer to the succeeding layer, hence maintaining information integrity and enabling the network to acquire knowledge from deeper layers. This is especially advantageous for the segmentation of brain tumors, as it is essential to capture delicate information from complex MRI scans.
ii) **Feature Reuse and Reduced Parameters:** ResNet employs bottleneck blocks, which are a modified version of residual blocks, to decrease the number of parameters in the network. This is accomplished by reducing the size of the feature maps prior to performing computationally intensive convolutional processes. The presence of shortcut connections in residual blocks enables the network to effectively utilize previously learnt features from prior layers. This not only enhances effectiveness but also fosters resilient learning, particularly when working with restricted medical imaging collections such as brain tumor images.
iii) **Transfer Learning and Adaptability:** ResNet-50, a widely used version, is frequently trained in advance on big image datasets such as ImageNet. Pre-training provides the network with a solid basis for identifying common image characteristics. The pre-trained ResNet can be adapted for brain tumor segmentation by fine-tuning it using a smaller dataset of labeled MRI scans. This utilizes the previously acquired features for the process of segmenting, while adjusting to the distinct attributes of brain structure and malignancies [12].

9.3.4 Benefits of Federated Learning in Brain Tumor Segmentation

Federated learning (FL) provides multiple advantages for the segmentation of brain tumors in medical imaging, by tackling significant obstacles and improving the overall procedure of detection and therapy [13]. Some of the main benefits are mentioned below:

i) Enhanced Data Privacy

FL encourages increased involvement and trust among stakeholders in addition to improving privacy and security. More reliable and precise machine learning applications are made possible by upholding patients' trust and adhering to regulations.

- **Compliance with Regulations:** FL guarantees adherence to privacy standards like HIPAA and GDPR by storing patient data only on the institution's local servers. This decentralized method reduces the likelihood of data breaches and unwanted access.
- **Patient Trust:** Preserving data confidentiality cultivates patient confidence in healthcare facilities, promoting patient involvement in research and data exchange efforts crucial for expanding medical understanding and enhancing therapies [14].

ii) Improved Model Performance

Federated Learning (FL) is transforming the healthcare industry by leveraging a variety of data sources to create accurate and dependable models while protecting patient privacy. This strategy opens the door for improvements in patient care and medical research by improving model performance, lowering biases, and building stakeholder trust.

- **Diverse Data Utilization:** FL enables the training of models using varied datasets from many institutions. This diversity contributes to the development of more resilient and universally applicable models, thereby mitigating biases that may emerge from the exclusive use of data from a single institution.
- **Enhanced Accuracy:** Enhanced access to a wider array of data enhances the model's capacity to precisely categorize brain tumors, resulting in improved diagnostic accuracy and more efficient treatment strategizing.

iii) Operational Efficiency

- **Reduced Training Time:** FL can decrease the total training time of models by dividing the computing workload among numerous institutions. Every institution has the ability to leverage its own local resources to contribute to the training process.
- **Resource Optimization:** Institutions can engage in collaboration without the necessity of conducting extensive data transfers, resulting in savings in terms of bandwidth and storage expenses. The optimal utilization of resources is especially advantageous for institutions with limited computational capacities.

iv) Accelerated Research and Innovation

- **Collaborative Advancements:** FL promotes the joint development and improvement of segmentation models by universities, promoting a collaborative atmosphere for research and innovation. Disseminating model updates and insights expedites the advancement of state-of-the-art AI technology in the field of medical imaging [15].
- **Continuous Improvement:** Institutions have the ability to regularly update their models with newly acquired data, thereby ensuring that the models progress and enhance their performance over time. This iterative procedure ensures that the models remain current with the most recent medical knowledge and data patterns.
- **Personalized Patient Care Tailored Treatments:** Enhanced segmentation models result in improved treatment planning and monitoring by providing more accurate and precise information. By doing a thorough segmentation of brain tumors, it is possible to create tailored therapeutic recommendations, leading to enhanced patient outcomes [16].
- **Improved Surgical Outcomes:** Precise demarcation of tumor boundaries is essential for surgical preparation and immediate assessment of tumor margins during surgery. FL improves the dependability of segmentation models, resulting in enhanced surgical outcomes and decreased likelihood of problems.

v) Enhanced Clinical Trials and Telemedicine

Federated Learning (FL), which complies with regulatory criteria while improving accessibility, dependability, and data privacy, is transforming clinical trials and telemedicine. By encouraging trust and cooperation among stakeholders, this decentralized method opens the door for machine learning applications that are more accurate and dependable, advancing medical research and enhancing patient care.

- **Dependable Clinical Trials:** FL enhances the dependability and generalizability of models, hence increasing the trustworthiness of AI-driven clinical trials. This improves the credibility of trial findings and expedites the progress of creating novel therapies.
- **Expanded Access to Expertise:** Enhancing segmentation models can greatly enhance the effectiveness of telemedicine by enabling remote discussions with professionals. Underserved patients are provided with high-quality diagnostic services and expert opinions, thereby enhancing healthcare equity.

FL provides significant advantages for the segmentation of brain tumors in medical imaging, improving data privacy, model performance, operational efficiency, research, and tailored patient care. FL allows for collaborative model creation while maintaining data confidentiality, which has the potential to drive major progress in medical diagnoses and treatment [17].

9.3.5 Comparison of Brain Tumor Segmentation Methods

Brain tumor segmentation is an essential task in medical imaging in the diagnosis and treatment planning of gliomas, which are among the most aggressive brain tumors. Numerous methods have been developed to automate this process, utilizing advancements in deep learning and neural networks. Based on the selected research publications, Table 9.2 compares several well-known approaches.

The contrast of these methods emphasizes the progress made in DL algorithms for the segmentation of brain tumors. Every method possesses distinct advantages, including rapidity, precision, and the capacity to address overfitting and data imbalance. The selection of the approach may vary based on the particular demands of the clinical application, such as the necessity for immediate processing or the accessibility of computational resources.

Table 9.2 A comparison of several well-known techniques.

Method	Approach	Advantages	Performance
Custom CNN model applied in FL approaches [18]	FL techniques like FedAvg and Ft-FedAvg were successfully applied for brain tumor classification on MRI images, demonstrating superior performance in accuracy and robustness compared to traditional methods.	Ft-FedAvg shown superior performance with regard to accuracy and robustness in comparison with the others.	FedAvg and Ft-FedAvg outperformed other FL approaches in brain MRI classification .FedAvg showed 85.55% success for 10 rounds in brain MRI classification.
CNN and U-Net [3]	FL enhances brain tumor segmentation by training on distributed data without sharing raw data.	Federated learning enhances brain tumor segmentation accuracy. Outperforms CNN- and RNN-based methods in accuracy and efficiency.	Improving specificity to 0.96 and dice coefficient to 0.89 with scalability for large-scale deployment.
Deep Neural Networks (DNNs) [19]	Uses an innovative Convolutional Neural Network (CNN) structure that leverages both local and global contextual characteristics. The last layer is a convolutional version of a fully linked layer.	Highly efficient, resulting in a 40-fold increase in speed compared to conventional procedures. The cascade architecture enhances accuracy by incorporating local label dependencies into the model.	Exhibited exceptional performance on the 2013 BRATS dataset, surpassing the current highest level of achievement while achieving a speed that is more than 30 times quicker.

(*Continued*)

Table 9.2 A comparison of several well-known techniques. (*Continued*)

Method	Approach	Advantages	Performance
Convolutional Neural Networks (CNNs) with Small Kernels [20]	Utilizes compact 3x3 kernels to create a more intricate architecture. Pre-processing processes include intensity normalization and data augmentation.	Attains high Dice Similarity Coefficient (DSC) values, which indicate precise segmentation. Successfully tested on the BRATS 2013 and 2015 datasets, achieving high rankings in segmentation competitions.	Obtained DSC (Dice Similarity Coefficient) values of 0.88, 0.83, and 0.77 for the full, core, and enhanced areas, respectively, using the BRATS 2013 dataset.
U-Net Based Fully Convolutional Network [21]	A refined U-Net design with skip connections and inception modules. A sequential cascade training approach is employed for segmenting subregions.	Provides thorough segmentation by generating separate segmentation maps for each slice. Exhibits significant improvements in comparison to traditional U-Net models.	Attained exceptional results in terms of the overall, crucial, and advancing tumor regions using the BRATS 2015 and 2017 datasets.

(*Continued*)

Table 9.2 A comparison of several well-known techniques. (*Continued*)

Method	Approach	Advantages	Performance
Hybrid CNN with Attention Mechanism [22]	The method described employs a Cascade Convolutional Neural Network (C-CNN) to combine local and global properties. Furthermore, it has a Distance-Wise Attention (DWA) mechanism.	Highly time-efficient and adept at mitigating overfitting. The DWA mechanism improves the model's concentration on the central site of the tumor.	Obtained average Dice Similarity Coefficient (DSC) scores of 0.9203, 0.9113, and 0.8726 for the entire tumor, the tumor region with enhanced activity, and the central region of the tumor, respectively, using the BRATS 2018 dataset.
Symmetric Neural Networks [23]	A Deep Convolutional Symmetric Neural Network (DCSNN) that incorporates symmetry masks in several layers.	A useful approach to segmentation in medical images is to prioritize symmetry, as it is a straightforward yet powerful form of previous knowledge.	Attained a mean Dice Similarity Coefficient (DSC) of 0.852 on the BRATS 2015 dataset, with a segmentation duration of roughly 10.8 seconds per patient instance.

9.3.6 Case Studies by Different Institutions

Case studies in Table 9.3 demonstrate various techniques and results, illustrating the wide range of uses and advantages of AI in the segmentation of brain tumors.

Table 9.3 AI techniques and results in brain tumor segmentation case studies.

Case study	Institution	Method	Outcome
AI-Assisted Brain Tumor Diagnosis [24]	Stanford University	Deep learning on MRI datasets	Improved precision in tumor detection, and decreased time required for diagnosis.
Brain Tumor Segmentation with U-Net [25]	University of Pennsylvania	Enhanced U-Net with skip connections and inception modules	Enhanced precision in segmenting the BRATS 2015 dataset.
Precision Medicine Initiative [26]	IBM Watson Health	Artificial intelligence is being used to analyze genomic data and MRI scans.	Customized therapy suggestions, enhanced patient care.
Automated Tumor Segmentation [27]	Mayo Clinic	CNN-based models	Precise demarcation of tumor boundaries for radiation therapy
Real-Time Intraoperative MRI Analysis [7]	Massachusetts General Hospital	DNNs and CNNs in operating rooms	Real-time assessment of tumor margins during surgery
Remote Diagnosis via Telemedicine [28]	Cleveland Clinic	Cloud-based neural network models	Enhanced availability of specialized medical services in places with limited access
AI-Driven Clinical Trials [29]	National Institutes of Health (NIH)	AI segmentation tools	Accurate and reliable tumor measures, improving the reliability of clinical trials.

The case studies shown in Table 9.2 demonstrate the varied applications and advantages of artificial intelligence in the process of segmenting brain tumors. As an illustration:

- Stanford University's application of deep learning algorithms on MRI datasets resulted in enhanced accuracy in tumor detection and reduced the duration of the diagnostic process.
- The University of Pennsylvania's improved U-Net, which includes skip connections and inception modules, achieved higher accuracy in segmenting the BRATS 2015 dataset.
- IBM Watson Health utilized artificial intelligence to analyze genomic data and MRI scans, resulting in personalized therapeutic recommendations that improved the quality of patient care.
- CNN-based models accurately delineated tumor boundaries at the Mayo Clinic for the purpose of radiation therapy.
- Massachusetts General Hospital employed Deep Neural Networks (DNNs) and Convolutional Neural Networks (CNNs) to promptly evaluate tumor boundaries during surgical procedures.
- The cloud-based neural network models developed by Cleveland Clinic enhanced the availability of specialized medical services by means of telemedicine.
- The National Institutes of Health (NIH) utilized artificial intelligence (AI) segmentation methods to attain precise and dependable measurements of tumors, hence improving the dependability of clinical trials.

9.4 Advantages and Challenges of AI-Based Methods

The integration of AI-based methods in brain tumor segmentation offers numerous advantages and presents significant challenges. This section explores both aspects to provide a comprehensive understanding of the impact of AI on this critical area of medical imaging [24].

9.4.1 Advantages

AI-based methods bring several key benefits to brain tumor segmentation, revolutionizing the process and enhancing clinical outcomes. These advantages include:

i) **Automation:** AI algorithms streamline the segmentation process through automation. An AI model that has been trained can process an MRI image as input and autonomously produce a segmentation map. This enables medical practitioners to allocate their time more effectively, prioritizing duties such as treatment planning and direct patient engagement.

ii) **Consistency:** AI algorithms offer reliable and impartial outcomes, irrespective of the operator's identity. The segmentation process is directed by the acquired patterns within the AI model, reducing the impact of individual judgments.

iii) **Precision:** AI models undergo training using extensive datasets consisting of several labeled MRI scans accompanied by tumor segmentations. The AI's wide exposure enables it to acquire knowledge about intricate patterns and characteristics that differentiate malignancies from healthy brain tissue. Consequently, AI models have the ability to attain a high level of accuracy in segmentation, which may surpass human performance in certain instances.

iv) **Scalability:** AI approaches demonstrate exceptional proficiency in successfully managing extensive datasets. The algorithms can be executed in parallel and deployed on high-performance computer platforms, enabling efficient processing of a vast quantity of scans.

9.4.2 Challenges

Despite the numerous advantages, AI-based methods also face several challenges that need to be addressed for successful implementation [30]. These challenges include:

i) **Data requirements:** Acquiring extensive and varied datasets can provide difficulties. Data scarcity might arise due to factors such as patient privacy rules, restricted availability of high-quality scans, and the labor-intensive process of human labeling.

ii) **Ethical Considerations:** The AI models' efficacy is directly dependent on the quality of the training data. The model's outputs may mirror biases that exist in the training data. It is crucial to reduce bias by carefully selecting data and evaluating models.

iii) **Regulatory Issues:** Acquiring regulatory endorsement for AI models can be intricate and time-consuming. This can hinder the implementation of these potentially life-saving techniques in clinical practice.

iv) **Integration:** Incorporating AI models into established clinical operations can provide difficulties. It may be necessary to upgrade the technical infrastructure and ensure interoperability with current medical record systems.

By understanding both the advantages and challenges of AI-based methods, stakeholders can better navigate the development and implementation of these technologies in brain tumor segmentation.

9.5 Federated Learning Workflow for Brain Tumor Segmentation

The FL brain tumor segmentation workflow is a systematic process designed to jointly train a high-performing AI model while maintaining data privacy. Data partitioning is the first step, in which each participating medical facility keeps its dataset. Instead of centralizing all data, each institution keeps its sensitive patient data locally, ensuring compliance with privacy regulations like GDPR and HIPAA. A decentralized approach significantly reduces the risk of data breaches and unauthorized access.

Following that, each company begins to initialize and train a local model with its dataset. This means using machine learning techniques to learn from the local data and identify the unique characteristics and trends that are unique to that organization. Because it allows each model to gain a thorough understanding of the content without divulging any raw information outside of the business, the local training phase is crucial. The institutions create model updates, which typically contain the model's gradients or parameters, after training the local models. These updates don't contain any raw patient data; instead, they provide an overview of the insights gleaned from the local data. The model updates are then securely moved to a central server. To strengthen privacy, techniques [31].

To create a global model, the central server gathers and aggregates these changes from each participant. The aggregation process often uses techniques like federated averaging, which combines the updates to improve the global model's performance. Compared to a model trained on a single dataset, this global model is more resilient and adaptable to many

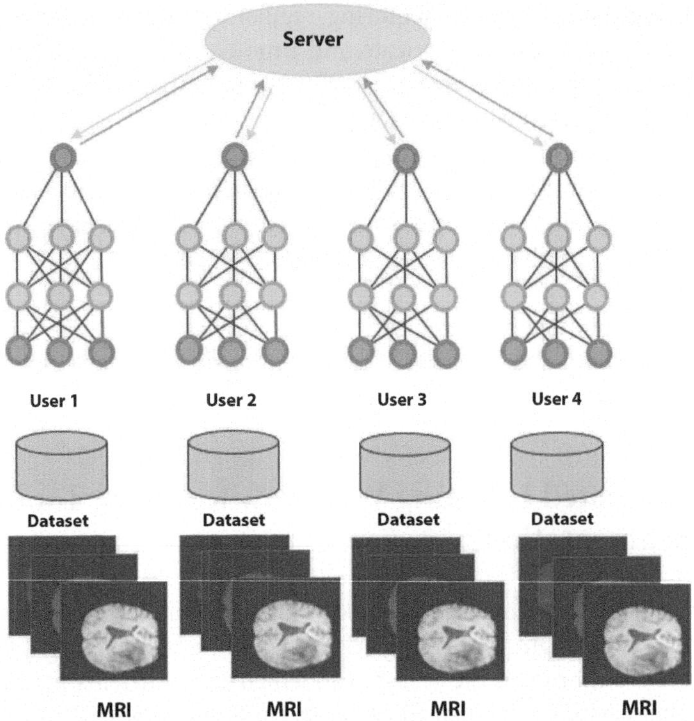

Figure 9.7 Federated learning model receiving local model weights from users, Source: [3].

scenarios since it uses the diverse data from multiple institutions. After modification, the Global model gets transferred to the collaborating institutions, whereby each institution proceeds with the training procedure after integrating the revised global parameters into its local model. Until the model reaches an acceptable level of performance, this iterative process of training on local data, updating the model, and aggregating the results worldwide is repeated [32].

By leveraging a variety of datasets and maintaining data privacy, the FL technique allows companies to collectively construct brain tumor segmentation models that are highly accurate and dependable. This collaborative strategy protects patient privacy while hastening the development of AI models. As showcased in Figure 9.7, the server in this framework compiles client-provided model updates to create a global model.

9.6 Notable Projects and Research

The use of FL in brain tumor segmentation and other medical imaging tasks has been considerably improved by several notable studies and research initiatives. These illustrations demonstrate how FL can improve diagnosis accuracy while maintaining data privacy [33]. Here are few prominent illustrations:

9.6.1 Federated Tumor Segmentation (FeTS) Initiative

A collaborative effort across multiple universities, the Federated Tumor Segmentation (FeTS) Initiative aims to improve brain tumor segmentation by applying federated learning. While protecting patient privacy, this program uses data from multiple sources to build models that accurately identify brain tumors. The FeTS Initiative has generated several pertinent publications on this subject and effectively demonstrated the viability of FL in producing segmentation models of outstanding quality.

9.6.2 Federated Learning for Healthcare (FL4HC)

The goal of the FL4HC project is to develop specific FL algorithms for medical applications, like brain tumor segmentation. This project aims to create FL frameworks that are scalable and durable, so that healthcare organizations may easily use them. The study carried out by FL4HC has aided in privacy-preserving techniques and improved model performance for the medical imaging industry.

9.6.3 AI for Health by NVIDIA Clara's

NVIDIA Clara uses FL tool to make it easier to create and use AI models in the healthcare industry. With Clara's FL Software Development Kit (SDK) organizations can work together to develop AI models without sharing private information. One of the organization's most impressive efforts is the division of brain tumors. Through various datasets, this effort enables institutions to train models, improving their accuracy and enabling them to be applied to many scenarios. NVIDIA Clara has improved secure aggregation techniques and created a strong FL platform with great strides.

9.6.4 The Role of FL in BraTS

Every year, a competition called the Brain Tumor Segmentation (BraTS) challenge is held to evaluate how well algorithms perform in the segmentation of brain tumors using standardized datasets. FL approaches have recently been incorporated into the challenge, allowing participants to build and assess federated models. Studies on these challenges have produced valuable insights into the effectiveness of FL in real-world healthcare settings.

9.6.5 Collaborative Research with Hospitals and Universities

Several hospitals and academic institutions are working together on research projects to explore the application of FL to **BraTS**. Research from esteemed establishments including Massachusetts General Hospital, University of Pennsylvania, and King's College London has demonstrated that segmentation accuracy may be improved through FL on datasets from several institutions, all the while maintaining patient privacy. These studies usually result in articles in esteemed medical and artificial intelligence journals, expanding the knowledge already known about the topic [34].

9.6.6 OpenFL by Intel

Intel developed Open Federated Learning (OpenFL), an open-source platform designed to advance FL research and development. Brain tumor segmentation is one of the many healthcare applications for which OpenFL offers comprehensive support. OpenFL provides academics and developers with a flexible and expandable platform that makes it easier to create and evaluate FL algorithms in medical imaging. OpenFL has been shown in studies and initiatives to be capable of producing effective federated models.

9.6.7 Google Health's Federated Learning Projects

Google Health has been actively exploring the use of FL in medical imaging, namely brain tumors segmentation. Their work focuses on building FL systems that can grow and handle large and diverse datasets. The advancement of secure aggregation methods, FL algorithms, and useful applications in clinical settings have all benefited from research conducted by Google Health.

These notable studies and research endeavors highlight the growing interest in and effectiveness in brain tumor segmentation. Medical imaging systems are being revolutionized by federated learning, which allows for collaborative model training while maintaining data privacy. This approach enhances the accuracy and dependability of these solutions, leading to better patient care and outcomes.

9.7 Conclusion

FLis a major step forward in brain tumor segmentation because it protects the privacy of personal information, makes use of a variety of datasets without requiring centralized storage, and guarantees regulatory compliance. Its ability to protect data privacy and enable collaborative model training across multiple institutions opens up new possibilities for improving segmentation accuracy and dependability. By enabling more precise diagnoses and tailored treatments, FL holds the potential to revolutionize personalized medicine and medical imaging in the future. To fully profit from these advantages, research and development communities in the science and healthcare domains should be motivated to look into and implement FL solutions that address current problems and propel future developments in other sectors, like medical imaging.

9.8 Future Scope

Future developments in Federated Learning (FL) for brain tumor segmentation have great potential. One novel area is the development of customized models, which improve local performance by tailoring the global model to the unique data features of institutions. Another promising technique is cross-modality learning, which incorporates data from multiple imaging modalities, including CT and MRI scans, to produce segmentation results that are more accurate and comprehensive. It is imperative to enhance privacy techniques, focusing on implementing robust privacy-preserving measures to provide even higher security for model updates. FL frameworks would be more computationally efficient and scalable to become extensively adopted. Thus, it will be easier for them to manage larger datasets and more complicated models, which will increase their use and effectiveness in clinical contexts.

References

1. N., C., *et al.*, Federated Learning for Smart Healthcare: A Survey. *ACM Comput. Surv. (CSUR)*, 55, 1–37, Feb. 2022, doi: 10.1145/3501296.
2. Federated learning-based AI approaches in smart healthcare: concepts, taxonomies, challenges and open issues. *Cluster Comput.*, 26, 2271–2311, 2022, Accessed: Jul. 13, 2024. [Online]. Available: https://link.springer.com/article/10.1007/s10586-022-03658-4.
3. Ullah, F., Nadeem, M., Abrar, M., Amin, F., Salam, A., Khan, S., Enhancing Brain Tumor Segmentation Accuracy through Scalable Federated Learning with Advanced Data Privacy and Security Measures. *Mathematics*, 11, 19, 1–27, Jan. 2023, Art. no. 19, doi: 10.3390/math11194189.
4. Mehta, M. and Shao, C., Federated learning-based semantic segmentation for pixel-wise defect detection in additive manufacturing. *J. Manuf. Syst.*, 64, 197–210, Jul. 2022, doi: 10.1016/j.jmsy.2022.06.010.
5. Kavitha, K. and Kumar, E.K., A Short Review on the Role of Various Deep Learning Techniques for Segmenting and Classifying Brain Tumours from MRI Images. *IJACSA*, 13, 9, 815–824, 2022, doi: 10.14569/IJACSA.2022.0130995.
6. Bhalodiya, J.M., Lim Choi Keung, S.N., Arvanitis, T.N., Magnetic resonance image-based brain tumour segmentation methods: A systematic review. *Digit. Health*, 8, 20552076221074122, Mar. 2022, doi: 10.1177/20552076221074122.
7. Işın, A., Direkoğlu, C., Şah, M., Review of MRI-based Brain Tumor Image Segmentation Using Deep Learning Methods. *Procedia Comput. Sci.*, 102, 317–324, Jan. 2016, doi: 10.1016/j.procs.2016.09.407.
8. Kaus, M.R., Warfield, S.K., Nabavi, A., Black, P.M., Jolesz, F.A., Kikinis, R., Automated segmentation of MR images of brain tumors. *Radiology*, 218, 2, 586–591, Feb. 2001, doi: 10.1148/radiology.218.2.r01fe44586.
9. Sajid, S., Hussain, S., Sarwar, A., Brain Tumor Detection and Segmentation in MR Images Using Deep Learning. *Arab J. Sci. Eng.*, 44, 11, 9249–9261, Nov. 2019, doi: 10.1007/s13369-019-03967-8.
10. Sharif, M.I., Li, J.P., Khan, M.A., Saleem, M.A., Active deep neural network features selection for segmentation and recognition of brain tumors using MRI images. *Pattern Recognit. Lett.*, 129, 181–189, Jan. 2020, doi: 10.1016/j.patrec.2019.11.019.
11. Sahaai, M.B., Jothilakshmi, G.R., Ravikumar, D., Prasath, R., Singh, S., ResNet-50 based deep neural network using transfer learning for brain tumor classification. *AIP Conf. Proc.*, 2463, 1, 020014, May 2022, doi: 10.1063/5.0082328.
12. Ammari, S., *et al.*, Influence of Magnetic Field Strength on Magnetic Resonance Imaging Radiomics Features in Brain Imaging, an *In Vitro* and *In Vivo* Study. *Front. Oncol.*, 10, 541663, 2020, doi: 10.3389/fonc.2020.541663.
13. Mammen, P.M., Federated Learning: Opportunities and Challenges. arXiv: arXiv:2101.05428, Jan. 13, 2021, doi: 10.48550/arXiv.2101.05428.

14. Nalawade, S., *et al.*, Federated Learning for Brain Tumor Segmentation Using MRI and Transformers, in: *Brainlesion: Glioma, Multiple Sclerosis, Stroke and Traumatic Brain Injuries*, A. Crimi and X.X.X.S. Bakas (Eds.), pp. 444–454, Springer International Publishing, Cham, 2022, doi: 10.1007/978-3-031-09002-8_39.
15. Federated Learning-Based Personalized Recommendation Systems: An Overview on Security and Privacy Challenges. *IEEE Trans. Consum. Electron.*, 70, 2618–2627, 2023, Accessed: Jul. 13, 2024. [Online]. Available: https://ieeexplore.ieee.org/abstract/document/10262054.
16. Mahlool, D.H. and Abed, M.H., Distributed brain tumor diagnosis using a federated learning environment. *Bull. Electr. Eng. Inf.*, 11, 6, 3313–3321, Dec. 2022, Art. no. 6, doi: 10.11591/eei.v11i6.4131.
17. Xu, J., Glicksberg, B.S., Su, C., Walker, P., Bian, J., Wang, F., Federated Learning for Healthcare Informatics. *J. Healthc. Inform. Res.*, 5, 1, 1–19, Mar. 2021, doi: 10.1007/s41666-020-00082-4.
18. Ay, S., Ekinci, E., Garip, Z., A brain tumour classification on the magnetic resonance images using convolutional neural network based privacy-preserving federated learning. *Int. J. Imaging Syst. Technol.*, 34, 1, e23018, 2024, doi: 10.1002/ima.23018.
19. Havaei, M., *et al.*, Brain tumor segmentation with Deep Neural Networks. *Med. Image Anal.*, 35, 18–31, Jan. 2017, doi: 10.1016/j.media.2016.05.004.
20. Pereira, S., Pinto, A., Alves, V., Silva, C.A., Brain Tumor Segmentation Using Convolutional Neural Networks in MRI Images. *IEEE Trans. Med. Imaging*, 35, 5, 1240–1251, May 2016, doi: 10.1109/TMI.2016.2538465.
21. Li, H., Li, A., Wang, M., A novel end-to-end brain tumor segmentation method using improved fully convolutional networks. *Comput. Biol. Med.*, 108, 150–160, May 2019, doi: 10.1016/j.compbiomed.2019.03.014.
22. Ranjbarzadeh, R., Bagherian Kasgari, A., Jafarzadeh Ghoushchi, S., Anari, S., Naseri, M., Bendechache, M., Brain tumor segmentation based on deep learning and an attention mechanism using MRI multi-modalities brain images. *Sci. Rep.*, 11, 1, 1–17, May 2021, Art. no. 1, doi: 10.1038/s41598-021-90428-8.
23. Chen, H., Qin, Z., Ding, Y., Lan, T., Qin, Z., Brain tumor segmentation with Deep Convolutional Symmetric Neural Network. *Neurocomputing*, 392, 314–324, Apr. 2019, doi: 10.1016/j.neucom.2019.01.111.
24. Wagaralkar, P., Bagwe, O., Amle, C., Khokale, D., Artificial Intelligence Assisted Brain Tumor Diagnosis. *Int. J. Adv. Res. Sci. Commun. Technol.*, 2, 254–258, Apr. 2022, doi: 10.48175/IJARSCT-3254.
25. Chetty, G., Yamin, M., White, M., A low resource 3D U-Net based deep learning model for medical image analysis. *Int. J. Inf. Technol.*, 14, 1, 95–103, 2022, doi: 10.1007/s41870-021-00850-4.
26. Hameurlaine, M. and Moussaoui, A., Survey of Brain Tumor Segmentation Techniques on Magnetic Resonance Imaging. *Nano Biomed. Eng.*, 11, 178–191, Jun. 2019, doi: 10.5101/nbe.v11i2.p178-191.

27. Murthy, M.Y.B., Koteswararao, A., Babu, M.S., Adaptive fuzzy deformable fusion and optimized CNN with ensemble classification for automated brain tumor diagnosis. *Biomed. Eng. Lett.*, 12, 1, 37–58, Feb. 2022, doi: 10.1007/s13534-021-00209-5.
28. Ezhilarasi, R. and Varalakshmi, P., Tumor Detection in the Brain using Faster R-CNN, in: *2018 2nd International Conference on 2018 2nd International Conference on I-SMAC (IoT in Social, Mobile, Analytics and Cloud) (I-SMAC) I-SMAC (IoT in Social, Mobile, Analytics and Cloud) (I-SMAC)*, pp. 388–392, Aug. 2018. doi: 10.1109/I-SMAC.2018.8653705.
29. Raza, R., Ijaz Bajwa, U., Mehmood, Y., Waqas Anwar, M., Hassan Jamal, M., dResU-Net: 3D deep residual U-Net based brain tumor segmentation from multimodal MRI. *Biomed. Signal Process. Control*, 79, 103861, Jan. 2023, doi: 10.1016/j.bspc.2022.103861.
30. Pati, S., *et al.*, The Federated Tumor Segmentation (FeTS) Challenge. arXiv: arXiv:2105.05874, May 13, 2021, doi: 10.48550/arXiv.2105.05874.
31. Sohan, M.F. and Basalamah, A., A Systematic Review on Federated Learning in Medical Image Analysis. *IEEE Access*, 11, 28628–28644, 2023, doi: 10.1109/ACCESS.2023.3260027.
32. Nazir, S. and Kaleem, M., Federated Learning for Medical Image Analysis with Deep Neural Networks. *Diagnostics*, 13, 9, 1–18, Jan. 2023, doi: 10.3390/diagnostics13091532, Art. no. 9.
33. Mahlool, D.H. and Abed, M.H., A Comprehensive Survey on Federated Learning: Concept and Applications, in: *Mobile Computing and Sustainable Informatics*, S. Shakya, K. Ntalianis, K.A. Kamel (Eds.), pp. 539–553, Springer Nature, Singapore, 2022, doi: 10.1007/978-981-19-2069-1_37.
34. Chowdhury, A., Kassem, H., Padoy, N., Umeton, R., Karargyris, A., A Review of Medical Federated Learning: Applications in Oncology and Cancer Research, in: *Brainlesion: Glioma, Multiple Sclerosis, Stroke and Traumatic Brain Injuries*, A. Crimi and X.X.X.S. Bakas (Eds.), pp. 3–24, Springer International Publishing, Cham, 2022, doi: 10.1007/978-3-031-08999-2_1.

10

Disease Prediction and Early Diagnosis Using Federated Models

Vibha Tiwari[1], B. K. Mishra[2*], Nitya Hari Das[2], Balwinder Singh[3] and Harmandeep Kaur[4]

[1]*Medi-Caps University, Indore, India*
[2]*Chandigarh University, Mohali, Punjab, India*
[3]*Doaba Group of Colleges PTU, Mohali, Punjab, India*
[4]*Rayat Bahra University, Mohali, Punjab, India*

Abstract
Federated learning has emerged as a promising approach to disease prediction and early diagnosis, addressing critical concerns about data privacy and security in healthcare settings. By allowing multiple healthcare institutions to collaboratively refine predictive models without compromising sensitive patient data, it ensures that privacy is maintained while improving the accuracy of diagnostic tools Recent advancements include personalized frameworks that consider the heterogeneity of medical data between hospitals, leading to better generalization and personal trade-offs. Additionally, the integration of federated learning with blockchain technology enhances security and privacy, enabling full data value mining while safeguarding local data sharing. Moreover, the application of different private stochastic gradient descent in federated averaging models has shown promising results in diabetes prediction, offering increased privacy levels without compromising model utility. These advancements collectively contribute to more efficient and secure disease prediction and early diagnosis processes in healthcare.

Keywords: Federated learning, healthcare, data privacy, machine learning, security

**Corresponding author*: bkmishra21@gmail.com

S. Rakesh Kumar, N. Gayathri and Seifedine Kadry (eds.) Federated Intelligent System for Healthcare: A Practical Guide, (233–252) © 2025 Scrivener Publishing LLC

10.1 Introduction

Federated Learning (FL) represents a paradigm shift in machine learning, enabling collaborative model training across geographically dispersed clients without compromising data privacy [1]. This innovative approach tackles the dual challenges of data silos and privacy concerns that have long hindered the development of robust, globally applicable models.

At its core, FL addresses the inherent complexities of distributed learning environments, particularly the issues of class imbalances and non-IID (non-independent and identically distributed) data distributions. These challenges often manifest as the client-drift phenomenon, where local models diverge, leading to sub-optimal convergence and performance degradation [2].

FL's sophisticated framework employs periodic model update aggregation and redistribution, coupled with advanced techniques such as adaptive self-distillation and data harmonization. This multi-faceted approach not only mitigates the effects of data heterogeneity but also enhances model generalization across diverse datasets. The real strength of FL is in the fact that it can leverage different and large datasets while keeping sensitive information secure and private. The advent of FL opens the door to revolutionary developments in areas such as next-generation telecoms, financial fraud detection, and tailored medicine by allowing institutions to work together without directly exchanging sensitive information.

Moreover, FL's framework is inherently adaptable, allowing for the integration of emerging technologies such as differential privacy and secure multi-party computation. This flexibility ensures that FL can evolve to meet increasingly complex data protection requirements while continuing to push the boundaries of what's possible in distributed machine learning.

As we navigate an increasingly data-driven world, FL stands at the forefront of efforts to balance the competing demands of data utilization and privacy protection. It offers a promising solution to one of the most pressing challenges in modern machine learning, potentially catalyzing a new era of collaborative, privacy-preserving AI development [3, 4]. Federated systems can significantly contribute to disease prediction and early diagnosis in several ways:

10.1.1 FL in Healthcare

FL is becoming popular in healthcare due to its application in data privacy, which is particularly important for handling sensitive patient medical

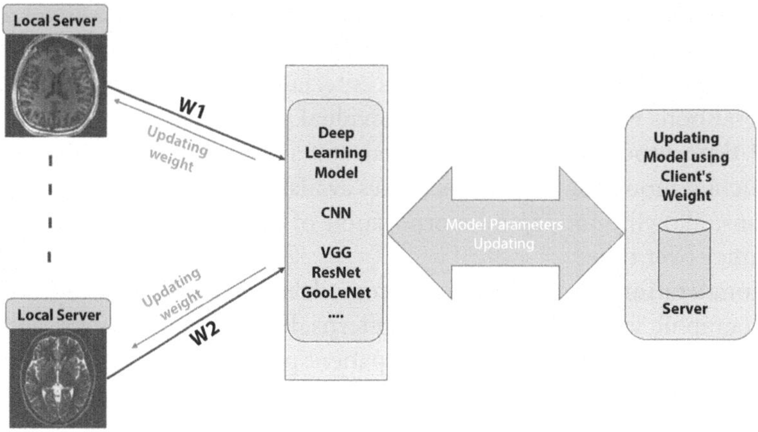

Figure 10.1 Architecture of FL for predicting brain tumor.

data, such as images, reports, electronic health records (EHRs), and so on [5]. FL allows healthcare organizations to jointly train ML models while keeping raw data localized and secure, safeguarding patient privacy. This approach has been implemented across various healthcare sectors, particularly in disease diagnosis [6]. Models trained on diverse, multi-institutional datasets have improved the accuracy of detecting conditions such as cancer, diabetic retinopathy, and other illnesses. Figure 10.1 illustrates the FL framework used to train various TL-based models, such as VGG16, ResNet50, and ResNet101, across two separate client servers. The clients exchange their trained weights, which serve as model parameters for the global model. Additionally, FL has enabled the secure sharing of EHR data, fostering the development of predictive models for patient outcomes and personalized treatment plans while maintaining privacy standards. In drug discovery, FL supports cross-institutional data collaboration, improving the identification of potential therapeutic compounds. Moreover, FL has facilitated the analysis of wearable device data, contributing to the early detection and monitoring of chronic diseases like heart disease and diabetes. By emphasizing privacy and security, FL encourages data collaboration while protecting sensitive medical information [7, 8]. Over the years, several key developments have significantly influenced the direction of FL in healthcare [9, 10].

Data sharing while preserving privacy: FL allows multiple healthcare institutions to collaborate on building predictive models without directly sharing sensitive patient data. This enables access to larger, more diverse datasets while maintaining patient privacy and data security.

Improved model accuracy: By leveraging data from multiple sources, federated systems can create more robust and generalizable models for disease prediction and early diagnosis. This is especially beneficial for rare diseases or conditions with limited data at individual institutions.
Real-time model updates: Federated systems can continuously update prediction models as new data becomes available across participating institutions, allowing for rapid incorporation of new insights and improved accuracy over time.
Personalization: FL can help develop models that account for regional or demographic variations in disease patterns, leading to more personalized and accurate predictions for specific patient populations.
Overcoming data silos: By enabling collaboration across institutions, federated systems help overcome the limitations of data silos in healthcare, potentially leading to faster breakthroughs in disease prediction and diagnosis.
Reduced bias: Access to diverse datasets from multiple sources can help reduce bias in predictive models, leading to more equitable and accurate disease predictions across different populations.
Enhanced early warning systems: Federated systems can facilitate the development of early warning systems for disease outbreaks by aggregating and analyzing data from multiple healthcare providers in real-time.

10.2 Related Works

A quick overview of deep learning and FL is provided in this part, followed by the system model.

10.2.1 Machine Learning (Deep Learning)

Feature extraction in deep learning typically makes use of deeper convolutional networks. In addition, deep learning models train themselves with the characteristics gathered by utilizing feedforward and backpropagation algorithms. Figure 10.2 depicts a generic deep learning model that makes use of a feedforward neural network. The feedforward function is defined as mathematical relationship between input vector x and parameter vector w i.e., $f(x,w) = y$. The training dataset $D = (x_i, y_i); i \in I$ is used for each instance of (x_i, y_i). Furthermore, the loss function l is defined as $L(D,w) = \sum(x_i, y_i)$ where D is dataset. During the backpropagation phase, techniques like ADAM optimizer employed to update the parameters.

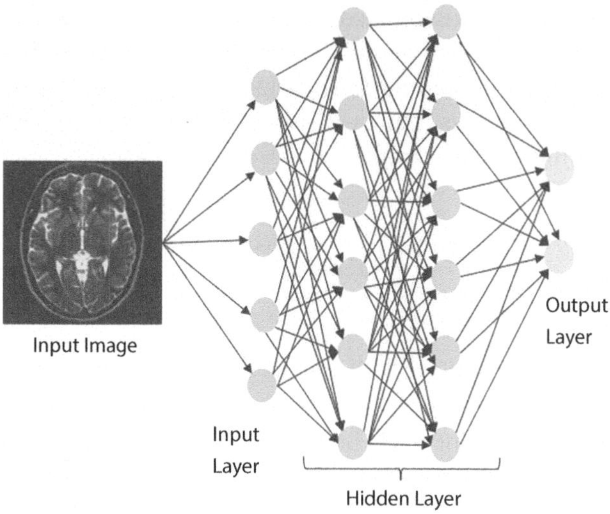

Figure 10.2 Basic deep learning model architecture.

where η is the hyperparameter's learning rate and w^t is an iteration vector. Also, D^t is used as a training dataset. The typical method for training data for a user or facility is shown in Equation 10.1.

$$W^{t+1} \leftarrow w^t - \eta \nabla_w L(D^t, w^t) \tag{10.1}$$

FL is a safe and distributed deep learning method that allows users train a shared model without compromising data secrecy. In addition, FL has implemented a system that allows them to get data from many sources, including hospitals, while protecting the privacy of those institutions. The FL model enhances the training model's quality while reducing the workload of a single participant's resources (i.e., power and memory). To rephrase, FL entails teaching the model to the local machines in a group and then sharing the trained model with them. Assume that every user $u \in U$ has their own private $D_u \subseteq D$ dataset. For the mini-batch dataset $D_t = \bigcup_{u \in U} D_u^t$ using SGD, the equation is as follows:

$$w^{t+1} \leftarrow w^t - \eta \frac{\sum_{u \in U} \nabla_w L(D_u^t, w^t)}{|U|} \tag{10.2}$$

The decentralized distributed ledger allows users to train a shared global model by sharing their local models. Users and healthcare facilities update the global model by uploading fresh data, such as gradients or weights. Figure 10.1 further shows that each user $u \in U$ has his/her own private dataset containing FL data samples.

$$F_i(w) = \frac{1}{D_i} \sum_{j \in D_i} f_j(w, x_i, y_i) \tag{10.3}$$

Using different location with dataset D, a global loss function $f_j(w, x_i, y_i)$ help to minimize the loss. To differentiate between the estimated and real model for each hospital, $f_j(w, x_i, y_i)$ the global model function of the $F(w)$ is described as

$$F(w) = \frac{1}{[M_i]} \sum_{i \in I} u_i . F_i(w) = \frac{1}{[M_i]} \sum_i \in I \sum_i \in D_i u_i . \frac{f_j(w, x_i, y_i)}{[D_i]} \tag{10.4}$$

In equation (10.1), i represents as a dataset (x_i, y_i) of the Meta data $I = 1, 2, 3, \ldots. n$ and u_i is the number of individual dataset models.

10.2.2 Horizontal FL

Horizontal FL (HFL) shown in Figure 10.3, represents a distributed ML paradigm aimed at enhancing model performance by harnessing data from decentralized devices or nodes. This technique, often applied in scenarios involving Internet of Things (IoT) devices or mobile devices, enables collaborative learning while preserving data privacy and security. HFL operates through horizontal federation, where data is partitioned horizontally across multiple nodes, allowing each node to process its portion of the data locally. This decentralized approach reduces the risk of data breaches and ensures that sensitive data remains on users' devices, addressing significant concerns regarding privacy and data security [5].

10.2.3 Vertical FL

It aims to enhance the efficacy of ML models by leveraging data from diverse distributed nodes or devices [6]. This method involves vertically partitioning

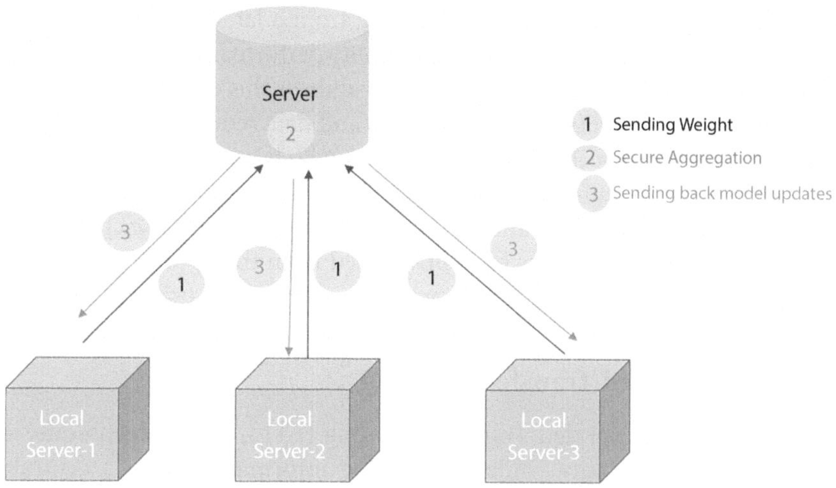

Figure 10.3 Horizontal FL.

the data of each node, ensuring that each node possesses a distinct set of attributes or characteristics, and subsequently training the model using collective data from all nodes, the details are shown in Figure 10.4. The pre-processing phase of VFL involves vertical data partitioning, dividing data from each node into distinct subsets corresponding to specific data categories [7]. Subsequently, the data is introduced into the model for training [8],

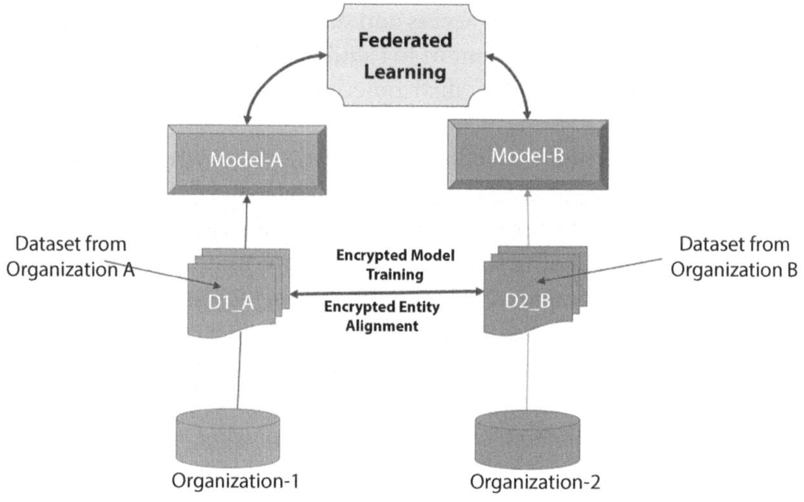

Figure 10.4 Vertical FL [11].

enhancing overall performance by learning from a larger and more varied dataset. Ensuring consistency and high-quality performance across all nodes poses a significant challenge in VFL [9]. To address this challenge, VFL typically implements quality control measures and data refinement techniques. The practicality and scalability of training in VFL is a recognized challenge [10]. Optimization and scaling approaches, such as parallel processing and distributed training, are commonly employed to overcome these challenges. The study presents equations for VFL derived from the optimization problem of minimizing the loss function while preserving data privacy [11].

10.2.4 Federated Transfer Learning

The objective of Federated Transfer Learning (FTL), an ML technique, is to ensure confidentiality while transferring information from a centralized model to a decentralized one [12]. Fan *et al.*, in their work on IoT Defender [13], propose a model which is centralized and it is used to train first, followed by the transmission of acquired knowledge to decentralized models trained on smaller datasets. That approach aims to enhance the performance and precision of distributed models by assimilating knowledge from the centralized model.

FTL has emerged as a promising technique for training more precise models while preserving individual privacy [14]. By leveraging knowledge learned from one domain to another, FTL improves model performance in new domains while safeguarding individual data privacy. This approach is particularly relevant in scenarios with sensitive or distributed data, reducing the possibility of unwanted access and data breaches [15]. The application of FTL has become prevalent in IoT and mobile device environments, addressing limitations posed by distributed nodes or devices with limited resources.

This approach facilitates secure and privacy-preserving learning processes by eliminating the need for centralized data storage [16].

Zheng, Xiao, *et al.* [15] explored the efficacy of FTL in knowledge transfer across domains, utilizing strategies such as fine-tuning, knowledge distillation, and model compression. In other studies, the authors examine the relationship between knowledge distillation and model compression, both involving the central model, to facilitate training of distributed models and enable local training [17, 18]. Additionally, Zhang, Wei, *et al.* present a comprehensive analysis of equations for FTL, exploring the mathematical formulations governing knowledge transfer in FL.

Their analysis underscores the importance of problem-specific settings and the nature of data in FTL equations [19].

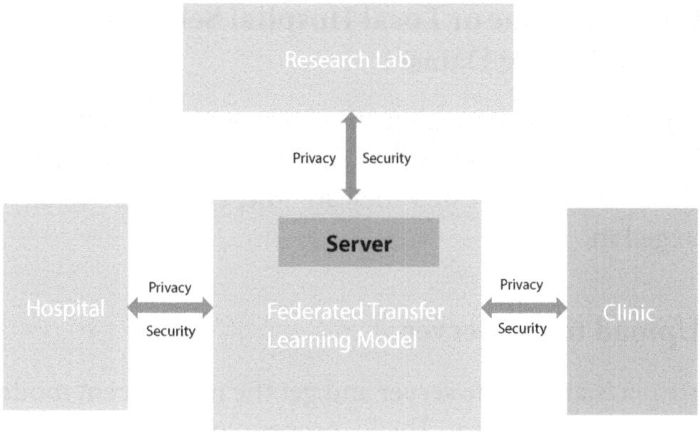

Figure 10.5 Federated transfer learning in the healthcare sector [20].

Figure 10.5 visually illustrates the application of FTL in healthcare, providing insights into its functionality and operation within the healthcare domain.

10.3 Proposed Method

The proposed model for healthcare application is using FL approach. This contains several key steps, such as data partitioning, local model training, and global model aggregation. A general overview of the typical steps involved in implementing FL in healthcare is presented in Figure 10.6 having following steps:

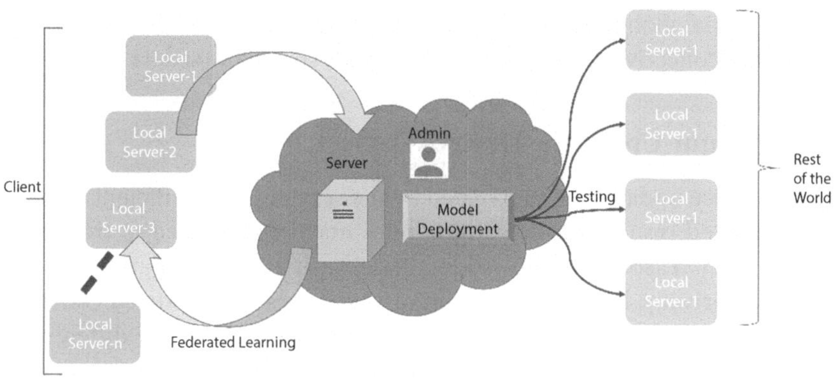

Figure 10.6 Proposed FL.

10.3.1 Local Machine or Local Hospital Selection for Collecting Dataset

The server selects users at random from a pool of those that qualify. As an example, to prevent any inconvenience to the user, mobile phones may only connect to the server when they are idle, connected to any network, and are plugged in.

10.3.2 Upload to the Server

Selected prospects access the server and get the most recent model weights along with a training program. The FL process combine multiple steps. The first step is global model initialization that performs random initialization or pre-training on public dataset, defines hyperparameters like learning rate and batch size. The second step requires current server and sends current global model to all participants. After that, it performs local training at each institution. Then each local machine or institution sends model updates to central server. Then the central server aggregates updates using Federated Average algorithm that includes weighted average of updates based on dataset sizes and update global model with aggregated changes. This process is repeated for a predefined number of times or continue until the model converges.

10.3.3 Client Computation

Each participating device executes the distributed training program on its local dataset. This program typically implements ADAM optimizer along with the Federated Averaging algorithm. The device then computes a model update based on the difference between the locally trained model and the initial global model. This update represents the device's contribution to the collective learning process without sharing raw data.

10.3.4 Sum-Up All the Devices Dataset

All the device updates are aggregated by the server. Once sufficient devices have reported results, the remaining ones may be discarded at this stage for efficiency reasons. Additional methods, such as secure aggregation for enhanced privacy, lossy compression of aggregates for improved communication efficiency, and noise addition and update clipping for differential privacy, all find their way into this stage from subsequent discussions.

Algorithm: General overview of the proposed work

Input: Training datasets D1, D2, . . . , Dm from m different healthcare institutions, Global model M, Number of communication rounds R, Local training epochs E, Learning rate η

Output: Trained global model M

Step:1 Data Partitioning: Partition the overall training data into m subsets, D1, D2, . . . , Dm, where Di represents the local dataset of the ith healthcare institution.

Step:2 Local Model Training: State For each communication round r from 1 to R:

a) Send the global model $M^{(r-1)}$ to all m institutions.

b) Each institution i initialize its local model $M_i^{(r)}$ with $M_i^{(r-1)}$

c) Each institution i trains $M_i^{(r)}$ on its local dataset D_i for E epochs using a local optimizer with learning rate η , resulting in updated model $M_i^{(r-1)}$

Step:3 Global Model Aggregation: Collect the updated models $M_1^{(r,E)}$, $M_2^{(r,E)}$, ...,$M_n^{(r,E)}$ from all m institutions.

10.3.5 Update Model

After all the clients in the current round have contributed their modifications, the server applies them locally to the shared model. The proposed model's pseudocode is displayed below.

Aggregate the local models to update the global model:

$$M(r) = \frac{1}{m}\sum_{i=1}^{m} M_i^{(r,E)} \tag{10.5}$$

10.4 Result Discussion

FL operates on a decentralized data distribution model, where data is dispersed across multiple devices or participants instead of being centralized in a single location, as seen in traditional ML methods. This distribution offers various advantages. Firstly, it enhances data privacy by allowing sensitive information to remain on individual devices, thus safeguarding it against unauthorized access. Secondly, decentralization ensures system resilience and security by eliminating a single point of failure. Lastly, FL exhibits scalability, as it can efficiently handle large datasets without necessitating centralized data storage solutions.

In FL, participants train local models on their respective data and share model parameters with a central aggregator, consolidating these parameters to construct a global prediction model. However, achieving optimal model performance in FL relies heavily on maintaining balanced data distribution among participants. Imbalanced data distribution can hinder model generalization and compromise its accuracy. Therefore, careful data distribution management is crucial to ensure representative sampling and robust model training.

Moreover, FL algorithms must account for the heterogeneity of data distribution across participants. This necessitates the adaptation of algorithms to accommodate varying data distributions, including differences in missing values, outliers, or other anomalies present in the data. By addressing these considerations, FL can effectively harness the collective knowledge of distributed data sources while mitigating the challenges posed by diverse data distributions.

10.4.1 Dataset Description

The primary dataset utilized for training the models in this research is taken openly available dataset [21]. The dataset consists of three different types of brain tumor disease along with one more set of images having without any tumor. The different types of MRI images are shown in Figure 10.6. The number of images is shown in Figure 10.7. Each participating hospital or research institution maintains its own dataset of MRI images. These datasets may vary in size, quality, and patient demographics. Images are typically stored in DICOM format, containing both pixel data and metadata. Data preprocessing (e.g., normalization, resizing) is performed locally at each institution.

Visualizing cancer diagnosis medical images is crucial to understanding and assessing their quality. The visualizations show how preprocessing methods affect the dataset's usefulness for training and assessing machine learning models. Removing duplicate images is essential for effective model training. Implementing this process is crucial to ensuring the uniqueness of each dataset image. Visualizing the dataset before and after duplication

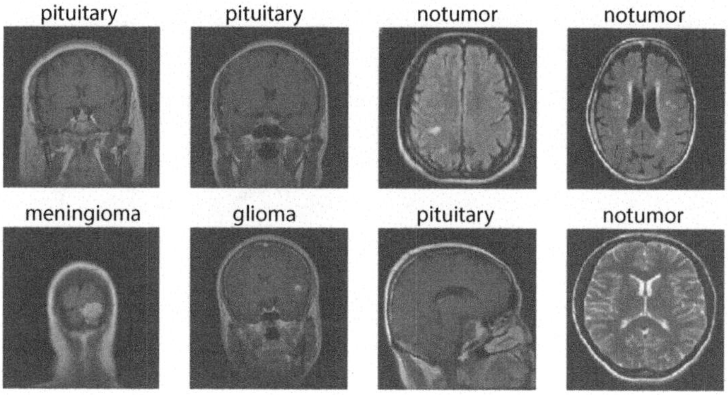

Figure 10.7 Types of brain tumor.

reduction helps verify its effectiveness. This improves dataset organization, eliminates errors, and makes the data more suitable for analysis.

The dataset is further divided into two parts; i.e., training and testing the federated model. To train the model, 81.3 % of data is captured and the remaining 18.7 % is kept for testing purpose. The details are shown in Figure 10.8.

For training the model, a Convolutional Neural Network based VGG16, designed for image analysis, offers the following features:

Input layer: Accepts MRI feature
Convolutional layers: Extract feature extraction
Pooling layers: Use max pooling to reduce spatial dimensions
Batch normalization: For training stability
Dropout: To prevent overfitting

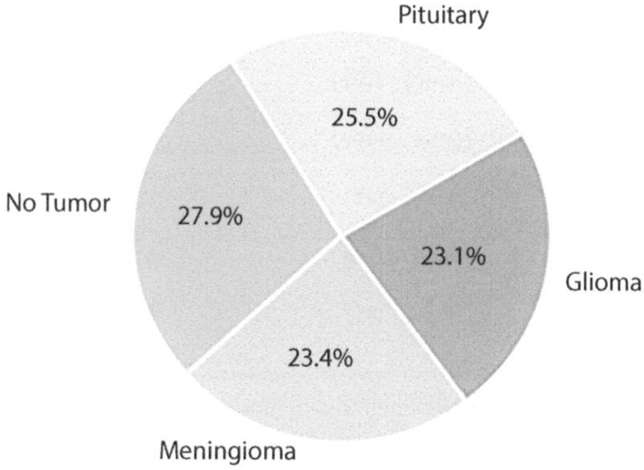

Figure 10.8 Number of different types of brain tumor images (in %).

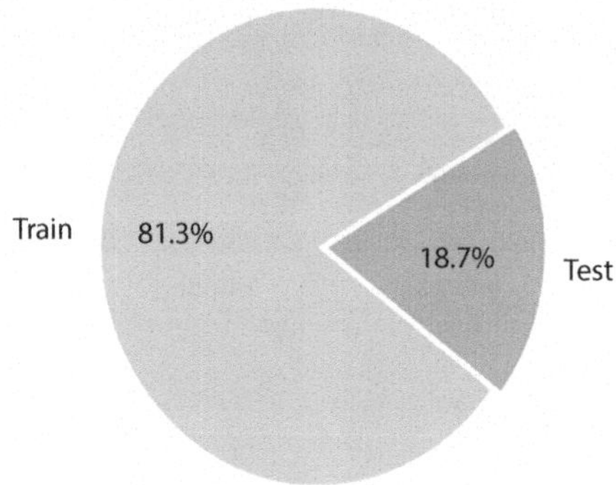

Figure 10.9 Dataset is divided into training and testing part.

Dense layers: For final classification or regression
Output layer: For multi-classification used softmax

The model training is conducted on Kaggle's cloud platform, leveraging GPU acceleration for improved performance. The entire codebase is implemented in Python, utilizing the PyTorch deep learning framework. For each model, the training process consists of 15 epochs, with a batch size of 25 samples per iteration.

```
model.summary()
```

```
Model: "sequential"
_________________________________________________________________
 Layer (type)                Output Shape              Param #
=================================================================
 vgg16 (Functional)          (None, 4, 4, 512)         14714688

 flatten (Flatten)           (None, 8192)              0

 dropout (Dropout)           (None, 8192)              0

 dense (Dense)               (None, 128)               1048704

 dropout_1 (Dropout)         (None, 128)               0

 dense_1 (Dense)             (None, 4)                 516

=================================================================
Total params: 15763908 (60.13 MB)
Trainable params: 8128644 (31.01 MB)
Non-trainable params: 7635264 (29.13 MB)
```

Figure 10.10 Model summary.

The Adam optimizer is employed with an initial learning rate of 0.01. To strike a balance between privacy preservation and classification performance, the privacy parameter σ (sigma) is set to 0.001, while also being evaluated as a hyperparameter. Figures 10.9 and 10.10 provide a comprehensive summary of the model architecture and configuration.

The confusion matrix shown in Figure 10.11. In this figure value of true positive and true negative of each category of dataset is given.

The performance evaluation of the federated model is shown in Figure 10.12. In this figure, the precision, recall, f1-score of each category of class is given. The average F1-score is also calculated and the result obtained is 98.03 % which is far better that other approach, shown in Figure 10.13.

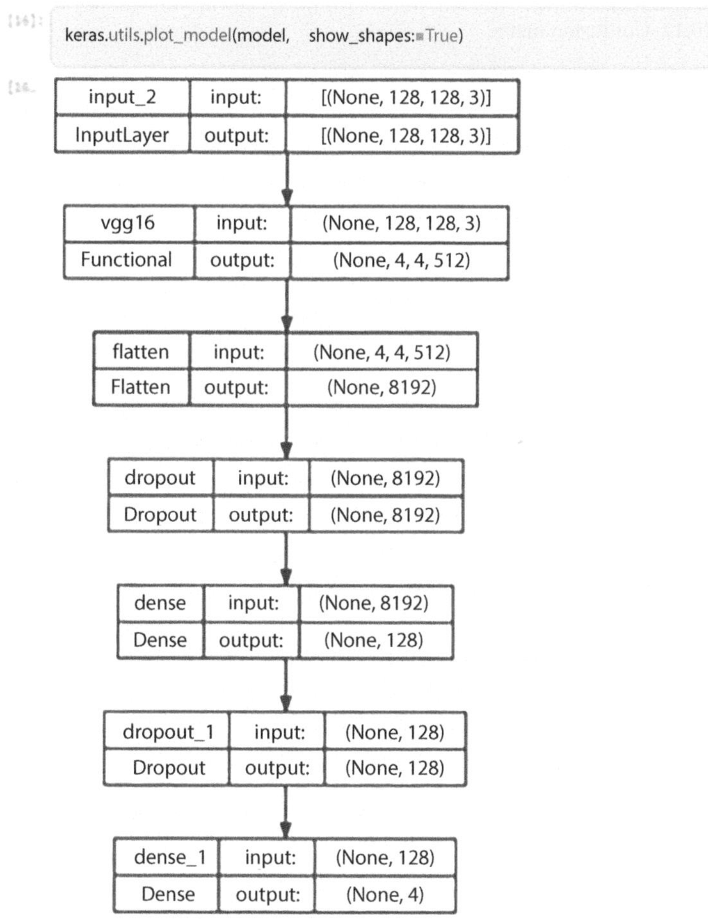

Figure 10.11 Model internal configuration.

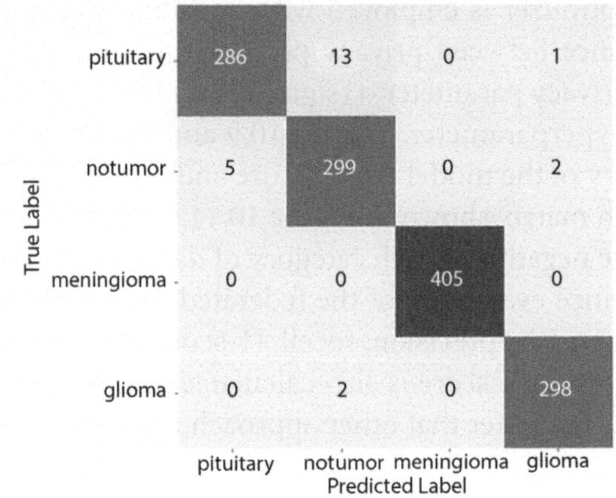

Figure 10.12 Confusion matix.

```
[21]: print(classification_report(y_true, y_pred))
```

```
              precision    recall  f1-score   support

      glioma       0.98      0.95      0.97       300
  meningioma       0.95      0.98      0.96       306
     notumor       1.00      1.00      1.00       405
   pituitary       0.99      0.99      0.99       300

    accuracy                           0.98      1311
   macro avg       0.98      0.98      0.98      1311
weighted avg       0.98      0.98      0.98      1311
```

Figure 10.13 Results in terms of precision, recall and f1-score.

10.5 Conclusion & Future Work

Federated Learning (FL) in healthcare is a rapidly evolving field with far-reaching implications. Its primary advantage lies in the creation of superior, generalized global models that have the potential to revolutionize disease diagnosis and, consequently, save countless lives. The true power of FL in healthcare stems from its ability to standardize and democratize access to cutting-edge diagnostic tools. By allowing healthcare institutions to contribute to, and benefit from a shared model regardless of their size, geographic location, or extent of participation, FL levels the playing field. This approach ensures that even smaller or remote facilities can leverage state-of-the-art diagnostic capabilities, potentially reducing healthcare disparities.

Advancements in secure gradient communication protocols are paving the way for truly privacy-preserving data collaboration. These innovations address one of the most significant challenges in healthcare data utilization: balancing the need for large-scale, diverse datasets with stringent privacy requirements and regulatory compliance. As these methods mature, they will facilitate secure and private data sharing across communication channels, fostering unprecedented collaboration while maintaining the highest standards of data protection.

The FL paradigm also introduces a dynamic aspect to model deployment and maintenance. Once the aggregated model is trained at the central server and distributed to local facilities, it retains the capacity for continuous refinement. This adaptability is crucial in the ever-changing landscape of healthcare. Local retraining can be performed as new data becomes available, allowing the model to evolve with emerging trends and patient populations. Moreover, this approach provides a robust mechanism for addressing model drift, ensuring that diagnostic accuracy remains high over time and across diverse patient groups.

As research in FL progresses, it promises to unlock new possibilities in personalized medicine, rare disease diagnosis, and global health initiatives. By enabling healthcare institutions worldwide to collaboratively build and maintain sophisticated diagnostic models without compromising patient privacy, FL stands poised to usher in a new era of data-driven, equitable, and highly effective healthcare practices.

References

1. Yashwanth, M., Nayak, G.K., Singh, A., Simmhan, Y., Chakraborty, A., Adaptive Self-Distillation for Minimizing Client Drift in Heterogeneous Federated Learning, arXiv preprint arXiv:2305.19600. 2023 May 31.
2. Stripelis, D., Ambite, J.L. Federated learning over harmonized data silos, in: *International Workshop on Health Intelligence*, pp. 27–41, Cham: Springer Nature Switzerland, 2023 Feb 13.
3. Tran, N.H., Bao, W., Zomaya, A., Nguyen, M.N.H., Hong, C.S., Federated Learning over Wireless Networks: Optimization Model Design and Analysis, in: *Proceedings-IEEE INFOCOM*, 2019, doi: 10.1109/INFOCOM.2019.8737464.
4. Shi, Y. and Xu, X., Deep Federated Adaptation: An Adaptative Residential Load Forecasting Approach with Federated Learning. *Sensors*, 22, 9, 3264, Apr 24, 2022.

5. Zhu, H. and Jin, Y., Multi-objective evolutionary federated learning. *IEEE Trans. Neural Netw. Learn. Syst.*, 31, 4, 1310–1322, 2019.
6. Li, L., Fan, Y., Tse, M., Lin, K.Y., A review of applications in federated learning. *Comput. Ind. Eng.*, 149, 106854, 2020 Nov 1.
7. Lau, H., Tsang, Y.P., Nakandala, D., Lee, C.K.M., Risk quantification in cold chain management: a federated learning-enabled multi-criteria decision-making methodology. *Ind. Manage. Data Syst.*, 121, 7, 1684–703, 2021 Jul 5.
8. Varasteh, M., Privacy Against Agnostic Inference Attacks in Vertical Federated Learning. arXiv preprint arXiv:2302.05545. 2023 Feb 10.
9. Thapa, C., Arachchige, P.C.M., Camtepe, S., Sun, L., SplitFed: When Federated Learning Meets Split Learning, in: *Proceedings of the 36th AAAI Conference on Artificial Intelligence, AAAI 2022*, 2022, doi: 10.1609/aaai.v36i8.20825.
10. Wang, Y., Cui, X., Gao, Z., Gan, B., Fed-SCNN: A Federated Shallow-CNN Recognition Framework for Distracted Driving. *Secur. Commun. Netw.*, 2020, 1, 6626471, 2020.
11. Ali, M.S., Ahsan, M.M., Tasnim, L., Afrin, S., Biswas, K., Hossain, M.M., Ahmed, M.M., Hashan, R., Islam, M.K., Raman, S., Federated Learning in Healthcare: Model Misconducts, Security, Challenges, Applications, and Future Research Directions--A Systematic Review. arXiv e-prints. 2024 May:arXiv-2405.
12. Chen, Y., Qin, X., Wang, J., Yu, C., Gao, W.,G Fedhealth: A federated transfer learning framework for wearable healthcare. *IEEE Intell. Syst.*, 35, 4, 83–93, 2020 Apr 22.
13. Fan, Y., Li, Y., Zhan, M., Cui, H., Zhang, Y., IoTDefender: A Federated Transfer Learning Intrusion Detection Framework for 5G IoT, in: *Proceedings-2020 IEEE 14th International Conference on Big Data Science and Engineering, BigDataSE 2020*, 2020, doi: 10.1109/BigDataSE50710.2020.00020.
14. Li, X., Chi, H.L., Lu, W., Xue, F., Zeng, J., Li, C.Z., Federated transfer learning enabled smart work packaging for preserving personal image information of construction worker. *Autom. Constr.*, 128, 103738, 2021 Aug 1.
15. Zheng, X., Shah, S.B., Ren, X., Li, F., Nawaf, L., Chakraborty, C., Fayaz, M., Mobile edge computing enabled efficient communication based on federated learning in internet of medical things. *Wirel. Commun. Mob. Comput.*, 2021, 1, 4410894, 2021.
16. Rieke, N., Hancox, J., Li, W., Milletari, F., Roth, H.R., Albarqouni, S., Bakas, S., Galtier, M.N., Landman, B.A., Maier-Hein, K., Ourselin, S., The future of digital health with federated learning. *NPJ Digit. Med.*, 3, 1, 1–7, 2020 Sep 14.
17. Can, Y.S., Ersoy, C., Privacy-preserving federated deep learning for wearable IoT-based biomedical monitoring. *ACM Trans. Internet Technol. (TOIT)*, 21, 1, 1–7, 2021 Jan 5.

18. Chen, Y., Lu, W., Wang, J., Qin, X., FedHealth 2: Weighted federated transfer learning via batch normalization for personalized healthcare. arXiv preprint arXiv:2106.01009. 2021 Jun 2.
19. Zhang, W., Li, X., Data privacy preserving federated transfer learning in machinery fault diagnostics using prior distributions. *Struct. Health Monit.*, 21, 4, 1329–44, 2022 Jul.
20. Joshi, M., Pal, A., Sankarasubbu, M., Federated learning for healthcare domain-pipeline, applications and challenges. *ACM Trans. Comput. Healthc.*, 3, 4, 1–36, 2022 Nov 3.
21. Abiwinanda, N., Hanif, M., Hesaputra, S.T., Handayani, A., Mengko, T.R. Brain tumor classification using convolutional neural network, in: *World Congress on Medical Physics and Biomedical Engineering 2018*, Prague, Czech Republic, vol. 1, no. 2019, pp. 183–189, Springer Singapore, June 3–8, 2018.

11

Navigating Bias and Ensuring Fairness in Federated Learning: An In-Depth Exploration of Data Distribution, IID, and Non-IID Challenges

Vajratiya Vajrobol[1]*, Nitisha Aggarwal[1], Pushkar Baranwal[1], Geetika Jain Saxena[2], Amit Pundir[2] and Sanjeev Singh[1]

[1]*Institute of Informatics and Communication, University of Delhi, Delhi, India*
[2]*Department of Electronics, Maharaja Agrasen College, University of Delhi, Delhi, India*

Abstract

Federated Learning (FL) presents a transformative approach to machine learning by enabling decentralized training across various devices while preserving data privacy. However, the inherent heterogeneity in data distribution among clients poses significant challenges, particularly in terms of bias and fairness. This research delves into the complexities of data distribution within Federated Learning, emphasizing the critical distinctions between Independent and Identically Distributed (IID) and Non-IID data. We explore how non-IID data exacerbates bias, impacts model performance, and challenges the stability of the training process. Furthermore, we address the necessity of understanding these distributions to design algorithms that ensure fair and equitable outcomes across diverse populations. By thoroughly examining these aspects, we aim to provide a comprehensive framework for mitigating bias and fostering fairness in Federated Learning systems.

Keywords: Federated learning, data distribution, IID, non-IID, data bias, fairness, bias mitigation, responsible AI

**Corresponding author*: tiya101@south.du.ac.in

S. Rakesh Kumar, N. Gayathri and Seifedine Kadry (eds.) Federated Intelligent System for Healthcare: A Practical Guide, (253–292) © 2025 Scrivener Publishing LLC

11.1 Introduction to Federated Learning and Data Distribution

A. Brief Overview of Federated Learning

Federated Learning (FL) is an innovative approach to machine learning that decentralizes the training process by allowing individual devices or local servers (often referred to as clients) to train models on their local data. Instead of pooling data into a central server, FL facilitates the creation of a global model by aggregating locally computed updates [1]. This method is particularly advantageous in scenarios where data privacy, security, and ownership are of paramount concern, such as in healthcare, finance, and mobile applications [2].

The basic workflow of Federated Learning involves several steps as explained in Figure 11.1:

1. Initialization

   - Global Model Initialization: A central server initializes a global model. This model could be a neural network or any machine learning algorithm, which is often initialized with random weights or pre-trained on some public or synthetic dataset.

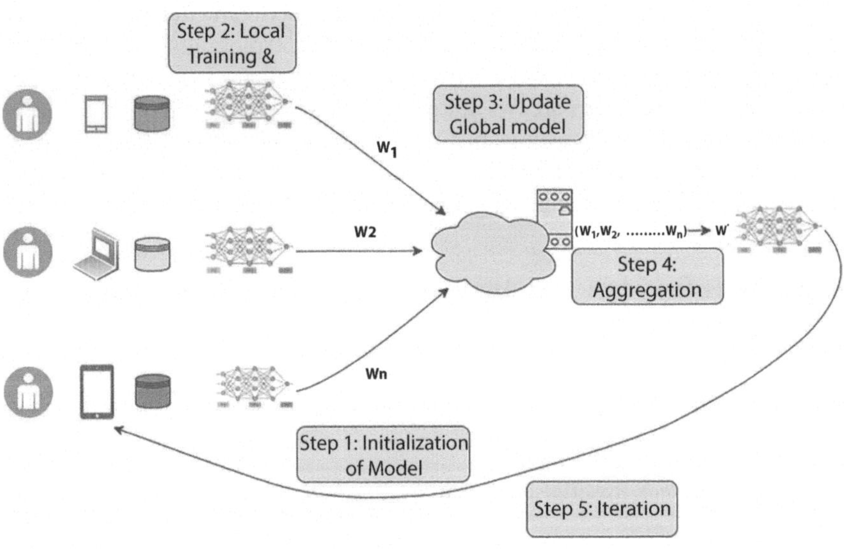

Figure 11.1 The process of federated learning.

- Distribution: The central server distributes this initial global model to a set of local devices or clients. These clients can be mobile phones, IoT devices, or any computing devices with locally stored data.

2. Local Training

   - Local Data: Each client utilizes its local dataset to train the global model. The datasets are private and never leave the local devices.
   - Training: The clients perform a specified number of training epochs on their local data. This training process involves calculating gradients and updating model weights using local data.
   - Client Computation: This step typically uses techniques like mini-batch Stochastic Gradient Descent (SGD) to update the model parameters.

3. Model Updates

   - Local Updates: After training, each client calculates model updates, which can be gradients or updated model weights, based on its local dataset.
   - Communication: These updates are subsequently sent back securely to the central server. The updates are generally smaller in size compared to raw data, making it feasible to transfer them over the network.

4. Aggregation

   - Secure Aggregation: The central server receives updates from multiple clients. To enhance security, various cryptographic techniques like secure multi-party computation can be utilized to ensure that individual updates remain confidential.
   - Weighted Aggregation: The server aggregates these updates to form a new global model. Aggregation can be implemented using techniques such as Federated Averaging (FedAvg), where the updates are averaged, often weighted by the number of data samples each client use in their local training.

5. Iteration

   - Redistribution: The updated global model is redistributed to the local clients.
   - Repetition: Steps 2 to 4 are performed for several iterations or until the model converges to a satisfactory performance level.

By iterating through these steps, Federated Learning enables the construction of a robust and generalized global model while maintaining data privacy and security. This approach is particularly useful in scenarios where data is sensitive, and direct data sharing is not feasible.

B. Importance of Addressing Bias and Ensuring Fairness in Federated Learning

Bias and fairness are critical issues in machine learning and are even more pronounced in the context of Federated Learning due to the varied nature of the data and clients. Bias in Federated Learning can stem from several sources:

- Data Distribution Bias: In Federated Learning, data distribution bias refers to the uneven distribution of data across the various clients or devices participating in the learning process. This bias may arise due to a multitude of factors, including variations in user demographics, geographical locations, device types, or usage patterns [3]. One manifestation of this bias is the presence of non-representative data, where certain clients possess a greater volume of data samples compared to others [4]. For instance, devices situated in densely populated regions might generate more data than those in rural areas, skewing the overall distribution [5]. Moreover, the data collected by different clients may exhibit distinct characteristics, such as language preferences or user behaviors, leading to discrepancies in the representation of various aspects of the dataset [6]. Additionally, under-representation of minority groups within client datasets can occur, impacting the performance of models trained on biased data. Historical biases inherent in the training data can also perpetuate into the Federated Learning process, further exacerbating data distribution bias [7]. Addressing this bias is critical for developing fair and accurate models in Federated Learning. Techniques such as data weighting, adaptive learning, and personalized federated learning can help mitigate the effects of biased data distribution by giving more weight to underrepresented clients or adapting the learning process to account for differences in data characteristics [8]. Furthermore, federated aggregation methods that account for the diversity of data distributions across clients can help produce more robust models that generalize effectively across diverse datasets [9, 10].

- Participation Bias: Participation bias in Federated Learning refers to the phenomenon where the participation rates of different clients vary, resulting in unequal contributions to the training process as shown in Figure 11.2. In Federated Learning, clients (which could be devices, users, or organizations) typically participate by contributing their local data or model updates to the central server for aggregation [11]. However, due to factors like connectivity issues, device availability, or user preferences, some clients may participate more frequently or consistently than others [12].

This participation bias can have important implications for the FL model. Clients that participate more frequently may have a disproportionate influence on the aggregated model, leading to a bias towards their data characteristics. Consequently, the aggregated model might perform effectively on

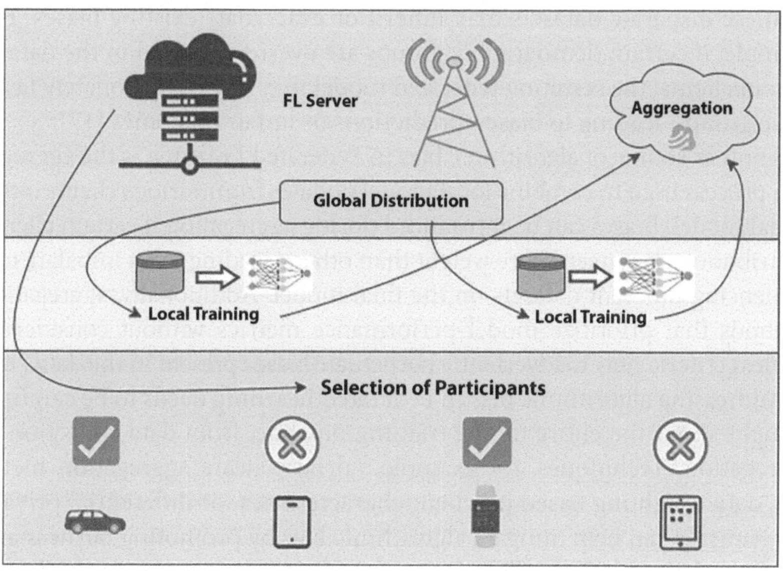

Figure 11.2 The explanation of participation bias.

data, resembling that of the more frequently participating clients but poorly on data from underrepresented clients. This can result in unfair outcomes and reduced generalization performance, as the model may fail to accurately represent the broader population or diverse user groups [13].

The techniques for adaptive client selection and weighted aggregation can help mitigate the impact of participation bias by giving more weight to updates from underrepresented clients [14, 15]. By promoting more equitable participation, Federated Learning systems can produce more robust and fair models that exhibit good generalization across diverse datasets and user populations.

- Algorithmic Bias: Algorithmic bias in Federated Learning refers to biases that are introduced or amplified during the training process of machine learning algorithms in a federated setting. These biases may arise from various sources, including biased data distributions across clients, unfair aggregation methods, or inherent biases in the learning algorithms themselves [16].

One aspect of algorithmic bias in Federated Learning is the propagation of biases present in the local datasets of individual clients. As each client may have its own unique data distribution influenced by factors such as user demographics, device types, or geographical locations, models trained on these disparate datasets may inherit or exacerbate existing biases. For example, if certain demographic groups are overrepresented in the data of certain clients, the resulting federated model may disproportionately favor these groups, leading to biased predictions or unfair outcomes [17].

Another source of algorithmic bias in Federated Learning is the aggregation process used to combine local model updates from various clients into a global model. Biases can be introduced during aggregation if certain clients' contributions are given more weight than others, leading to an imbalance in influencing different datasets on the final model. Additionally, aggregation methods that prioritize model performance metrics without considering fairness criteria may inadvertently perpetuate biases present in the data [18].

Addressing algorithmic bias in Federated Learning needs to be carefully thought about the entire model training pipeline, from data collection to aggregation. Techniques, for example, fairness-aware aggregation methods, data weighting based on client characteristics, or differential privacy mechanisms can help mitigate algorithmic bias by promoting fairness and equity in the resulting models. Furthermore, regular monitoring and evaluation of models for bias using appropriate fairness metrics are essential to ensure that Federated Learning systems produce unbiased and ethically sound outcomes [19].

Ensuring fairness in Federated Learning involves addressing these biases to create models that perform equitably across different populations and use cases. This includes developing methods to ensure that the model is accurate and fair, providing consistent performance across diverse groups.

C. Introduction to Data Distribution

Data distribution is a fundamental concept in Federated Learning that significantly impacts the training process and the resulting model's performance. In traditional centralized machine learning, data is often assumed to be Independent and Identically Distributed (IID). However, in Federated Learning, this assumption is often not valid because of the decentralized nature of data collection and storage.

In federated learning, data distributions can be categorized into two primary types: IID (Independent and Identically Distributed) and non-IID (Non-Independent and Identically Distributed) as illustrated in Figure 11.3.

IID (Independent and Identically Distributed) refers to a scenario where each data point is drawn from the same probability distribution independently of the others. In machine learning, this assumption simplifies the training process and often results in more stable and predictable model performance.

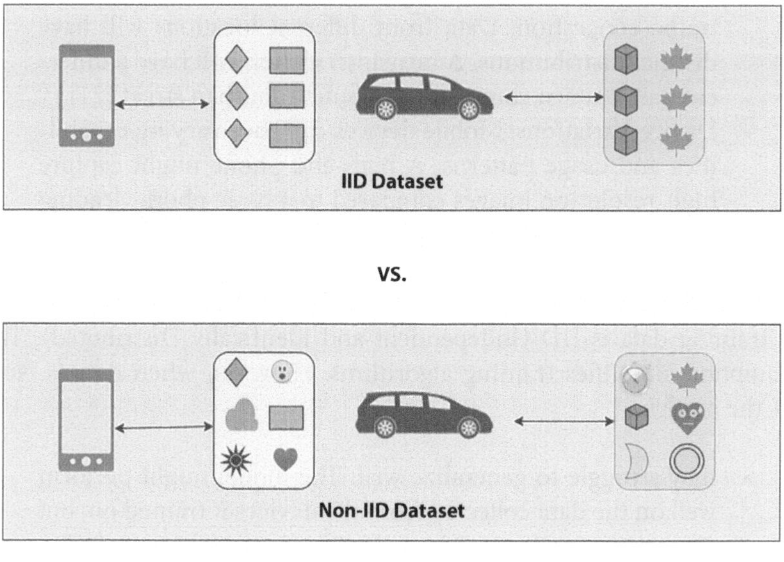

Figure 11.3 IID and non-IID dataset.

Non-IID (Non-Independent and Identically Distributed) refers to a scenario where the data used to train the model on different devices deviates from two key assumptions:

1. Independence: Data points on a single device are not necessarily independent. This means there could be correlations or dependencies between the data points a user or device possesses. For instance, a user's browsing history might influence the types of ads they see, creating a connection between data points.
2. Identical Distribution: The probability distributions of the data points differ across devices. Imagine training a model to predict traffic flow. Traffic data from a busy intersection is likely to follow a different distribution than data from a quiet neighborhood.

There is a breakdown of how Non-IID data arises in federated learning:

- User-Specific Data: Consider a recommendation system. Each user has a unique purchase history and browsing habits that influence the recommendations they receive. This data is specific to each user and will not be representative of the entire user base [20].
- Location-Based Data: Imagine training a model to predict traffic congestion. Data from different locations will have distinct distributions. A busy intersection will have a different data pattern compared to a quiet suburban street [21].
- Device Variations: Mobile devices can have varying capabilities and usage patterns. A high-end phone might capture high-resolution images compared to a basic phone, leading to variations in the data collected [22].

The challenge with Non-IID data is that federated learning often assumes the training data is IID (Independent and Identically Distributed). This assumption simplifies training algorithms. However, when data is Non-IID, the model:

- may struggle to generalize well: The model might perform well on the data collected from the devices it trained on, but struggle with unseen data with different distributions [17].

- can lead to less efficient training: The training process might become slower or less effective due to the mismatch between data distributions across devices [23].

Researchers are actively working on techniques to address Non-IID challenges in federated learning, such as weighting updates from different devices based on their data distribution or federated distillations where a central model guides local training [24].

D. Significance of Understanding Data Distribution in Federated Learning
Understanding data distribution is vital in Federated Learning for several reasons:

1. Algorithm Design: Designing effective Federated Learning algorithms requires an understanding of how data distribution affects training dynamics and model performance [25].
2. Model Generalization: Ensuring that models generalize well across diverse data distributions is critical for their robustness and reliability [26].
3. Fairness and Equity: Addressing disparities in data distribution is essential for developing fair models that do not disproportionately disadvantage certain groups [27].
4. Resource Allocation: Efficiently allocating computational resources and communication bandwidth requires knowledge of the underlying distribution of the data [28].

By grasping the complexities of data distribution, researchers can develop more effective and fair Federated Learning systems, ultimately leading to better and more equitable outcomes in real-world applications.

11.2 Understanding Data Bias in Federated Learning

A. Definition of Data Bias
Data bias in terms of machine learning refers to the systematic deviation of the data from an accurate representation of the population or phenomenon being studied. This deviation can lead to models that make unfair or incorrect predictions for certain groups or scenarios. In Federated Learning, data bias becomes even more complex due to the decentralized and heterogeneous nature of data collected from different clients. Understanding and

addressing these biases is crucial for developing robust, fair, and effective Federated Learning models [29].

B. Sources of Data Bias in Federated Learning

1. Non-representative Data Distribution Across Devices

Non-representative data distribution occurs when the data collected on different devices do not accurately reflect the overall population or intended application of the model. This can happen due to various factors, such as geographical differences, socio-economic factors, or differing usage patterns of devices [30].

2. Skewed Data Collection Processes

Skewed data collection processes refer to the inherent biases introduced during the data collection phase. For instance, some devices might collect more data than others due to better connectivity, more active users, or specific user behaviors, leading to an overrepresentation of certain data types and an underrepresentation of others [31].

3. Labelling Bias

Labelling bias occurs when the labels assigned to the data are not accurate or consistent across the dataset. This can happen due to human error, subjective judgments, or cultural differences in interpretation. In Federated Learning, where data labeling might be done locally on devices, these inconsistencies can propagate and lead to biased models [32].

4. Historical Bias in Training Data

Historical bias refers to the biases that already exist within the data due to historical inequalities or prejudices. This kind of bias poses a significant challenge because it is deeply embedded in the data and can perpetuate existing inequities if not addressed properly. In Federated Learning, historical bias in local datasets can contribute to systemic bias in the global mode [33].

C. Examples Illustrating Data Bias in Federated Learning

1. Healthcare: In a Federated Learning system for medical diagnosis, data collected from urban hospitals may dominate the training process, resulting in models that perform poorly on data from rural clinics, where patient demographics and disease prevalence may differ [34, 35].

2. Finance: A Federated Learning model trained on financial data might reflect biases if certain regions or socio-economic groups are overrepresented in the data. This could result in credit scoring models that unfairly disadvantage underrepresented groups [36].
3. Mobile Applications: In a scenario where a language prediction model is trained using data from mobile devices, the model may be biased if most of the data comes from users in a specific region, leading to poorer performance for users from other regions with different linguistic patterns [37, 38].

11.3 Implications of Data Bias in Federated Learning

Data bias in Federated Learning (FL) has far-reaching implications that significantly affect model performance, user group outcomes, and ethical considerations. Understanding these impacts is essential for developing robust and fair FL systems.

The presence of data bias can drastically impair model performance. Biases in local datasets can lead to skewed model updates, causing the global model to perform poorly [3]. For example, if a subset of devices contributes data that is not representative of the broader population, the aggregated model might overfit to the characteristics of this biased data [39]. This can result in reduced generalization, where the model fails to perform well on data from other devices with different distributions. Consequently, the model's accuracy, precision, and overall effectiveness can be compromised, limiting its utility in real-world applications.

The consequences of data bias for diverse user groups are especially concerning. Biases in FL models can lead to unequal performance across different demographic groups, exacerbating existing inequalities [40]. For instance, in a healthcare application, a biased FL model might provide accurate diagnoses for certain populations while offering poor predictions for others, potentially leading to inadequate or harmful medical advice [41]. Similarly, in financial services, biased models could result in unfair credit scoring or loan approval processes, disadvantaging underrepresented groups. Ensuring equitable performance across diverse user groups is crucial for fostering trust and inclusivity in FL systems.

Ethical considerations and potential harm stemming from data bias cannot be overlooked. Biased models can perpetuate and amplify societal prejudices, leading to discriminatory outcomes that harm vulnerable populations [42]. This raises significant ethical concerns regarding fairness, justice, and responsibility in AI systems. Organizations deploying FL must be vigilant in identifying and mitigating biases to prevent harm and uphold ethical standards. Implementing fairness-aware algorithms and conducting thorough bias audits are essential steps in this direction.

Non-IID (Non-Independent and Identically Distributed) challenges are a core aspect of data bias in Federated Learning. Non-IID data distribution refers to scenarios where data across clients are neither independent nor identically distributed. Each client's data may reflect unique characteristics based on user behavior, geographical location, or device type. This heterogeneity can introduce significant challenges for FL model training and convergence.

Non-IID data distribution impacts model performance and convergence in several ways. The diversity in local data distributions can lead to conflicting model updates, making it difficult for the global model to converge to an optimal solution [17]. Training on Non-IID data can cause instability and slow down the convergence process, as the model oscillates between the varying local updates [43]. This can result in longer training times and increased computational costs. Furthermore, models trained on Non-IID data may exhibit inconsistent performance, excelling on some clients' data while failing on others [24].

Real-world examples illustrate the challenges posed by Non-IID data in Federated Learning. In mobile applications, user behavior and preferences vary widely, leading to Non-IID data distributions. For instance, a text prediction model trained on data from different regions may struggle to handle regional language variations and usage patterns [44]. Similarly, in personalized health monitoring systems, data collected from individuals with different lifestyles, health conditions, and medical histories can result in highly Non-IID datasets, challenging the model's ability to provide accurate and generalized predictions [45].

In conclusion, data bias in Federated Learning has profound implications for model performance, user group outcomes, and ethical standards. Addressing the challenges of Non-IID data is critical for developing fair and effective FL systems. By understanding and mitigating these biases, researchers and practitioners can ensure that FL models deliver equitable and reliable outcomes, benefiting all users while upholding ethical principles.

11.4 Fairness in Federated Learning

Fairness in machine learning refers to the principle that a model should provide equitable and unbiased outcomes across all demographic groups and individual users [46]. It aims to ensure that the model's predictions do not disproportionately benefit or harm any group, maintaining ethical standards and social responsibility in machine learning applications. In the context of Federated Learning (FL), achieving fairness becomes even more complicated due to the decentralized nature of data and the diversity of client devices involved in the training process.

One of the main challenges in achieving fairness in Federated Learning is the lack of central control over data [47]. Unlike traditional machine learning, where data is centrally collected and pre-processed to mitigate biases, FL relies on data that remains distributed across various devices. Each device may collect and store data that is inherently biased or non-representative of the broader population [48]. This distributed data collection leads to variability in data quality and distribution, making it difficult to apply uniform fairness constraints across the entire dataset. Consequently, models trained in an FL setup might inadvertently perpetuate or even amplify existing biases present in the local datasets of individual clients [49].

Communication limitations between devices further complicate the pursuit of fairness in FL. Federated Learning relies on iterative interaction between client devices and a central server to aggregate model updates. However, communication constraints, such as limited bandwidth, connectivity issues, and latency [10], can hinder the efficient and timely exchange of model updates. These constraints may lead to uneven participation of clients in the training process, where only certain devices consistently contribute to the model updates [50]. This uneven participation can introduce biases, as the aggregated model might overrepresent the data from frequently participating devices while underrepresenting others, resulting in an unfair model that does not generalize well across all user groups.

Considering fairness from a global perspective is crucial in addressing these challenges. A global perspective involves ensuring that the FL model performs equitably across all participating clients, regardless of their local data characteristics. This requires the development of fairness-aware algorithms that can detect and mitigate biases during the training process [49]. Methods such as re-weighting client contributions, bias correction, and fairness constraints need to be integrated into the FL framework to promote equitable outcomes [51]. Additionally, adopting a holistic approach that considers the societal and ethical implications of model predictions is necessary to ensure that the benefits of FL are distributed fairly among all users.

In summary, achieving fairness in Federated Learning involves addressing significant challenges related to the shortage of central control over data and communication limitations between devices. By considering fairness from a global perspective and integrating fairness-aware techniques into the FL framework, researchers and practitioners can work towards developing models that provide equitable and unbiased outcomes, ensuring that Federated Learning technology aligns with ethical standards and promotes social good.

11.5 Approaches to Address Data Bias and Ensure Fairness

Addressing data bias and ensuring fairness in Federated Learning (FL) requires a multifaceted approach that combines several techniques and strategies. This chapter explores several methods designed to mitigate bias and promote fairness in FL systems.

- Federated Averaging with Differential Privacy

Federated Averaging (FedAvg) is a foundational algorithm in FL that combines local model upgrades from multiple devices into a global model as shown in Figure 11.4. To enhance privacy and reduce bias, differential

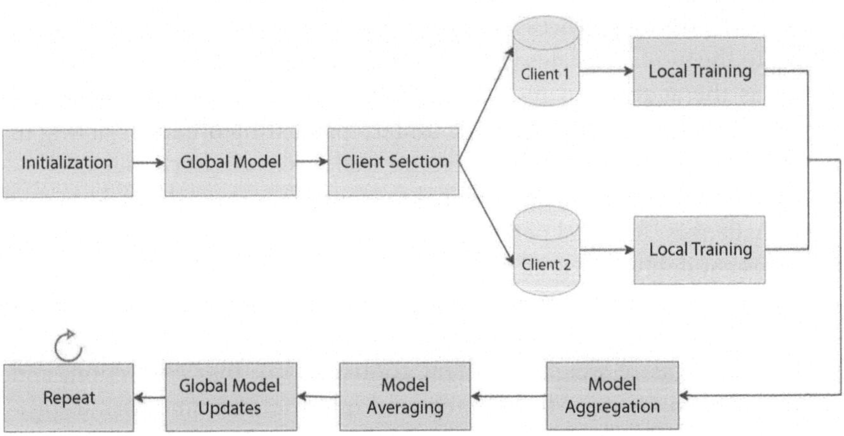

Figure 11.4 FedAvg process.

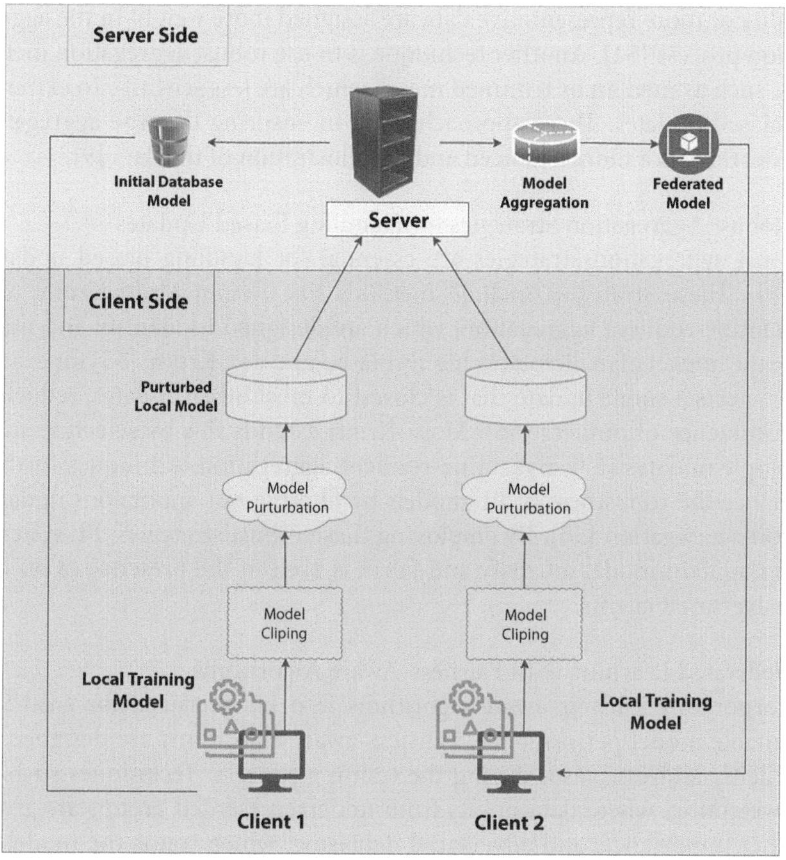

Figure 11.5 Federated averaging with differential privacy.

privacy can be integrated into FedAvg. Differential privacy introduces noise to the data, serving the purpose at individual data points remain anonymous while still enabling accurate model training [52]. This method helps protect user privacy and reduce the risk of biased data, contributing disproportionately to the global model. By applying differential privacy, FL systems can achieve an equilibrium between data utility and privacy, fostering trust and fairness in the model outcomes as shown in Figure 11.5.

- Model Aggregation Techniques to Reduce Bias

Model aggregation techniques are crucial for minimizing bias in FL. These techniques involve combining model updates from multiple clients in a manner that mitigates the influence of biased data [53]. One effective approach is weighted averaging, where updates from clients with higher quality or more representative data are assigned more weight in the aggregation process [54]. Another technique is to use robust aggregation methods, such as median or trimmed mean, which are less sensitive to extreme or biased updates. These approaches aid in ensuring that the aggregated model reflects a more balanced and fair illustration of the data [9].

- Robust Aggregation Strategies for Handling Biased Updates

Robust aggregation strategies are essential for handling biased updates in FL. These strategies include methods like Krum, Multi-Krum, and Byzantine-resilient aggregation, which are designed to identify and mitigate the impact of malicious or highly biased updates. Krum, [55] for example, selects a single update that is closest to most other updates, reducing the influence of outliers [56]. Multi-Krum extends this by selecting such multiple updates [57]. Byzantine-resilient aggregation techniques further enhance the robustness of FL models by filtering out anomalous updates before aggregation [58]. By employing these robust strategies, FL systems can maintain model integrity and fairness even in the presence of biased or adversarial clients.

- Federated Learning with Fairness-Aware Algorithms

Incorporating fairness-aware algorithms into FL is crucial for ensuring equitable model performance. Fairness-aware algorithms are designed to explicitly address biases during the training process. Techniques such as re-weighting, where data points from underrepresented groups are given higher importance, and adversarial debiasing, which trains the model to minimize bias-related disparities, are effective in promoting fairness [59]. Additionally, incorporating fairness constraints directly into the optimization objective ensures that the model learns to balance accuracy with fairness. These approaches help create FL models that provide more equitable outcomes across diverse user groups [60].

- Considerations for Incorporating Fairness Metrics in Evaluation

Evaluating FL models using fairness metrics is significant to ensure that they perform equitably across diverse groups. Metrics for fairness such as demographic parity, equal opportunity, and disparate impact ratio provide insights into the model's performance from a fairness perspective. Incorporating these metrics into the evaluation process allows researchers and practitioners to detect and address biases in the model [61, 62]. Regular monitoring and assessment using fairness metrics ensure that FL systems maintain ethical standards and do not perpetuate or exacerbate existing inequalities.

• Mitigating Non-IID Challenges
Handling Non-IID data distribution is one of the most significant challenges in FL. Several methods can help mitigate the effects of Non-IID data on model training and performance. One approach is to use personalized federated learning, where local models are designed to the specific data distributions of individual clients after the global aggregation step. This personalization helps improve model performance for diverse users. Another technique is federated meta-learning, which trains a meta-model to adapt quickly to new and diverse data distributions [63]. Additionally, clustering clients with comparable data distributions and aggregating their updates separately can enhance the robustness of the global model to Non-IID data [64].

Considerations for adapting FL algorithms to Non-IID scenarios include ensuring that the algorithms can dynamically adjust to changing data distributions [21]. This involves developing adaptive learning rates and optimization techniques that can manage the variability in data. Regularly updating the global model and incorporating feedback loops that allow for continuous learning and adaptation are also crucial. By tackling the complexities of Non-IID data, FL systems can achieve more consistent and fair performance across diverse client populations.

11.6 Evaluating and Mitigating Bias in Federated Learning

Ensuring fairness and mitigating bias in Federated Learning (FL) involves not only developing robust algorithms but also employing appropriate metrics and techniques to assess and address biases. This chapter outlines various metrics for assessing bias and explores methods for detecting and mitigating bias throughout the FL pipeline.

A. Metrics for Assessing Bias in Federated Learning Models
Assessing bias in FL models is crucial for understanding their fairness and identifying areas for improvement. Two primary categories of fairness metrics include group fairness metrics and individual fairness metrics.

• Group Fairness Metrics
Group fairness metrics evaluate how well a model performs across different demographic groups. These metrics aim to ensure that no group is disproportionately advantaged or disadvantaged by the model's predictions [65]. Common group fairness metrics include:

- Demographic Parity (DP): Ensures that the positive outcome rate is equal across different groups. In simpler terms, everyone has the same chance of getting a positive outcome, regardless of their demographic group [66]. The equation is as follows;

$$P(\hat{Y}=1 \mid A=a)=P(\hat{Y}=1 \mid A=b)$$

- $\hat{Y}$: Predicted outcome (1 indicates a positive outcome)
- A: Sensitive attribute (e.g., race, gender)
- a, b: Specific values of the sensitive attribute (e.g., a could represent male and b could represent female)

This equation shows that the probability of the model predicting a positive outcome ($\hat{Y}$) should be the same for all demographic groups (A), regardless of their specific characteristic (a or b).

- Equal Opportunity (EO): Focuses on the true positive rate, ensuring that every group has an equal opportunity of receiving a positive outcome, given that the outcome is indeed positive. The equation is as follows:

$$P(\widehat{Y}=1 \mid Y=1, A=a)=P(\widehat{Y}=1 \mid Y=1, A=b)$$

- $\hat{Y}$ is the predicted label.
- Y is the actual label.
- A is the sensitive attribute (e.g., race, gender).

This equation indicates that the probability of correctly predicting a positive outcome ($\hat{Y}=1$) given the actual outcome is positive (Y=1) should remain consistent across different values of the sensitive attribute A. In other words, the true positive rate of the model should be the same for all groups defined by A.

It is important to distinguish Equal Opportunity from Demographic Parity (DP). While they both aim to achieve fairness, they focus on different aspects:

Demographic Parity: Ensures everyone has an equal chance of getting a positive outcome, regardless of their group.

Equal Opportunity: Ensures individuals with a positive outcome has an equal chance of having it correctly predicted, regardless of their group
- Equalized Odds: Extends equal opportunity by ensuring that both true positive rates and false positive rates are equal across all groups [67].

By Combining the concepts of EO (True Positive Parity) and additional fairness for false positives:

- True Positive Parity: $P(\hat{Y}=1 \mid Y=1, A=a)=P(\hat{Y}=1 \mid Y=1, A=b)$ (same as EO)
- False Positive Parity: $P(\hat{Y}=1 \mid Y=0, A=a)=P(\hat{Y}=1 \mid Y=0, A=b)$

This metric ensures fairness in both true positives (who benefits from a positive prediction) and false positives (who is wrongly classified as positive).

- Disparate Impact Ratio (DIR): Compares the rate of favorable outcomes between the most and least favored groups.

$$\text{DIR} = \text{Favorable Outcome Rate } (A = a) \,/\, \text{Favorable Outcome Rate } (A = b)$$

- A: Sensitive attribute (e.g., race, gender)
- a, b: Specific values of the sensitive attribute
- Favorable Outcome Rate: The rate of outcomes considered desirable in a specific context (positive predictions, actual positive outcomes, etc.)

A DIR close to 1 suggests similar rates of favorable outcomes for both groups, potentially indicating fairness in that specific context. However, DIR does not explicitly identify a "most favored group."

The definition of "favorable outcome" depends entirely on the context. What is desirable for one group might not be desirable for another.

- **Example 1: Loan Approval**
    - Favorable outcome for applicant: Loan approved (positive prediction)
    - Favorable outcome for lender: Loan rejected (negative prediction)
    - We can't assume A=a always represents the "most favored group" without knowing the context (applicant vs. lender).

- **Example 2: Spam Filter**
  - Favorable outcome for email system: Identified as spam (positive prediction)
  - Favorable outcome for recipient: Not identified as spam (negative prediction)
  - Again, the "favorable" outcome depends on the group (email system vs. recipient).

To identify the least favored group, it's essential to first comprehend the specific scenario and what constitutes a "favorable outcome" for each group defined by the sensitive attribute. This definition can vary significantly. For instance, in a loan approval system, a positive outcome for the applicant (loan approved) might be negative for the lender (risky loan). Conversely, in a spam filter, a positive outcome for the email system (identified as spam) would be negative for the recipient (important email flagged incorrectly). Once we determine the "favorable outcome" for each group, the group with the lower Favorable Outcome Rate is considered the least favored group in that specific context.

- Individual Fairness Metrics

Individual fairness metrics make sure that similar individuals receive similar predictions. These metrics assess fairness at a more granular level, focusing on the consistency of model performance for individuals with similar characteristics [68]. Key individual fairness metrics include:

  - Consistency: Measures the degree to which similar individuals receive similar outcomes from the model [69].

This metric focuses on how similar the model's predictions are for individuals with similar characteristics. There is no single equation, but we can represent it as a distance function:

$$d\,(\hat{Y}\,(a), \hat{Y}\,(b)) \leq f(d(X(a), X(b)))$$

- $\hat{Y}\,(a), \hat{Y}\,(b)$: Predicted outcomes for individuals a and b
- X(a), X(b): Feature vectors (characteristics) of individuals a and b

- d: Distance function measuring similarity between outcomes (e.g., difference in scores)
- f: Function relating the distance between features (X) to the expected distance between outcomes (Y^)

Here, a smaller distance between features (d(X(a), X(b))) should correspond to a smaller distance between predicted outcomes $(d(\hat{Y}(a), \hat{Y}(b)))$. The specific form of function f depends on the chosen distance metrics and the specific fairness notion.
- Fairness Through Awareness: Ensures that the model avoids making decisions based on sensitive attributes, such as race or gender unless these attributes are explicitly part of the decision-making criteria and justified [70].

$$P(\hat{Y}|X, A)=P(\hat{Y}|X)$$

- $\hat{Y}$: Predicted outcome.
- **X**: Feature vector, which includes all features except the sensitive attribute.
- **A**: Sensitive attribute (e.g., race, gender, age).

This condition implies that the predicted outcome $(\hat{Y})$ should not be dependent on the sensitive attribute (A), given the feature vector (X). In other words, the model should not use the sensitive attribute to influence its predictions.

B. Bias Detection and Mitigation Techniques
To ensure fairness in FL, it is essential to detect and mitigate bias at various stages of the model development pipeline. Bias mitigation techniques can be classified into pre-processing, in-processing, and post-processing methods.

- Pre-Processing Methods

Pre-processing methods aim to reduce bias in the data before it is used for model training. These methods include:

- Data Balancing: Ensures that the training data is representative of all demographic groups. This can be achieved through

oversampling underrepresented groups or under sampling overrepresented groups [71].
- Data Transformation: Modifies the data to remove or reduce bias. Techniques like re-weighting data points or generating synthetic data to balance the dataset are commonly used [29].
- Data Anonymization: Removes sensitive attributes that could introduce bias while retaining the essential features needed for accurate predictions [72].

• In-Processing Methods

In-processing methods the focus is on modifying the model training process to mitigate bias. These methods include:

- Fairness Constraints: Incorporate fairness constraints directly into the model's objective function, ensuring that the model optimizes for both accuracy and fairness during training [73].
- Adversarial Debiasing: Uses adversarial training techniques where an adversary network attempts to detect bias in the model's predictions. The main model is trained to minimize both prediction inaccuracies and the adversary's ability to detect bias [74].
- Regularization Techniques: Apply regularization terms to the model's objective function that penalize biased predictions, encouraging the model to produce fairer outcomes [75].

• Post-Processing Methods

Post-processing techniques adjust the model's predictions to ensure fairness after the training phase of the model. These methods include:

- Recalibration: Adjusts the decision thresholds for different groups to equalize performance metrics such as true positive rates and false positive rates [76].
- Output Perturbation: Adds controlled noise to the model's predictions to achieve fairness. This technique ensures that the adjusted predictions meet fairness criteria without significantly impacting overall accuracy [77].
- Fairness-aware Re-ranking: Re-orders the model's predictions to ensure that the final outputs are fair across different groups. This technique is particularly useful in ranking and recommendation systems [78].

In summary, assessing and mitigating bias in Federated Learning involves a combination of metrics and techniques that span the entire model development pipeline. By employing group and individual fairness metrics, and implementing pre-processing, in-processing, and post-processing methods, researchers, and practitioners can create FL models that are not only effective but also fair, ensuring equitable outcomes for all users.

11.7 Case Studies and Examples

A. Real-World Examples of Bias in Federated Learning
Bias in Federated Learning (FL) manifests in various ways, reflecting the complexities and diversities of real-world data. One notable example is in the healthcare sector, where FL models trained on data from predominantly urban hospitals may exhibit bias against rural populations [79]. These models could exhibit subpar performance on rural data due to differences in disease prevalence, patient demographics, and healthcare practices [80]. There are many case studies presented as follows:

Case Study 1: Federated Learning used for Electronic Health Records

Background: Electronic Health Records (EHRs) are digital representations of patients' medical histories, inclusive of diagnoses, medications, and treatment plans, stored securely in electronic format. They streamline healthcare delivery by providing centralized access to comprehensive patient information across healthcare providers and settings.
Implementation: The study proposes a comprehensive federated learning (FL) approach combined with adversarial debiasing and a fair aggregation technique tailored for the healthcare domain, particularly in the context of electronic health records (EHRs) [81].

Bias and Fairness Considerations:

1. Data Representativeness: EHR data may not accurately represent the entire patient population, leading to biased models that perform differently across demographic groups. For example, data from certain demographics or geographical regions may be underrepresented, skewing model predictions and exacerbating disparities in healthcare outcomes.
2. Bias Sources: Biases in EHR data can arise from several sources, including historical inequities in healthcare delivery, socioeconomic factors, cultural differences, and

systemic healthcare practices. These biases can manifest in diagnostic errors, unequal treatment recommendations, and disparities in access to healthcare services.

Mitigation Strategies:

- Data Preprocessing: Cleaning and augmenting data to reduce bias and improve representativeness.
- Algorithmic Fairness: Designing AI models that incorporate fairness considerations during training and inference.
- Fairness-Aware Learning: Using techniques like adversarial training, regularization, and bias-aware loss functions to mitigate bias in predictions.
- Post-processing: Adjusting model outputs to ensure fairness using techniques like calibration or reweighing.

Case Study 2: Federated Learning for Medical Imaging

Background: Medical imaging involves advanced technologies like MRI, CT scans, and X-rays to visualize internal body structures and diagnose conditions non-invasively. These images provide detailed anatomical and functional information crucial for medical diagnosis, treatment planning, and monitoring of patients' health. Advances in artificial intelligence are enhancing medical imaging by improving accuracy, efficiency, and interpretation of these complex data sets.
Implementation: Federated learning (FL), medical images are utilized across decentralized healthcare institutions to train machine learning models without centrally aggregating sensitive patient data. Each institution retains control over its data, ensuring privacy [82].

Bias and Fairness Considerations:

1. Label Bias: Label bias in medical imaging can arise from various sources, potentially leading to inaccurate or biased machine learning model training. Here are some examples of label bias specific to medical imaging:
   - Subjective Annotation: Annotations provided by radiologists or medical experts may vary based on individual interpretations, leading to inconsistencies in labeling.
   - Clinical Context: Labels assigned to medical images can be influenced by clinical context, such as patient history or symptoms, which might introduce biases.

- Technological Variability: Differences in imaging equipment or techniques across medical institutions can affect image quality and interpretation, impacting the accuracy of labels.

2. Data Heterogeneity bias: Medical imaging refers to the differences and diversity found in datasets gathered from different sources or institutions. This type of bias can significantly affect the performance and reliability of machine learning models trained on such heterogeneous data. There are some key aspects of data heterogeneity bias in medical imaging:
   - Equipment Differences: Variations in imaging equipment (e.g., MRI machines, CT scanners) across medical institutions can lead to differences in image resolution, noise levels, and overall quality, affecting the consistency of data.
   - Patient Demographics: Datasets collected from different demographics (e.g., age groups, ethnicities) may exhibit variations in disease prevalence, anatomical variations, or physiological characteristics, influencing the distribution of features in the data.
   - Clinical Protocols: Differences in clinical protocols and practices among institutions can affect the collection and annotation of medical images, introducing variability in labeling and diagnostic criteria.
   - Temporal Changes: Data gathered over time may reflect changes in medical practices, technological advancements, or evolving diagnostic criteria, leading to temporal variations in the data distribution.

Mitigation Strategies:

- Addressing Data Heterogeneity: Designed methods to handle data diversity and label scarcity simultaneously, enhancing the model's adaptability across varied medical datasets.
- Improved Label Efficiency: Demonstrated enhanced label efficiency and robustness to non-IID data compared to conventional supervised learning approaches and existing federated learning algorithms.
- Real-World Evaluation: assess the model's performance under realistic federated conditions, ensuring robustness and reliability in practical healthcare applications.

Case Study 3: Federated Learning for Student Predictive Analytics

Background: The prediction in this context denotes the procedure of using student modeling techniques to forecast student outcomes based on their measured activities and behaviors.
Implementation: The Multi-Layer Personalized Federated Learning (MLPFL) methodology improves the accuracy of these predictions by creating personalized models for different student subgroups [83].
Bias and Fairness Considerations:

- Demographic Disparities: Unequal representation of various demographic groups (e.g., gender, race, socioeconomic status) in the data can lead to biased models that favor more represented groups.
- Historical Data Collection Practices: Biases can be introduced through past practices in data collection, where specific groups might be underrepresented or misrepresented.
- Systemic Inequalities: Existing inequalities within the educational system (e.g., access to resources, quality of instruction) can be reflected in the data, leading to biased outcomes.
- Sampling Bias: The data used to train models might not accurately represent the entire student population, thereby bias results towards the characteristics of the sampled group.
- Measurement Bias: Inaccuracies or inconsistencies in student performance and behavior which are measured and recorded can introduce bias into the data.
- Labeling Bias: Subjective or inconsistent labeling of student outcomes and performance metrics can lead to biased model predictions.
- Cultural Bias: Cultural variations that influence learning preferences and educational the results may not adequately reflect in the data, resulting in biased models that fail to accommodate these differences.

Mitigation Strategies:

- Introducing Constraints During Model Training: Implementing fairness constraints to ensure equitable outcomes among diverse student groups.
- Data Augmentation and Rebalancing: Using techniques to balance the representation of various demographic groups within the training data.

- Algorithmic Fairness Techniques: Applying methods such as fairness-aware algorithms that actively work in reducing the bias during the training process.
- Regular Bias Audits: Conducting ongoing evaluations of model performance to detect and address biases.
- Inclusive Data Collection Practices: Ensuring that data gathering methods are intended to capture a broad and inclusive sample of the student population.

B. Successful Implementations of Fairness-Aware Federated Learning Models

Despite the challenges, successful implementations have been achieved for fairness-aware FL models that address these biases. For example, a federated healthcare application successfully implemented fairness-aware algorithms to ensure that the model performed equally well across different demographic groups [81, 84]. By integrating fairness constraints during the model training process and using techniques such as re-weighting and bias correction, the application achieved a more balanced performance [18]. Similarly, in the finance sector, FL methods have been designed to detect and mitigate biases by ensuring that credit scoring algorithms do not disproportionately disadvantage certain socio-economic groups. These models employ techniques like federated adversarial training and fairness regularization to enhance fairness without compromising accuracy [85].

C. Case Studies and Examples: IID vs. Non-IID

1. Comparative Evaluation of Federated Learning Models Under IID and Non-IID Scenarios

In real-world applications, data often exhibits non-IID characteristics, where each client or institution possesses datasets with distinct distributions. This variability poses significant challenges for training machine learning algorithms, particularly in contexts such as healthcare where preserving patient privacy is paramount. Federated learning (FL) has emerged as a promising approach to address these issues by facilitating collaborative model training across decentralized data sources while avoiding the centralization of sensitive information. This comparative analysis focuses on evaluating FL models under both IID and non-IID scenarios, emphasizing how data distribution impacts model performance and highlighting FL's robustness and adaptability in diverse data environments. Specifically, the research applies FL to diagnose depression while safeguarding patient privacy, proposing a multi-view FL framework that facilitates collaborative training across different institutions without sharing raw data. The study integrates late fusion techniques to handle inconsistencies in time series data sourced from user interactions on mobile devices and HDRS scores. Results demonstrate FL's efficacy, showcasing a 10%-15% accuracy improvement for IID data compared to local training methods, while maintaining acceptable performance with up to a 13% decrease in accuracy for non-IID data. This underscores FL's potential to enhance clinical applications in mental health by ensuring data security and privacy while achieving effective diagnostic outcomes [86].

Another study focuses on developing a privacy-preserving system using Federated Learning (FL) to identify Major Depressive Disorder (MDD) based on EEG signals. This approach is crucial due to the sensitive nature of medical data and patients' privacy concerns. The study utilizes a 3-channel EEG dataset (MODMA) with 26 individuals diagnosed with MDD and 29 non-MDD individuals to train deep learning (DL) models such as Long Short-Term Memory (LSTM), Bidirectional LSTM (Bi-LSTM), Gated Recurrent Unit (GRU), and One Dimensional Convolutional Neural Network (1D-CNN). Among these models, Bi-LSTM emerges as the most effective, achieving training accuracy of 93.58% and testing accuracy of 92.92% in a standalone DL setup.

Transitioning to Federated Learning, the privacy-preserving FL model based on Bi-LSTM achieves promising results with an IID dataset, obtaining training accuracy of 95.99%, AUC 99.35%, and testing accuracy of 95%. For non-IID datasets, the FL model maintains strong performance with 94.86% training accuracy and 98.9% AUC. These results show the feasibility and efficacy of FL in training DL models across distributed data sources while safeguarding patient privacy. The study underscores the potential of FL-based EEG analysis for clinical applications in diagnosing MDD, providing accurate predictions that could assist healthcare professionals in early intervention and treatment planning [87].

Indeed, the study highlights a common observation in FL research where models trained on IID data tend to achieve higher performance compared to models trained on non-IID data. This discrepancy arises because FL assumes data from different clients or institutions having similar distributions, which is often not the case in real-world scenarios.

In many practical applications, including medical diagnostics such as identifying Major Depressive Disorder (MDD) using EEG signals, the data gathered from various sources can exhibit varying distributions due to variations in patient demographics, instrumentation, and environmental factors. These non-IID characteristics present challenges in FL, affecting model convergence, accuracy, and generalizability.

Despite the performance gap between IID and non-IID data scenarios observed in this study and other real-world cases of FL, researchers continue to explore strategies to mitigate these challenges. Techniques such as data augmentation, adaptive learning rates, model personalization, and advanced aggregation methods are being investigated to improve FL's effectiveness in handling non-IID data without compromising privacy.

Moreover, the findings emphasize the importance of adapting FL frameworks to accommodate real-world data complexities while maintaining robust privacy-preserving procedures. The focus of future research is on developing more sophisticated FL algorithms and protocols tailored to heterogeneous data distributions to enhance the applicability and reliability of FL in various domains, including healthcare and beyond.

2. Lessons Learned from Practical Implementations

Implementing federated learning (FL) in real-world scenarios, particularly for applications involving sensitive data like medical diagnostics, has provided several key insights and lessons:

- Data Heterogeneity Challenges: Real-world data from various sources often exhibit non-IID characteristics due to varying demographics, instrumentation differences, and environmental factors. This variety presents significant challenges for FL algorithms, impacting model convergence, accuracy, and generalizability across different client datasets.
- Performance Discrepancy: Models trained on IID data typically surpass those trained on non-IID data. FL assumes similar data distributions across clients, which is seldom the case in practice. Addressing this performance gap requires creating resilient techniques that can handle data heterogeneity effectively without compromising privacy.
- Privacy-Preserving Strategies: FL inherently protects data privacy by keeping sensitive information decentralized. However, ensuring robust privacy-preserving mechanisms remains critical. Techniques such as differential privacy, secure aggregation, and federated averaging with noise injection are essential to maintain confidentiality while aggregating model updates.
- Algorithmic Adaptations: Researchers are exploring adaptive learning rates, model personalization approaches, and advanced aggregation methods to improve FL's effectiveness in heterogeneous data environments. These adaptations

aim to strengthen model performance on non-IID data while respecting the privacy constraints imposed by FL frameworks.
- Need for Standardization and Guidelines: Establishing standardized protocols and guidelines for FL implementations, particularly in healthcare and other regulated industries, is crucial. Clear frameworks can ensure compliance with data protection regulations while fostering trust among stakeholders.

In conclusion, while Federated Learning (FL) holds great potential in preserving privacy and facilitating collaborative machine learning across distributed data sources, addressing the challenges posed by data heterogeneity is crucial for its widespread adoption and success in real-world applications, especially in sensitive domains such as healthcare.

11.8 Ethical Considerations and Responsible AI

Federated Learning (FL) presents promising advancements in maintaining data privacy and facilitating collaborative machine learning across distributed networks. So, the implementation of FL systems raises several ethical concerns that must be addressed to ensure responsible AI practices. Establishing ethical guidelines for FL research and deployment is essential to navigate the complex landscape of data privacy, user consent, and equitable model performance [88]. Researchers and practitioners must adhere to principles that prioritize the rights and interests of all parties involved, ensuring that data privacy is not compromised and that user consent is obtained transparently and ethically [89].

One critical aspect of ethical FL involves addressing potential unintended outcomes that may arise during the implementation of FL systems. For instance, the presence of biases in local datasets might lead to unfair model outcomes, exacerbating existing inequalities [14]. It is crucial to implement mechanisms that detect and mitigate biases, ensuring that the models are fair and do not disproportionately harm any group. Additionally, the robustness and security of FL systems must be rigorously tested to prevent adversarial attacks and data breaches, which could have severe ethical and legal ramifications.

Promoting transparency and accountability in FL systems is another fundamental ethical consideration [90]. Transparency involves openly communicating the objectives, processes, and limitations of FL models to all stakeholders, including users, researchers, and regulatory bodies. This helps build trust and allows stakeholders to make informed decisions about their participation in FL initiatives. Accountability, conversely, requires establishing clear lines of responsibility for the results of FL systems [91]. This includes setting up governance structures that monitor and evaluate the performance and impact of FL models, ensuring that any negative consequences are promptly addressed and rectified.

In conclusion, ethical considerations in Federated Learning encompass a broad range of issues, from developing ethical guidelines and addressing unintended consequences to promoting accountability and transparency. By prioritizing these aspects, the FL community can ensure that the advantages of this technology are realized in a manner that is fair, responsible, and aligned with societal values.

11.9 Future Directions and Research Challenges

As Federated Learning (FL) continues to evolve, addressing fairness and bias remains a critical area of ongoing research. Emerging research on fairness in FL seeks to develop methods that ensure equitable model performance across diverse client populations. This involves developing algorithms that can detect and mitigate biases arising from heterogeneous data sources and ensuring that the advantages of FL are distributed fairly among all users [92, 93]. Researchers are exploring several techniques, such as fairness-aware aggregation methods and bias-correction mechanisms, to enhance the fairness of FL models [49].

Despite these advancements, numerous open challenges and areas for improvement persist. One significant challenge is the inherent complexity of FL systems, which must balance the competing demands of data privacy, computational efficiency, and model accuracy [94]. Developing FL models that can robustly handle non-IID data remains a critical hurdle. Non-IID data might lead to biased updates and unstable training processes, making it difficult to achieve consistent and fair model performance. Additionally, ensuring the scalability of FL systems as the number of participating devices grows is an ongoing concern [95].

Interdisciplinary collaboration plays an essential role in addressing these challenges. Integrating insights from disciplines such as machine learning, data privacy, ethics, and law can lead to more holistic solutions for bias and fairness in FL [96]. For instance, collaboration with social scientists can assist in identifying and mitigating societal biases reflected in the data, while legal experts can guide adherence to data protection regulations. Such interdisciplinary efforts are essential for developing FL systems that are not only technically sound but also socially responsible and legally compliant.

Handling data distribution diversity is a critical future direction for Federated Learning. Research challenges in this area include creating models that are robust to diverse data distributions and can adapt to dynamic changes in data over time [98]. Innovations and techniques, such as federated meta-learning and personalized federated learning, are being explored to address these challenges [74, 97]. These approaches aim to develop models that can effectively generalize across diverse clients and adapt to new data distributions as they emerge. Furthermore, the development of adaptive methods that can dynamically adjust to changing data distributions in real-time is essential for the sustained success of FL. These algorithms need to efficiently manage the trade-offs between model accuracy, fairness, and computational resources.

In summary, the future of Federated Learning hinges on overcoming significant research challenges related to fairness, bias, and data distribution diversity. Emerging research, interdisciplinary collaboration, and innovative techniques are essential to developing robust and equitable FL systems. As these efforts continue, they will pave the way for more effective and responsible deployment of Federated Learning technologies, ensuring that their benefits are equitable and accessible to all users.

11.10 Conclusion

In conclusion, Federated Learning presents an effective approach across distributed data sources for collaborative model training. It also brings to light significant challenges related to data bias and fairness. Throughout this exploration, we have delved into the intricacies of data distribution bias, algorithmic bias, and the implications of participation bias in Federated Learning. We have identified various techniques and strategies, from fairness-aware algorithms to robust aggregation methods, aimed at mitigating bias and promoting fairness in FL models. Ongoing efforts to address these challenges are paramount for the continued advancement and ethical deployment of Federated Learning technologies. As Federated Learning continues to gain traction across various domains, there is a pressing need for collaboration among researchers, developers, and policymakers to ensure that FL systems uphold fairness and mitigate bias. Moreover, the role of federated approaches in accommodating diverse data sources while maintaining fairness cannot be overstated. By embracing federated methodologies, we can harness the power of distributed data while safeguarding against biases and promoting equitable outcomes for all stakeholders. As we move forward, it is imperative that we remain vigilant, proactive, and committed to the principles of fairness and transparency in Federated Learning.

References

1. AbdulRahman, S., Tout, H., Ould-Slimane, H., Mourad, A., Talhi, C., Guizani, M., A survey on federated learning: The journey from centralized to distributed on-site learning and beyond. *IEEE Internet Things J.*, 8, 7, 5476–5497, 2020 Oct. https://doi.org/10.1109/JIOT.2020.3030072.
2. Xu, J. *et al.*, Federated Learning for Healthcare Informatics. *J. Healthc. Inf. Res.*, 5, 1–19, 2021, https://doi.org/10.1007/s41666-020-00082-4.
3. Abay, A., Zhou, Y., Baracaldo, N., Rajamoni, S., Chuba, E., Ludwig, H., Mitigating bias in federated learning, 2020. arXiv preprint arXiv:2012.02447.
4. Beresewicz, M. *et al.*, *An overview of methods for treating selectivity in big data sources*, Eurostat: Publications Office of the European Union, 2018. https://www.sipotra.it/wp-content/uploads/2018/07/An-overview-of-methods-for-treating-selectivity-in-big-data-sources.pdf.
5. Graham, M. *et al.*, Uneven geographies of user-generated information: Patterns of increasing informational poverty. *Ann. Assoc. Am. Geogr.*, 104, 4, 746–764, 2014.
6. Olteanu, A. *et al.*, Social data: Biases, methodological pitfalls, and ethical boundaries. *Front. Big Data*, 2, 13, 2019.
7. Schwartz, R. *et al.*, Towards a standard for identifying and managing bias in artificial intelligence, 3, US Department of Commerce, National Institute of Standards and Technology, 2022. https://www.dwt.com/-/media/files/blogs/artificial-intelligence-law-advisor/2022/03/nist-sp-1270--identifying-and-managing-bias-in-ai.pdf.
8. Tan, A.Z. *et al.*, Towards personalized federated learning. *IEEE Trans. Neural Netw. Learn. Syst.*, 34, 12, 9587–9603, 2022.
9. Pillutla, K. *et al.*, Robust aggregation for federated learning. *IEEE Trans. Signal Process.*, 70, 1142–1154, 2022.
10. Khan, L.U. *et al.*, Federated learning for internet of things: Recent advances, taxonomy, and open challenges. *IEEE Commun. Surv. Tutor.*, 23, 3, 1759–1799, 2021.
11. Yang, C. *et al.*, Characterizing impacts of heterogeneity in federated learning upon large-scale smartphone data. *Proceedings of the Web Conference 2021*, 2021.

12. Soltani, B. *et al.*, A survey on participant selection for federated learning in mobile networks. *Proceedings of the 17th ACM Workshop on Mobility in the Evolving Internet Architecture*, 2022.
13. Tan, L. *et al.*, AdaFed: Optimizing participation-aware federated learning with adaptive aggregation weights. *IEEE Trans. Netw. Sci. Eng.*, 9, 4, 2708–2720, 2022.
14. Djebrouni, Y. *et al.*, Bias mitigation in federated learning for edge computing. *Proceedings of the ACM on Interactive, Mobile, Wearable and Ubiquitous Technologies*, 2024.
15. Chen, P., Wu, L., & Wang, L., AI fairness in data management and analytics: A review on challenges, methodologies and applications. *Appl. Sci.*, 13, 18, 10258, 2023.
16. Crowson, M. G., Moukheiber, D., Arévalo, A. R., Lam, B. D., Mantena, S., Rana, A., Celi, L. A., A systematic review of federated learning applications for biomedical data. *PLOS Digit. Health*, 1, 5, e0000033, 2022.
17. Lu, Z. *et al.*, Federated learning with non-iid data: A survey. *IEEE Internet Things J.*, 11, 11, 19188–19209, 2024.
18. Li, Z. *et al.*, Revisiting weighted aggregation in federated learning with neural networks. *International Conference on Machine Learning*, 2023.
19. Du, W. *et al.*, Fairness-aware agnostic federated learning. *Proceedings of the 2021 SIAM International Conference on Data Mining (SDM)*, 2021.
20. Michieli, U. and Ozay, M., Are all users treated fairly in federated learning systems? *Proceedings of the IEEE/CVF conference on computer vision and pattern recognition*, 2021.
21. Zhang, C., Xie, Y., Bai, H., Yu, B., Li, W., Gao, Y., A survey on federated learning. *Knowl.-Based Syst.*, 216, 106775, 2021.
22. Aledhari, M., Razzak, R., Parizi, R. M., Saeed, F., Federated learning: A survey on enabling technologies, protocols, and applications. *IEEE Access*, 8, 140699–140725, 2020.
23. Ma, X., Zhu, J., Lin, Z., Chen, S., Qin, Y., A state-of-the-art survey on solving non-iid data in federated learning. *Future Gener. Comput. Syst.*, 135, 244–258, 2022.
24. Zhu, H., Xu, J., Liu, S., Jin, Y., Federated learning on non-IID data: A survey. *Neurocomputing*, 465, 371-390, 2021.
25. Banabilah, S., Aloqaily, M., Alsayed, E., Malik, N., Jararweh, Y., Federated learning review: Fundamentals, enabling technologies, and future applications. *Inf. Process. Manage.*, 59, 6, 103061, 2022.
26. Ji, S., Tan, Y., Saravirta, T., Yang, Z., Liu, Y., Vasankari, L., Walid, A., Emerging trends in federated learning: From model fusion to federated x learning. *Int. J. Mach. Learn. Cybern.*, 15, 3769–3790, 2024.
27. Rajkomar, A., Hardt, M., Howell, M. D., Corrado, G., Chin, M. H., Ensuring fairness in machine learning to advance health equity. *Ann. Intern. Med.*, 169, 12, 866–872, 2018.

28. Qin, Z., Li, G. Y., Ye, H., Federated learning and wireless communications. *IEEE Wireless Commun.*, 28, 5, 134–140, 2021.
29. Shahbazi, N., Lin, Y., Asudeh, A., Jagadish, H. V., Representation bias in data: A survey on identification and resolution techniques. *ACM Comput. Surv.*, 55, 13s, 1–39, 2023.
30. Drainakis, G., Pantazopoulos, P., Katsaros, K. V., Sourlas, V., Amditis, A., Kaklamani, D. I., From centralized to Federated Learning: Exploring performance and end-to-end resource consumption. *Comput. Netw.*, 225, 109657, 2023.
31. Sittijuk, P. and Tamee, K., Performance measurement of federated learning on imbalanced data. *2021 18th International Joint Conference on Computer Science and Software Engineering (JCSSE)*, 2021.
32. Chakraborty, J. *et al.*, Bias in machine learning software: Why? how? what to do? *Proceedings of the 29th ACM joint meeting on european software engineering conference and symposium on the foundations of software engineering*, 2021.
33. Bagga, S. and Piper, A., Measuring the effects of bias in training data for literary classification. *Proceedings of the 4th Joint SIGHUM Workshop on Computational Linguistics for Cultural Heritage, Social Sciences, Humanities and Literature*, 2020.
34. Bagula, A., Mandava, M., & Bagula, H., A framework for healthcare support in the rural and low income areas of the developing world. *J. Netw. Comput. Appl.*, 120, 17–29, 2018.
35. Pai, D.R. and Dissanayake, C.K., Predictive analytics methods for investigating inpatient volume in rural hospitals. *Healthcare Anal.*, 2, 100113, 2022.
36. Marda, V., Artificial intelligence policy in India: a framework for engaging the limits of data-driven decision-making. *Philos. Trans. R. Soc. A Math. Phys. Eng. Sci.*, 376, 2133, 20180087, 2018.
37. Cai, D. *et al.*, Federated few-shot learning for mobile nlp. *Proceedings of the 29th Annual International Conference on Mobile Computing and Networking*, 2023.
38. Wu, X., Xu, L., Zhu, L., Local Differential Privacy-Based Federated Learning under Personalized Settings. *Appl. Sci.*, 13, 7, 4168, 2023.
39. Stisen, A. *et al.*, Smart devices are different: Assessing and mitigatingmobile sensing heterogeneities for activity recognition. *Proceedings of the 13th ACM conference on embedded networked sensor systems*, 2015.
40. Ferrara, E., Fairness and bias in artificial intelligence: A brief survey of sources, impacts, and mitigation strategies. *Science*, 6, 1, 3, 2023.
41. Aldahiri, A., Alrashed, B., Hussain, W., Trends in using IoT with machine learning in health prediction system. *Forecasting*, 3, 1, 181–206, 2021.
42. Varona, D. and Suárez, J.L., Discrimination, bias, fairness, and trustworthy AI. *Appl. Sci.*, 12, 12, 5826, 2022.
43. Li, X., Huang, K., Yang, W., Wang, S., Zhang, Z., On the convergence of fedavg on non-iid data, 2019. arXiv preprint arXiv:1907.02189.

44. Marulli, F. *et al.*, Exploring a federated learning approach to enhance authorship attribution of misleading information from heterogeneous sources. *2021 International Joint Conference on Neural Networks (IJCNN)*, 2021.
45. Rajendran, S., Pan, W., Sabuncu, M. R., Chen, Y., Zhou, J., Wang, F. E. I., Learning across diverse biomedical data modalities and cohorts: Challenges and opportunities for innovation. *Patterns.*, 5, 2, 2024, 100913, 2024.
46. Mehrabi, N., Morstatter, F., Saxena, N., Lerman, K., Galstyan, A., A survey on bias and fairness in machine learning. *ACM Comput. Surv. (CSUR)*, 54, 6, 1–35, 2021.
47. Ozdayi, M.S. and Kantarcioglu, M., The impact of data distribution on fairness and robustness in federated learning. *2021 Third IEEE International Conference on Trust, Privacy and Security in Intelligent Systems and Applications (TPS-ISA)*, 2021.
48. Scheltjens, V. *et al.*, Target Informed Client Recruitment for Efficient Federated Learning in Healthcare, 2024. https://www.researchsquare.com/article/rs-3825499/v1.
49. Siddique, S., Haque, M. A., George, R., Gupta, K. D., Gupta, D., Faruk, M. J. H., Survey on machine learning biases and mitigation techniques. *Digital*, 4, 1, 1–68, 2023.
50. Imteaj, A. and Amini, M.H., FedPARL: Client activity and resource-oriented lightweight federated learning model for resource-constrained heterogeneous IoT environment. *Front. Commun. Netw.*, 2, 657653, 2021.
51. Shah, M. and Sureja, N., A Comprehensive Review of Bias in Deep Learning Models: Methods, Impacts, and Future Directions. *Arch. Comput. Methods Eng.*, 1–13, 2024.
52. Wu, X., Liang, Z., Wang, J., Fedmed: A federated learning framework for language modeling. *Sensors*, 20, 14, 4048, 2020.
53. Djebrouni, Y., Towards bias mitigation in federated learning. *16th EuroSys Doctoral Workshop*, 2022.
54. Jesus, P., Baquero, C., Almeida, P. S., A survey of distributed data aggregation algorithms. *IEEE Commun. Surv. Tutor.*, 17, 1, 381–404, 2014.
55. Shi, J. *et al.*, Challenges and approaches for mitigating byzantine attacks in federated learning. *2022 IEEE International Conference on Trust, Security and Privacy in Computing and Communications (TrustCom)*, 2022.
56. Jeong, H., Son, H., Lee, S., Hyun, J., Chung, T. M., FedCC: Robust federated learning against model poisoning attacks, 2022. arXiv preprint arXiv:2212.01976.
57. Nanayakkara, S. I., Pokhrel, S. R., Li, G., Understanding global aggregation and optimization of federated learning. *Future Gener. Comput. Syst.*, arXiv–2303, 2024.
58. Gabrielli, E., Belli, D., Miori, V., Tolomei, G., Protecting Federated Learning from Extreme Model Poisoning Attacks via Multidimensional Time Series Anomaly Detection, 2023. arXiv e-prints, arXiv-2303.

59. Dhabliya, D., Dari, S. S., Dhablia, A., Akhila, N., Kachhoria, R., Khetani, V., Addressing Bias in Machine Learning Algorithms: Promoting Fairness and Ethical Design. *E3S Web Conf.*, 491, 02040, 2024.
60. Shi, Y. *et al.*, Towards fairness-aware federated learning. *IEEE Trans. Neural Netw. Learn. Syst.*, 35, 9, 11922–11938, 2023.
61. Pagano, T. P., Loureiro, R. B., Lisboa, F. V., Peixoto, R. M., Guimarães, G. A., Cruz, G. O., Nascimento, E. G., Bias and unfairness in machine learning models: a systematic review on datasets, tools, fairness metrics, and identification and mitigation methods. *Big Data Cognit. Comput.*, 7, 1, 15, 2023.
62. MacCarthy, M., Standards of fairness for disparate impact assessment of big data algorithms. *Cumb. L. Rev.*, 48, 67, 2017.
63. Yang, L., Huang, J., Lin, W., Cao, J., Personalized federated learning on non-IID data via group-based meta-learning. *ACM Trans. Knowl. Discov. Data*, 17, 4, 1–20, 2023.
64. Gong, B., Xing, T., Liu, Z., Xi, W., Chen, X., Adaptive client clustering for efficient federated learning over non-iid and imbalanced data. *IEEE Trans. Big Data*, 2022.
65. Bird, S. *et al.*, Fairlearn: A toolkit for assessing and improving fairness in AI, Microsoft, Tech. Rep. MSR-TR-2020-32, 2020. https://www.microsoft.com/en-us/research/uploads/prod/2020/05/Fairlearn_WhitePaper-2020-09-22.pdf.
66. Jiang, Z. *et al.*, Generalized demographic parity for group fairness. *International Conference on Learning Representations*, 2022.
67. Shen, A., Han, X., Cohn, T., Baldwin, T., Frermann, L., Optimising equal opportunity fairness in model training, 2022. arXiv preprint arXiv:2205.02393.
68. Ilvento, C., Metric learning for individual fairness, 2019. arXiv preprint arXiv:1906.00250.
69. Lahoti, P., Gummadi, K. P., Weikum, G., Operationalizing individual fairness with pairwise fair representations, 2019. arXiv preprint arXiv:1907.01439.
70. Dwork, C. *et al.*, Fairness through awareness. *Proceedings of the 3rd innovations in theoretical computer science conference*, 2012.
71. Lavalle, A., Mate, A., Trujillo, J., Teruel, M. A., A data analytics methodology to visually analyze the impact of bias and rebalancing. *IEEE Access*, 11, 56691–56702, 2023.
72. Caruccio, L., Desiato, D., Polese, G., Tortora, G., Zannone, N., A decision-support framework for data anonymization with application to machine learning processes. *Inf. Sci.*, 613, 1–32, 2022.
73. Zafar, M.B. *et al.*, Fairness constraints: Mechanisms for fair classification. *Artificial Intelligence and Statistics*, 2017.
74. Yang, J., Soltan, A. A., Eyre, D. W., Yang, Y., Clifton, D. A., An adversarial training framework for mitigating algorithmic biases in clinical machine learning. *npj Digital Med.*, 6, 1, 55, 2023.
75. Boursier, E. and Flammarion, N., Penalising the biases in norm regularisation enforces sparsity. *Adv. Neural Inf. Process. Syst.*, 36, 57795–57824, 2023.

76. Jeni, L.A. *et al.*, Facing imbalanced data–recommendations for the use of performance metrics. *2013 Humaine association conference on affective computing and intelligent interaction*, 2013.
77. Oesterling, A. *et al.*, Fair machine unlearning: Data removal while mitigating disparities. *International Conference on Artificial Intelligence and Statistics*, 2024.
78. Liu, W. *et al.*, Personalized fairness-aware re-ranking for microlending. *Proceedings of the 13th ACM conference on recommender systems*, 2019.
79. Agrawal, V., Kalmady, S.V., Manoj, V.M., Manthena, M.V., Sun, W., Islam, M.S., Hindle, A., Kaul, P., Greiner, R., Federated Learning and Differential Privacy Techniques on Multi-hospital Population-scale Electrocardiogram Data, in: *Proceedings of the 2024 8th International Conference on Medical and Health Informatics*, pp. 143–152, 2024 May 17.
80. Rauniyar, A., Hagos, D. H., Jha, D., Håkegård, J. E., Bagci, U., Rawat, D. B., Vlassov, V., Federated learning for medical applications: A taxonomy, current trends, challenges, and future research directions. *IEEE Internet Things J.*, 11, 5, 7374–7398, 2023.
81. Poulain, R. *et al.*, Improving fairness in ai models on electronic health records: The case for federated learning methods. *Proceedings of the 2023 ACM conference on fairness, accountability, and transparency*, 2023.
82. Yan, R. *et al.*, Label-efficient self-supervised federated learning for tackling data heterogeneity in medical imaging. *IEEE Trans. Med. Imaging*, 42, 7, 1932–1943, 2023.
83. Chu, Y.-W. *et al.*, Multi-layer personalized federated learning for mitigating biases in student predictive analytics. *IEEE Trans. Emerging Top. Comput.*, 2024.
84. Chen, R. J., Chen, T. Y., Lipkova, J., Wang, J. J., Williamson, D. F., Lu, M. Y., Sahai, S., Mahmood, F., Algorithm fairness in ai for medicine and healthcare, 2021. arXiv preprint arXiv:2110.00603.
85. Jovanovic, Z., Hou, Z., Biswas, K., Muthukkumarasamy, V., Robust integration of blockchain and explainable federated learning for automated credit scoring. *Comput. Netw.*, 243, 110303, 2024.
86. Xu, X., Peng, H., Sun, L., Bhuiyan, M. Z. A., Liu, L., He, L., Fedmood: Federated learning on mobile health data for mood detection, 2021. arXiv preprint arXiv:2102.09342.
87. Gupta, C. and Khullar, V., Privacy Preserving Collaboratively Training Framework for Classification of Major Depressive Disorder using Non-IID Three Channel Electroencephalogram. *Procedia Comput. Sci.*, 235, 56–69, 2024.
88. Mothukuri, V., Parizi, R. M., Pouriyeh, S., Huang, Y., Dehghantanha, A., Srivastava, G., A survey on security and privacy of federated learning. *Future Gener. Comput. Syst.*, 115, 619–640, 2021.

89. Someh, I., Davern, M., Breidbach, C. F., Shanks, G., Ethical issues in big data analytics: A stakeholder perspective. *Commun. Assoc. Inf. Systems*, 44, 1, 34, 2019.
90. Diakopoulos, N., Accountability, transparency, and algorithms, in: *The Oxford handbook of ethics of AI*, 2020.
91. Rieke, N., Hancox, J., Li, W., Milletari, F., Roth, H. R., Albarqouni, S., Cardoso, M. J., The future of digital health with federated learning. *npj Digital Med.*, 3, 1, 1–7, 2020.
92. Seyyed-Kalantari, L., Zhang, H., McDermott, M. B., Chen, I. Y., Ghassemi, M., Underdiagnosis bias of artificial intelligence algorithms applied to chest radiographs in under-served patient populations. *Nat. Med.*, 27, 12, 2176–2182, 2021.
93. Johnson, G.M., Algorithmic bias: on the implicit biases of social technology. *Synthese.*, 198, 10, 9941–9961, 2021.
94. Li, Q., Wen, Z., Wu, Z., Hu, S., Wang, N., Li, Y., He, B., A survey on federated learning systems: Vision, hype and reality for data privacy and protection. *IEEE Trans. Knowl. Data Eng.*, 35, 4, 3347–3366, 2021.
95. Neto, H. N. C., Hribar, J., Dusparic, I., Mattos, D. M. F., Fernandes, N. C., A survey on securing federated learning: Analysis of applications, attacks, challenges, and trends. *IEEE Access*, 11, 41928–41953, 2023.
96. Franco, D., Oneto, L., Navarin, N., Anguita, D., Toward learning trustworthily from data combining privacy, fairness, and explainability: an application to face recognition. *Entropy.*, 23, 8, 1047, 2021.
97. Vettoruzzo, A. *et al.*, Personalized federated learning with contextual modulation and meta-learning. *Proceedings of the 2024 SIAM International Conference on Data Mining (SDM)*, 2024.
98. Nguyen, D. C., Ding, M., Pathirana, P. N., Seneviratne, A., Li, J., Poor, H. V., Federated learning for internet of things: A comprehensive survey. *IEEE Commun. Surv. Tutor.*, 23, 3, 1622–1658, 2021.

Index

Wiley The manufacturer's authorized representative according to the EU General Product Safety Regulation is Wiley-VCH GmbH, Boschstr. 12, 69469 Weinheim, Germany, e-mail: Product_Safety@wiley.com.

Printed and bound by CPI Group (UK) Ltd, Croydon, CR0 4YY
19/08/2026
02201086-0001